Divine Impassibility

Divine Impassibility

An essay in philosophical theology

RICHARD E. CREEL

Professor of Philosophy and Religion
Ithaca College, New York

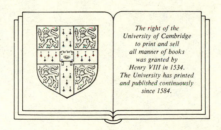

The right of the
University of Cambridge
to print and sell
all manner of books
was granted by
Henry VIII in 1534.
The University has printed
and published continuously
since 1584.

CAMBRIDGE UNIVERSITY PRESS

Cambridge
London   New York   New Rochelle
Melbourne   Sydney

Published by the Press Syndicate of the University of Cambridge
The Pitt Building, Trumpington Street, Cambridge CB2 1RP
32 East 57th Street, New York, NY 10022, USA
10 Stamford Road, Oakleigh, Melbourne 3166, Australia

First published 1986

Printed in Great Britain at the University Press, Cambridge

Library of Congress catalogue card number: 85-4741

British Library cataloguing in publication data
Creel, Richard E.
Divine impassibility: an essay in
philosophical theology.
1. God – Attributer
I. Title
212'.01   BT102
ISBN 0 521 303176

Dedicated
WITH LOVE AND ADMIRATION
to
Richard and Grace Creel, my parents
and
Earl and LaFran Wallick, my wife's parents

Contents

Preface

THE EVENT from which this volume grew was my encounter with Charles Hartshorne's attack on Thomas Aquinas' doctrine of divine impassibility, i.e., the doctrine that God is not influenced by the world or what goes on in it. The more I pondered this emotionally charged intellectual impasse between Aquinas and Hartshorne, the more intrigued I became with the subtlety and far-reaching significance of this issue. The next natural step was to read other writers on this topic. After working my way through many of them without getting a clear sense that the dispute over divine impassibility had a center of gravity, I came to realize why that is so. The issue of impassibility has four distinct aspects to it, but some authors are oblivious to some of these aspects, and other authors confuse the different aspects with one another. As a consequence some authors generate confusing statements about impassibility because they use "impassibility" to refer now to one aspect of impassibility, now to another, all the while thinking they are speaking of one and only one thing; other authors speak past one another by addressing different aspects of the problem while assuming that they are speaking about one and the same thing because they are all speaking about "impassibility." To help reduce confusion and miscommunication of this sort, I have in the first chapter of this volume provided a framework for clear and systematic discussion of divine impassibility, setting in relief its four basic aspects: nature, will, knowledge, and feeling.

The remainder of this volume was to have consisted simply of my reflections on whether God should be thought of as passible or impassible in nature, will, knowledge, and feeling. I do carry out that intention, coming down on the side of impassibility at some points and passibility at other points. I quickly discovered, however, that in order to enter adequately into contemporary discussion of divine impassibility, I had to venture into several related issues or risk having my positions dismissed for want of metaphysical underpinnings. For example, Charles Hartshorne was the respondent to a presentation to the Society for the Philosophy of Religion of an early version of Chapter 2 (on impassibility of the divine will). In his response he dismissed my position on impassibility of the divine will because it is predicated on the assumption that God knows all possibilities — an assumption that Hartshorne rejects in its classical form.

This rejection made it clear that my position in Chapter 2 would receive serious consideration by process philosophers only if it were backed up by an effort to show the plausibility of the classical position on God's knowledge of possibilities. Hence the development of Chapter 3: "Continuity, possibility, and omniscience."

I also discovered the issue of divine impassibility to be intimately related to issues of time, eternity, evil, freedom, and creation. As a consequence my last four chapters and some of the intervening chapters take up ways in which positions on divine impassibility affect or are affected by positions on these other issues. As a consequence this volume has become a more fully developed philosophical treatment of the concept of God than I had anticipated. To be sure, these few chapters are nowhere near exhaustive of topics in philosophical theology, but they are a conscientious attempt to deal constructively with a recurrent cluster of problems that stand at the heart of current debate among classical theologians, analytical philosophers, and process thinkers.

I hope that this volume will help to return the topic of impassibility to the forefront of philosophical theology and lead to advances beyond our previous grasp of this issue. It would also be nice if my substantive contributions prove to have some enduring value. Whether or not that proves to be the case, I am sufficiently familiar with the English literature on divine impassibility to be confident that the reader will find herein a useful contribution to the format for discussion of this very important topic.

Acknowledgments

I BEGAN MY WORK on the topic of divine impassibility in the context of a 1979 National Endowment for the Humanities Summer Seminar under the leadership of William Alston, and continued it as a participant in the 1980 Institute on Medieval Philosophy led by Norman Kretzmann. I am grateful to Alston and Kretzmann for the inspiration, wisdom, and challenge that they have provided to me over these six years and to NEH and the Council for Philosophical Studies for bringing us together. Finalization of this essay is being supported by an Ithaca College 1984 Summer Research Grant.

As I reflect back to 1979 I am particularly grateful to Michael McLain of Rhodes College. Michael provided extensive, painstaking commentary on the tortuous first paper that I wrote on impassibility. After I began to clarify the structure of my approach to the topic, it became evident that I needed a deeper, more adequate understanding of contemporary process philosophy. For generous help in that regard I am particularly grateful to James Keller of Wofford College and Lewis Ford of Old Dominion University. A host of others have helped in various ways, especially Stephen Bickham, William Dinges, Rem Edwards, Art Falk, James Felt, Douglas Greene, Charles Hartshorne, Delmas Lewis, Bruce Reichenbach, Michael Slusser, and Theodore Vitali.

Those at Ithaca College to whom I am particularly indebted are Lana Morse, my secretary, who typed this manuscript while serving three departments; John Henderson and Everett Morse, reference librarians who secured rare volumes and tracked down missing data; and Steve Schwartz, a friend who is also a philosophical presence.

I am grateful also to Robert Williams and Mary Baffoni of the Cambridge University Press. Robert, the editor at the Press, supported my initial manuscript and exercised sensible, constructive leadership in its development. Mary showed exquisite editorial skill in spotting omissions, mistakes, and infelicities.

Finally, I thank my wife, Diane, who started out only to proof-read but wound up making valuable substantive contributions, and I acknowledge my children, Rick and Chris, active social creatures who think it strange to see a healthy human voluntarily spend the better part of each lovely summer glued to books and a typewriter.

I

The issue of divine impassibility

THE DOCTRINE of divine impassibility has been keenly disputed in the Christian tradition from the early centuries of the church to the present day. St Augustine asked rhetorically, "who can sanely say that God is touched by any misery?" (Mozley 1926: 105). And in a treatise on patience he wrote, "far be it from us to imagine that the impassible nature of God suffers any vexation. For as He is jealous without any envy, is angry without any perturbation, is pitiful without any grief, repents without having any evil in him to correct, so He is patient without any suffering" (Mozley 1926: 107). In the early twentieth century Baron Friedrich von Hügel continued this line of thought when he wrote:

> Now God is that Perfect Love, Unmixed Joy, Entire Delectation. He is all this, not as a bundle of separate qualities, however consummate each quality may be, but as a living, spiritual, Personalist Reality, Who Himself is all this overflowingly. I believe this to be a true account of the fundamental religious experience and apprehension. But if so, we will not admit the presence of any Evil, be it Sin or even only Sorrow, be they actual or even only potential, in Him Who thus dwarfs for us all our little human goodness and earthly joy by His utter Sanctity and sheer Beatitude. And all this Goodness and Joy God does not become, does not acquire: He simply *is* it. (Hügel 1926: 208)

Later in the same essay von Hügel reports a mystical experience in which his awareness moved from the suffering of humanity to the joy of Christ weighed down by suffering to a vision of the unqualified joy of God:

> Joy, pure joy, an Ocean of it, unplumbed, unplumbable, with not one drop of Evil within it – not one drop of Sin or Suffering or of the possibility of either. And I did not want it otherwise – far, far from it! God was too much our Friend for us not to rejoice that He does not suffer; and this Joy of God is too much our sustenance, it too much shows us, contrastingly, our indigence, a sight of ourselves which constitutes our specific dignity, for me, for any of those great lovers of His, to wish His Joy mixed or limited or conditional. And yet this Pure Joy was utterly compassionate, utterly sympathetic... (Hügel 1926: 212)

The strength of conviction, intelligence, and sensitivity of Augustine and von Hügel can hardly be questioned, yet we find equally strong statements by respectable figures at the other end of the spectrum of opinions on divine impassibility. A. M. Fairbairn has written, "Theology has no falser idea than that of the impassibility of God" (Mozley 1926: 146); Douglas

White states, "The doctrine of the impassibility of God, taken in its widest sense, is the greatest heresy that ever smirched Christianity; it is not only false, it is the antipodes of truth" (Mozley 1926: 151); Charles Hartshorne writes: "The immutable, impassible God of classical theism has nothing in him conceivably analogous to love" (Hartshorne 1953: 152); H. P. Owen concedes, "This is the most questionable aspect of classical theism" (Owen 1971: 24).

All of these rejections of divine impassibility seem to be motivated by a clash between the conviction that God should be thought of as a loving person and the further conviction that an impassible being cannot be a loving person. Surely it is true that within the broad tradition of biblical theism the experience and idea of God as personal and loving is pervasive. See, for example, the book of Hosea or the Johannine literature. Hence, for biblical theists, if there is a conflict between God being loving and being impassible, it is impassibility that must be modified or ejected. To go at the point another way, it is conceivable that one could affirm that God is love and deny that God is impassible yet remain a Christian, but it is inconceivable that one could affirm that God is impassible and deny that God is love, yet remain a Christian. Jung Young Lee makes the point this way in his *God Suffers For Us: A Systematic Inquiry into a Concept of Divine Passibility*: "the divine nature governs the quality of divine attribute and not vice versa. Thus, if *Agape* is the divine nature and passibility is a divine attribute, the latter must conform to the former" (Lee 1974: 7). Hence, whether God is impassible is negotiable (for biblical theists), but whether God is love is not.

I agree with the spirit of Lee's position. However, I am not so confident as our passibilist authors that divine love and divine impassibility are incompatible, and I have failed to find an analysis of the issue of divine impassibility that is sufficiently systematic to give one confidence that the complexities thereof have been adequately unravelled, clarified and dealt with. Hence, in the next section of this essay I will survey numerous understandings of the nature of impassibility, then provide a core definition of impassibility, and finally distinguish four aspects of impassibility in terms of which I believe an adequate investigation of the question of divine impassibility can be conducted. After these preliminaries, I will attempt to do the impossible – or at least that which appears to be so. Christopher Bache, who wrote in a 1978 Brown University dissertation, 'The Logic of Religious Metaphor', that the concepts of love and impassibility appear "as irreconcilable as saying of a geometric figure that it has four corners and no sides," went on to say, "Nevertheless... I do not think we can at this point preclude the possibility that some resourceful philosophical theologian will eventually bring meaning out of what looks like sheer incompatibility" (Bache 1978: 267). After establishing in the remainder of this chapter what I believe to be an adequate framework for investigating the issue of the impassibility of God, I shall attempt in succeeding chapters to be a "resourceful philosophical theologian," showing that there is no incompatibility where to some it seems so obvious that there is.

WHAT IS IMPASSIBILITY?

My procedure in answering the question to which this section is addressed will be first to present a wide and representative selection of quotations on divine impassibility. Next I will show that from this array it is possible to abstract a core definition. Then I will distinguish four respects in which this central concept applies to God.

A. A survey of opinions

Robert M. Grant in *The Early Christian Doctrine of God* reveals that "impassible" (*apathēs*) had more than one meaning in the early post-apostolic era. To Origen it mean, *inter alia,* lacking all emotion. It also meant to him that God's bliss was entirely unperturbed and motionless. Consequently Origen concluded at one point in his career that God did not and could not suffer. For Clement of Alexandria *apathēs* took on another meaning: insusceptibility to distraction by the pleasures of the flesh. Clement wrote of God the Son, "he could never abandon his care for mankind through the distractions of any pleasure, since after he had taken on the flesh, which is by nature subject to passion, he trained it to habitual impassibility" (Grant 1966: 112). Let us separate and label these meanings of impassibility.

I_1 shall be taken to mean "lacking all emotion." We will not specify the intension or extension of "emotion" except to say, in accord with the Greek and Christian traditions, that it does not include bliss.[1] I_2 shall mean something like "being in a state of mind which is entirely unperturbable and motionless," whatever that state of mind might be, whether it involves emotion or does not.[2] I_2 seems to be what Origen had in mind when he wrote later in his career, "The Father himself is not impassible. If he is asked, he takes pity and experiences grief, he suffers something of love..." (Grant 1966: 30). I_3 shall mean "insusceptible to distraction from resolve by the pleasures of the flesh," or, more generally, "insusceptible to distraction from resolve."

Clearly these three definitions of impassibility are not equally implausible to predicate of a loving being. I_3, for example, seems quite compatible with being loving; a saint who can minister to prostitutes without being unravelled by passion is generally admired. Similarly we admire a doctor who can block out the pain-filled cries of a child he is trying to help. Indeed, we might even say that the doctor has not only a duty to help the child, but a duty not to let the child's struggling and tears interfere with the effectiveness of his helping. However, if the doctor seemed to maintain his poise in such a situation because he was emotionally indifferent to the child, i.e., was I_1 impassible, we would probably think he was in some way deficient as a person. In Chapter 7 we will examine whether an I_2 being could be loving.

G. L. Prestige, another scholar of early Christian thought, writes in his *God in Patristic Thought*, "Just as God is supreme in power and wisdom, so is He morally supreme, incapable of being diverted or overborne by forces and passions such as commonly hold sway in the creation and among mankind. The word chosen [by the early church fathers] to express this moral transcendence is 'impassible'" (Prestige 1952: 6). Shortly thereafter he says, "Impassibility then implies perfect moral freedom, and is a supernatural endowment properly belonging to God alone. God, says Clement... is impassible, without anger and without desire" (Prestige 1952: 7). In the first quotation Prestige is referring to I_3, but in the last sentence of the second quotation he switches to I_2 (or perhaps I_1; it is not clear). Then he cautions that "It is clear that impassibility means not that God is inactive or uninterested, not that He surveys existence with Epicurean impassivity from the shelter of a metaphysical insulation, but that His will is determined from within instead of being swayed from without" (Prestige 1952: 7). Here we have another sense of impassibility: I_4, according to which God's will is determined entirely by himself and neither caused nor modified from without.

Robert S. Franks states in *The Encyclopedia of Religion and Ethics* that the question of the passibility or impassibility of God is the question of his "capacity or incapacity of being acted upon" (Franks 1951: 658). This is the most general conception of impassibility so far. Let's call it I_5: incapable of being acted upon.

Bertrand Brasnett in *The Suffering of the Impassible God* says that if God were dependent upon the universe, then he would be passible (Brasnett 1928: 3). He adds that God impassibly created the universe because, "In no sense did created things constrain God to create them" (Brasnett 1928: 4). Prestige was getting at the same point when he said that the doctrine of impassibility protected the independence of God, for, were it possible to claim validly that any action "was wrung from Him either by the needs or by the claims of His creation, and that thus whether by pity or by justice His hand was forced, he could no longer be represented as absolute; He would be dependent on the created universe and thus at best only in possession of concurrent power" (Prestige 1952: 7). Brasnett and Prestige here seem to have I_4 in mind. But then Brasnett concludes, "had any force or power availed to keep him from creating then God would have been passible, because stayed from his purpose by something other than Himself" (Brasnett 1928: 5). Here we implicitly meet yet another sense of divine impassibility, I_6: God cannot be stayed from achieving his purpose by anything other than himself.

J. K. Mozley begins *The Impassible God*, an historical study, by saying simply that he will be doing a survey of what people have believed with regard to "God's incapacity for suffering" (Mozley 1926: 1). Context makes it clear that this is a species of I_1, rather than a version of I_5. We will broaden it a bit and call it I_7: lacking all negative emotions. A more recent thinker, Peter Bertocci, states that the truth about God that has been captured in the doctrine of impassibility is that, "His own inner happiness is not disturbed" (Bertocci 1951: 458). This seems clearly a version of I_7.

H. P. Owen has written of impassibility both in his article, "God Concepts of", in the *Encyclopedia of Philosophy* and in his book *Concepts of Deity*. In the latter Owen says that impassibility "can mean that God is incapable of suffering change from either an external or an internal cause. But," he adds, "the word means particularly that he cannot experience sorrow, sadness or pain" (Owen 1971: 23). The latter statement appears to be a version of I_7, but the former statement, which expands upon I_5, shall be I_8: cannot be changed by an external or internal force. Carl F. H. Henry expressed this position when he wrote, "God is perfect and, if perfect, can only change for the worse, and hence he will not change himself nor can he be compelled to change by anything outside himself" (Henry 1982: V, 304).

Whereas Grant, Prestige, and Mozley put the issue of divine impassibility into historical contexts, Jung Young Lee provides us with a systematic analysis in his *God Suffers For Us: A Systematic Inquiry into a Concept of Divine Passibility*. Lee, in the spirit of I_7, writes that "The terms 'passibility' and 'impassibility' are used to designate the capacity or incapacity of God to experience suffering" (Lee 1974: 4). Lee goes beyond Owen by distinguishing suffering from pain, attributing the latter to the body and the former to personal relationships, adding in the tradition of Gregory of Thaumaturgus (died AD270) that, though God suffers, God's suffering is voluntary and redemptive.[3]

Later in the volume Lee explains that "Divine *apatheia* means simply that there is an absence of feeling or passion in the divine nature. It implies, in other words, that God is free of any emotional life" (Lee 1974: 28). This later proves to be a version of I_1 (though it initially sounds stronger), and

Lee points out that impassibility in this sense was an ethical goal of the Stoics. The Stoics believed that God is impassible and that humans ought to become so because passion is "a bondage of human misery, servitude and imperfection" (Lee 1974: 30). Emotions are thought of as states of mind that are incompatible with perfect peace of mind, as pertains to I_2, or that tempt one from the path of moral duty, as pertains to I_3. Emotions and passions are thought of as irrational and susceptible to being triggered by things outside the self.

Lee adds that if God is to be thought of as impassible yet perfect, and therefore exquisitely blissful (again note: bliss is not thought of as an emotion), God must be thought of as entirely adequate unto himself. Hence, "The concept of *apatheia* is closely related to the Greek idea of *autarkeia*, which literally means 'sufficiency' or 'contentment'" (Lee 1974: 30). "The divine *autarkeia* simply signifies the nature of this God who is so wholly complete that He wants nothing" (31). Consequently, the impassible God "is often identified with the immovable and absolute Deity who is indifferent to His creature . . ." (48). Such a God "neither shares nor participates in the community of suffering humanity" because he needs nothing from the world (67). Lee, then, operates with a conception of impassibility that involves I_1, I_2, I_3, and I_7.

Finally we turn to Charles Hartshorne. Chronologically Hartshorne is not the most recent critic of divine impassibility, but he may well be the most influential living critic of this doctrine. Moreover, I have found his arguments to be the most challenging because of the passion of his convictions, the intelligence of his arguments, the fact that he limits his arguments to reason (making no appeal to revelation), and most important because of the connection of his critique of impassibility to a comprehensive and cohesive alternative conception of God and the world. Hence, in what follows I will not merely present Hartshorne's conception of impassibility; I will present it in the context of his arguments against it so that later we will have a background of specific arguments to which to respond.

Hartshorne says that contemporary theology has discovered of God "that he is the most powerful possible being, yet not in every sense 'impassive', incapable of being acted upon . . ." (Hartshorne 1941: 29). We have here in explicit fashion what seems to be Hartshorne's most basic conception of what it means to be impassive or impassible: incapable of being acted upon. This conception seems identical with I_5.

Two other important aspects of Hartshorne's conception of impassibility come out when he laments that some people have rejected theism because of its paradoxes; these people "held untenable the idea of a mind not subject to change or interaction with other beings . . . or knowing all suffering although it did not itself suffer..." (Hartshorne 1941: 44). The latter point, that God does not suffer, seems to be a version of I_7 and the former point, that God does not interact with other beings, follows from I_5 because, if God cannot be acted upon, then he cannot be interacted with.

Later in *Man's Vision of God* Hartshorne seems to be speaking of impassibility when he says that, according to the philosophical tenets of classical theism, "God is purely active, in no respect or relation passive to anything..." (95). God is absolutely independent of causal influence from the world, but the world is absolutely dependent on God (96). Hartshorne insists, however, that omnipotence does not entail impassivity. "A strong man is open to many an influence that leaves a cat beautifully 'impassive.' Weakness is in being influenced in the wrong directions or disproportionately, as by a friend more than by a stranger in a dispute in which both have equal right to be heard. Love is exalted as much through its passive as through its active side" (105–6). Here we see I_5 again: the cat is incapable of being acted upon or influenced in certain ways, but such impassibility is obviously a defect because it is a form of insensitivity. To be sure, being passible is problematic when it is combined with fallibility and moral weakness, but it is part of God's character that he is neither fallible nor morally weak; hence, we need not be concerned that God is passible to the world.

Hartshorne further critiques the classical conception of God by reasoning that, "Love involves sensitivity to the joys and sorrows of others, participation in them – but we cannot infect God with our sufferings (since he is cause of everything and effect of nothing), and our joys can add nothing to the immutable perfection of God's happiness" (114). The religious significance of God's impassivity is that "one can do nothing for God, and our worst sins harm God as little as the finest acts of sainthood can advance him" (114). As Lee might put it, God's impassivity presupposes his *autarkeia*.

Hartshorne goes on to say that process theology, as distinguished from classical theology, "ascribes to God, with full deliberateness, supreme sensitivity, that is, passivity, not as contradictory of supreme activity, but as a necessary aspect of it" (114). We can infer from this that Hartshorne thinks of divine impassivity as supreme insensitivity. Hence, an impassible God would be insensitive to the feelings, desires, circumstances, and prayers of his creatures. In a similar vein Hartshorne says that, in his own conception of God,

The dependence of God is his "passivity," and this passivity truly belongs to him... so that it is by virtue of his passive being, his sensitivity, that our activity can exist, and the divine passivity is the one passivity upon which all activity is unfailingly exercised...

Thus activity has as its only universal correlate the adequate, unstinted, unique sensitivity of God, just as passivity has as its only universal correlate the activity – equally unique in scope – of God. We "give" God his passive being in the sense that, by definition, this being, which is social, can receive determinate form, aesthetic realization, only in partial dependence upon others.   (282–3)

By contrast it follows that impassivity is independence, and independence is ignorance because knowledge of actuality is gained only from being influenced by it, but to be influenced is to be dependent, so an impassible God would be ignorant of the world. (We will return to the issue of impassibility and God's knowledge of the world in Chapter 5.)

In our final quotation from *Man's Vision of God*, Hartshorne asks a question:

The most trivial of physical particles will go where we push it, but will it feel our joy or sorrow, echo our thoughts, assume the *qualitative* form we wish some fellow being to share with us? Not to any noticeable extent. It resists with superhuman "power" of self-sufficiency, with admirable persistence, in its own course of activity. None but God, the opposite extreme from the particle, can be infinitely passive, the endurer of all change, the adventurer through all novelty, the companion through all vicissitudes. He is the auditor of all speech who should be heard because he has heard, and who should change our hearts because in every iota of our history we have changed his.

(297–8)

Again by contrast it follows that an impassive God would be even less responsive to us than "the most trivial of physical particles," his heart unchanged by our most heartfelt pleas.

That Hartshorne's position has remained constant can be seen in several of his later books. In *The Divine Relativity* he suggests a "mental experiment," viz., read aloud an eloquent poem in the presence of a glass of water. "The molecules of water," he tells us, "will be utterly 'impassible' (the theological term) to the words of the poem as words, and not even much affected by the mere physical sounds" (Hartshorne 1948: 49). Later in the same work he says, "Mere 'matter', supposed to be the most passive of entities, must really be the most *im*passive, if passivity means ability to reflect difference in other things. The closer we get to a 'merely material' individual, the closer we come to something for which nearly all changes in the universe make no appreciable difference at all" (77). Here we see another corollary of I_5: the more impassive a being is, the less able it is to reflect difference in other things. A being absolutely impassive to the world would be absolutely oblivious to differences in it and, since knowledge depends on awareness of difference (otherwise one would not be aware of how a thing is in distinction from how it is not), an impassible God would be totally ignorant of the world, as was Aristotle's God.

In *The Logic of Perfection* Hartshorne describes the activity/passivity of

God upon/to creatures as "an ideal form of give and take" (44). By contrast, an impassible God who is pure act cannot enter into give and take with the world. Hence, to be impassible pure act means that one may give but not take, therefore being uninfluenced by the world. Returning to physical particles, Hartshorne writes, "A man can sympathize with any living thing he sees suffering or enjoying, or imagines to do so, and this sympathy modifies the man; whereas an atom goes comparatively stolidly, 'impassively' about its business though whole nations groan in agony" (137). *Ceteris paribus*, an impassive God would be totally unaffected by such a tragic state of affairs.

Finally, in *A Natural Theology for Our Time* Hartshorne claims that, according to classical theism, "God may act, but cannot be acted upon" (68). Hence, there is zero interaction between God and anything else. Continuing to speak of immunity to influence, Hartshorne asks, "What can one do to change the number two? Also, past events are henceforth immune to influence. Deceased individuals are indeed 'impassible.' But living individuals...?" (75). As many a grief-stricken person has discovered, it does no good to talk to, shake, or beseech the dead. They are unresponsive, impassible. Toward the end of his *Natural Theology* Hartshorne says that the new metaphysics, unlike the old, "makes no leap from time to mere eternity, from the relative to the merely absolute, from interacting individuals to an impassible one, from the wholly dependent to the wholly self-sufficient" (135). Here Hartshorne rejects both the doctrine of divine *autarkeia* and the doctrine of divine impassibility.

In summary, to say that God is impassive, is, according to Hartshorne, to say that God is incapable of being acted upon or influenced (I_5). Corollaries to this are that (1) God cannot know us, (2) God cannot interact with us, (3) God cannot sympathize with us, and (4) God cannot hear or respond to our prayers.

B.   A core definition and four applications

Let us review and then examine these eight definitions of impassibility in relation to one another:

I_1 "lacking all emotions" (bliss not an emotion)
I_2 "in a state of mind that is imperturbable"
I_3 "insusceptible to distraction from resolve"
I_4 "having a will determined entirely by oneself"
I_5 "cannot be affected by an outside force"
I_6 "cannot be prevented from achieving one's purpose"
I_7 "has no susceptibility to negative emotions"
I_8 "cannot be affected by an outside force or changed by oneself."

I_1 implies but is not implied by I_2. A being that lacks all emotions would be imperturbable, but it does not follow that an imperturbable being would lack all emotions. We can imagine a being that is imperturbably optimistic or imperturbably sad. The members of I_1, however, could not all be housed in I_2 because only things in a state of mind can belong to I_2 whereas I_1 would include such things as stones and numbers, which have neither minds nor emotions and therefore would be only trivially imperturbable. I_3's members can also be divided into two groups: one group whose members are capable of being distracted from resolve but who are also capable of resisting distractions and perhaps of becoming voluntarily impervious to them, and another group whose members are by nature impervious to distraction from resolve. I_3 can be subsumed under I_2 because I_3 focuses on impassibility of purpose alone whereas I_2, interpreted broadly, would include other states of mind, such as knowing and feeling, in addition to intention and willing.

I_3 is also closely related to I_4. I_4 states that nothing external to an impassible being enters into determining its will; I_3 adds that once such a being determines its will, nothing can distract it from proceeding according to its decision. $I_2, I_3,$ and I_4, in turn, prove to be corollaries of I_5, which stipulates that *nothing* about God can be determined or changed from without. I_6 is also a corollary of I_5 in God's case, though it is not entailed for other beings. The difference turns upon God's omnipotence. I_5 implies that an I_5 being with a purpose cannot be prevented by an outside force from achieving that purpose, but I_5 does not exclude the possibility that because of an internal defect or deficiency an I_5 being could fail to achieve its purpose. An omnipotent I_5 being, however, could not be prevented by anything external or internal from achieving its purpose. For God, then $I_{2,3,4,6}$, can all be subsumed under I_5.

I_7 and I_1 are species of the genus of things that lack by nature some quality of emotion. We can distinguish (a) things that by nature lack all emotions, (b) things that by nature lack negative emotions but have positive emotions, and (c) things that by nature lack positive emotions but have negative emotions. The complement of this genus would be (d): things that by nature lack neither positive nor negative emotions. (c) would be an unfortunate nature for any being to have, and so it is unworthy of ascription to God. Aristotle's God was blissfully (a), but (a) excludes the emotion of love for the world, and so it falls short of the biblical conception of highest reality. The biblical picture of God is (d), but the classical tradition in theistic thought has construed that picture to be figurative rather than literal. Process thought, as we shall see, returns to the biblical picture of God as (d), though it touches up that picture to exclude what it considers to be inappropriate emotions such as jealousy and hatred. Classical theism, by contrast, describes God as (b): blissful and loving, experiencing by nature no negative feelings (I_7), and impassible to having such feelings caused by an outside force (I_5). I_1, then, is too narrow to fit a supremely perfect being, and I_7 proves to be a species of I_5.

I_5 is a species of I_8 because I_8 goes beyond I_5 by excluding not only that which is outside God from changing him, but also that which is within God, including presumably his own will. But, if we identify I_8 as a more general form of impassibility than I_5, we lose the distinction between impassibility and immutability. An immutable being, i.e., a being that is unchangeable *simpliciter*, is certainly a being that is impassible, i.e., not subject to change or influence by external factors; but an impassible being is not necessarily immutable – it might change itself. Conversely, a passible being could not be immutable, but a mutable being might be impassible.

It seems, then, that the most consistent element of meaning across these definitions of impassibility is I_5, i.e., that which is impassible is that which cannot be affected by an outside force. Hence, impassibility is imperviousness to causal influence from external factors. It should be clear from Section A, however, that this minimal definition of impassibility is not adequate for one confidently to answer the question, "Is x impassible?" From the quotations in Section A it is obvious that there are diverse respects in which a being may be passible or impassible; consequently, when we are answering the question "Is x impassible?", we should clarify whether we are focusing on the impassibility of the being in every respect or in some specific respect.

What are the specific respects in which a being might be impassible? An examination of the positions in Section A plus reflection on the respects in which a personal being might be impassible yield a fourfold result that strikes me as exhaustive for an incorporeal being such as God. Specifically, an incorporeal personal being could conceivably be impassible with regard to his *nature*, his *will*, his *knowledge*, or his *feelings*. To say that God is impassible with respect to his nature would be to say that his nature cannot be affected by an outside force. To say that God is impassible with respect to his will would be to say that his will cannot be affected by an outside force. To say that God is impassible with respect to his feelings would be to say that God's feelings, or the quality of his inner life, cannot be affected by an outside force. To say that God is impassible with respect to his knowledge would be to say that what he knows cannot be affected by an outside force.

It should be clear now that the question with which we are concerned does not come down to a choice between two simple alternatives: Is God passible or impassible? It comes down to a choice among sixteen permutations. Consider the possibilities, using "i" to stand for impassible, "p" to stand for passible, "N" to stand for "in nature," "W" to stand for "in will," "K" to stand for "in knowledge," and "F" to stand for "in feeling":

N	W	K	F
i	i	i	i
p	i	i	i
i	p	i	i
i	i	p	i
i	i	i	p
p	p	i	i
p	i	p	i
p	i	i	p
i	p	p	i
i	i	p	p
i	p	i	p
p	p	p	i
p	p	i	p
p	i	p	p
i	p	p	p
p	p	p	p

We will evaluate these alternatives in the following chapters.

A final complication is in order. I have been saying "cannot be changed," but we need as well to introduce "will not be changed" because some authors say that in certain respects God's passibility or impassibility is within the power of his own choosing, so that, whereas he is impassible in all respects in the sense that he could prevent himself from being changed by any outside force, he could choose to make himself passible in certain respects. Gregory of Thaumaturgus and Jung Lee, for example, claim that God has chosen freely to make himself emotionally vulnerable to the sins and sufferings of his creatures. This complication makes things messier, but its relevance will become clear in Chapter 7, on impassibility and feeling. Now let us examine each aspect of God's possible impassibility by examining and evaluating critiques by passibilists.

2

Divine impassibility in nature and will

THIS SECTION can be brief because all the authors whom I have read either claim or imply that the nature of God is impassible. That is, they claim that God's nature or essence cannot be affected by external force, or, for that matter, by himself. Hence, his essence is not only impassible but also immutable, i.e., completely beyond the possibility of change. It is clear from discussions of this point that even passibilists, i.e., people who believe that God is passible in at least one respect, do not believe that talk about God's impassibility is entirely without warrant. The point of passibilists has not been that impassibilism does not apply to God at all, but that it has been generalized beyond its appropriate application. Indeed, passibilists generally seem eager to assure readers of their ortho-doxy by affirming that they do believe in God's impassibility – but only with respect to his nature. That God exists, is loving, just, and unsurpass-able, cannot be changed, not even by God. Hartshorne writes:

> If we abstract from God's contingent qualities, with respect to the rest of his reality we can view classical theism as largely correct. Here indeed is the uncaused cause, impassible, immutable, and all the rest of it. Only it is not God, nor – in spite of Thomism – is it an actuality, "pure" or otherwise; rather, it is a mere abstraction, from the contingent and caused actuality of the divine life.
>
> (1967: 44; see also 1941: 111, and 1965: 32)

Passibilists, then, always seem to speak about God according to the following formula: "in nature impassible: in x passible."

This universal agreement on "in nature impassible" seems entirely appropriate because no being whose very nature is vulnerable to change could be worthy of unconditional worship. If the nature of God were subject to change by outside force, then God would not be omnipotent; if God were able to change his own nature, then he could not be trusted without concern; but by definition "God" refers to one who is categori-cally omnipotent and trustworthy. Hence, as Carl F. H. Henry has put it, "A creator and sustainer of the world who is vulnerable to mutability, a redeemer and judge of mankind *whose essential nature might waver* and whose purpose may vacillate, is not a deity in whom we can ever be religiously at rest" (Henry 1982: 288). Further, insofar as by "nature" we mean "essence," no thing's nature can be changed. The essence of a thing is immutable; only its accidents are mutable. To be sure, its essence might be made to be actual or not actual, but it cannot be changed. Even here, though, God is an exception because the divine essence cannot be made to become actual or non-actual; it is necessarily actual or necessarily non-actual. Here, then, passibilists and impassibilists stand united; from here on their paths diverge sharply.

IMPASSIBLE IN WILL

J. K. Mozley reports that, according to some writers around the turn of this century, God is impassible in nature but passible in will (1926: 35). That is, God's will can be influenced by forces outside himself; the prayers of humans, for example, might influence God's will – not in the sense of forcefully changing it, but, as Jung Lee points out, in the sense of occasioning a change of will on God's part.[1] (One might think here of Jesus' parable of the importunate widow who prevailed over the judge asleep at his home). By contrast, Bertrand Brasnett, a contemporary of Mozley's, seems to be opposed to passibility of the divine will when he states in *The Suffering of the Impassible God* that God's purpose "is utterly his own, unswayed by one hair's-breadth by any cause or influence other than his own." But later he makes it clear that he is speaking of God's purpose regarding ultimate goals, not intermediate goals and means thereto. God's intention to establish a kingdom of justice, peace, and good, for example, is rightly thought of as impassible. But if we also think of God's will as impassible with regard to the bringing about of these ends, we get an unpleasant picture of God as static and impersonal. "We may picture God," Brasnett writes, "as having a definite end in view which he is resolute to attain, but as varying his means in accordance with the demands of circumstances"; "on this view," he adds, "we have a very real and living idea of God functioning in time, changing his methods to meet varying needs..." (94). On a thoroughly impassibilist view, Brasnett implies, we would have an idea of God as unreal and dead.

Charles Hartshorne and Nelson Pike carry this analysis further and conclude that if God cannot respond to changing circumstances then he cannot respond to humans, and if he cannot respond to humans he cannot interact with them, and if he cannot interact with them he cannot have a personal relationship with them. Indeed, Hartshorne argues that it is questionable whether a volitionally impassible God could reasonably be considered to be a person. Hartshorne's most basic understanding of the meaning of divine impassibility is I_5: hence, an impassible God would be "resisted and acted upon by no other power," and that means he would be in no way changed by the changes that take place in the world. But, if God is changed neither by himself nor by the world, a serious problem results. "A changeless being can have no purposes," Hartshorne writes, "for purposes refer to the future and the future is related to the present by change" (1971: 159). That is, a being that purposes to bring about something in time must continually adapt to the continually changing present in order to bring about the achievement aimed at. But obviously a volitionally impassible being cannot adapt to changing circumstances; therefore a volitionally impassible being cannot be said to have a purpose relative to the world. It would be a category mistake to say that it did.

The very concept of having a purpose relative to a changing situation entails an intention to adapt to changing circumstances in order to achieve one's end. But an impassible being cannot have such an intention; therefore an impassible being cannot have a purpose. Hartshorne seems to mean the same thing elsewhere when he says, "An immutable purpose is meaningless..." The clincher to all this is that surely "the possessor of all perfections, of all positive perfections, of all positive predicates, must not be without purpose" (1941: 115). Therefore God, the possessor of all positive predicates and perfections, cannot be volitionally impassible. To go at this from another direction, surely if God is love, he purposes in general that his creatures shall enjoy as much happiness as is possible; but, if God is impassible, he cannot have any purpose, much less this one. *Ergo* we must choose between divine love and divine impassibility, and it is clear that love is a more important attribute of a supreme person than is volitional impassibility.

Furthermore, impassibility implies not only that God could have no purpose, it also implies that God could not have a personal relationship with us. Later in *Man's Vision of God* Hartshorne notes that the one-sided causality of God according to the classical conception is "wholly non-social, non-mutual" (275). Obviously such a God could not enter into the normal give and take of a personal relationship (1962: 44). Whatever such a God does, it is not in response to what is happening in the world; it is totally unilateral. Indeed, Hartshorne suggests, if the classical God is to be thought of as a person at all, it is as a dead person. Perhaps the most striking characteristic of the deceased is that they do not respond to being talked to, pled with, slapped or shaken. If God is impassible, then he is beyond our reach; for all practical purposes, he is dead – and surely one cannot have a personal relationship with a dead person. Just as clearly, such a picture of God is the opposite of the biblical picture of a living, dynamic, responding God.

Nelson Pike develops this line of argument in *God and Timelessness*. To be sure, his primary concern is with the philosophical problems of the concept of a timeless person; but, in the passages relevant to this essay, he makes it clear that certain problems result because a timeless being is immutable, and the aspect of immutability to which he is referring is clearly that of insusceptibility to external influence. Indeed, one wonders why Pike did not explicitly use the term "impassible" to identify more precisely his topic of concern in the following statements. He says, for example, "a timeless being could not be affected or prompted by another. It could not respond to needs, overtures, delights or antagonisms of human beings" (Pike 1970: 128). Speaking explicitly of an "immutable" being he says, "Such an individual could not be affected or prompted by another. To be affected or prompted by another is to be changed by the other. The actions of [such a being] could not be interpreted as a *response* to something else. Responses are located in time *after* that to which they are responses" (128). Clearly Pike is concerned here not with the genus, immutability, but with the species, impassibility. He goes on to say that it is doubtful that such a being could legitimately be considered to be a person. If we did stretch the term so far, he writes, "I doubt if one could become emotionally involved with such a person. I don't think one could take him as a friend – or as an enemy. Further, I don't think that a timeless person could be emotionally involved with another. To be emotionally involved, one must be able to *respond* in some way to the actions or inactions of others. A timeless individual could not respond" (128). Pike concludes his deliberations on this topic by agreeing with many passibilists that we should think of God's immutability as limited to his character. "If God is immutable," he writes, "He cannot change as regards his perfect power, wisdom, benevolence, etc.; but God might, e.g., change His mind. More importantly, God might be moved or prompted by the prayers of the faithful" (178). This kind of analysis of God's immutability, Pike claims, is "closer to the intentions of the biblical and confessional authors" and to "the notion of a being that is worthy of worship" than is the traditional analysis which claims that God is immutable in all respects (179). Now we need to evaluate these claims and arguments by Hartshorne, Pike, *et al.*

Critique

I believe that Hartshorne and Pike are wrong to conclude that a being impassible in will could not be a loving person. Given Pike's claim that a response necessarily comes after that to which it is a response, it appears at first that H. P. Owen is also in agreement when he states, "That God responds to men must be admitted by all Christian theists; for the admission is required by belief in petitionary prayer." However, in spite of the initial appearance, it is clear that Owen is not in agreement with Pike because he elaborates his statement in the following way:

That God responds to men must be admitted by all Christian theists; for the admission is required by belief in petitionary prayer. But "response" does not imply "change." On the contrary, Christians are committed to the belief that God's response to their prayers is determined by his changeless desire for, and knowledge of, their good. Nothing that creatures do, and nothing that happens to them, can cause any increase (or decrease) in this desire and knowledge. Christian prayer presupposes that God's mind and will are immutable. Even if we say... that God does not know future free choices in their concrete actuality, he knows them perfectly as possibilities; he is (as the Creator) wholly sovereign over them; so that he is necessarily and timelessly adapted to them and to all their consequences. (Owen 1971: 87)

It seems to me that in this passage Owen has set forth an idea that can be qualified and elaborated into a successful defense of the classical claim that God is impassible in will yet loving in nature.

Before we turn to development of this idea, let us look at two other expressions of it. The first is by another British thinker, Peter T. Geach. Geach employs the game of chess to show that we are free but that, nonetheless, due to God's complete knowledge of the game of life, his will cannot be thwarted. Geach writes:

A parable I have found useful is this: a chess master, without looking at the board, plays a score of opponents simultaneously; his knowledge of chess is so vastly superior to theirs that he can deal with any moves they are going to make, and he has no need to improvise or deliberate. There is no evident contradiction in supposing that God's changeless knowledge thus governs the whole course of the world, whatever men may choose to do. (Geach 1972: 325)

In a later work, *Providence and Evil*, Geach expands on his point:

God is the supreme Grand Master who has everything under his control. Some of the players are consciously helping his plan, others are trying to hinder it; whatever the finite players do, God's plan will be executed; though various lines of God's play will answer to various moves of the finite players. God cannot be surprised or thwarted or cheated or disappointed. God, like some grand master of chess, can carry out his plan even if he has announced it beforehand. "On that square," says the Grand Master, "I will promote my pawn to Queen and deliver checkmate to my adversary": and it is even so. No line of play that finite players may think of can force God to improvise: his knowledge of the game already embraces all the possible variant lines of play, theirs does not. (58)

Later in *Providence and Evil* Geach says explicitly that God "knows all possibilities of development," and he adds: "I should admit that my account made God's knowledge limited only if I had to ascribe to God such things as surprise, frustration, regret, and improvisation: but of course I deny that I need ascribe them to God" (141). Geach goes too far, I shall argue later, in claiming that God has "complete control over what actually happens" at all times, but his understanding of God's knowledge of possibilities and of its significance for divine providence seems basically correct.

An even more recent expression of the position that I believe is correct can be found in 'Properties, Modalities, and God' by Thomas V. Morris. Morris, reacting to a passibilist statement by Richard Swinburne (1977: 214), writes, "The position I am presenting is perfectly consistent with the divine intentions being indexed to, or conditional upon, contingencies arising in the created universe." Morris asks, "Why can't it always and immemorially have been the case that God intends to do A if B arises, or C if D comes about?" This understanding of God would accommodate those instances in which it appears that God has changed his will in response to a development in the world, such as the Ninevites repenting, when in fact God has not changed his will but rather has willed immemorially a change from "the Ninevites are going to be punished" to "the Ninevites are not going to be punished" should the Ninevites repent (Morris 1984: 47–8). The distinction between willing a change and changing one's will is pointed up nicely in Thomas Aquinas' *Summa Theologiae* Ia, q. 19, a.7: "The will of God is altogether immutable. But notice in this connection that changing one's will is different from willing a change in things. For a person whose will remains unalterable can will that something should happen now and its contrary happen afterwards."[2] Hence, should the Ninevites repent, "there would be no change in God's intentions, just a change with regard to which of his immemorial intentions he would in fact enact. And this would be wholly due to their conditional form, not to any change of mind on God's part" (Morris 1984: 48). Morris adds, in line with Geach, that because of God's exhaustive knowledge of possibility, "No development would take God by surprise and force him to improvise in his governance of the world" (48). Now let us develop this idea in Owen, Geach, and Morris, in relation to some of the criticisms of impassibilism by Hartshorne and others.

Could a being impassible in will be loving? I do not see why not. If, for example, we distinguish between the disposition and the exercise of love, it seems entirely possible that a being impassible in will could be loving in disposition, i.e., could be disposed such that it would act lovingly toward any existing entity. To say that such a being was loving by nature or was love would be to say that it would love itself, and, should there be other individuals in existence, it would also love them. Hartshorne appears to agree with the possibility that a being could be loving by nature in the dispositional sense. Note the following statement: "We say, God is holy, not that he is holiness. Only 'love' is an abstraction which implies the final concrete truth. God 'is' love, he is not merely loving, as he is merely righteous or wise (though in the supreme or definitive way)" (Hartshorne 1941: 111). Clearly, then, according to Hartshorne God's love is impassible and even immutable. No one and nothing caused him to acquire it, can cause him to lose it, or can increase or diminish it. Love is God's very nature, and to love is to care about and act for the good of the beloved.

Were Hartshorne to accept my argument that a God impassible in will could be loving in disposition, he would almost certainly add that the love of such a being would be empty, worthless sentiment because if God's loving will cannot be affected by anything external, then it cannot be affected by the changing circumstances, desires, and needs of our lives; consequently, it cannot be related to our lives in realistic, relevant ways. In such an instance it would seem sheer mockery to tell people that God loved them, as though by turning to God they could affect his will or expect him to reach out to them in the circumstances of their need. For the following reasons, however, I do not believe these conclusions follow.

We have already established that a God impassible in will could be loving in disposition. It would follow from this that God would provide for the welfare of any existent creatures, and given, on the classical model, that God in his omniscience always knows all possibilities, it would be possible for him prior to the creation of the world to be decided as to how to respond to all possible free actions in the world that he creates (though the word "respond" now becomes misleading, as we will see).[3] In brief, in his omniscience God always knows all possible circumstances and actions of free agents, and in his love and wisdom he can be eternally resolved as to how to respond to each of those possibilities. Hence, God's actions never need be chosen because of or in response to creaturely actualities. God could have been eternally resolved that if p_1 (a specific person) does a_1 (a specific act) at t_1 (a specific time), then he, God, would do a_2 at t_2. It follows from this that God can make and enact loving decisions without the actual world having any influence upon what he decides and wills.

Hartshorne accepts part of the preceding point but not all of it. In *Man's Vision of God* he writes, "In so far as God has *resolved* what the future shall be, he never relents or changes his resolution" (112). But Hartshorne's acceptance of this point is limited, like Brasnett's, to general resolutions such as the resolution to promote the growth of knowledge. He does not allow that God's resolutions could extend to specific acts as well as to general goals and principles. Presumably he omits this possibility because he believes that God cannot know all possibilities in the classical sense and therefore cannot know in advance of a creaturely free act all that is necessary for deciding a proper response to it.[4]

If the classical position is correct that God *can* have such knowledge, it follows that God can make for the world specific as well as general resolutions independently of the occurrence of worldly events. From this it follows that God could provide lovingly for the world though his will be invulnerable to influence from the world. Whether the assumption is true on which these conclusions are predicated, viz., the classical assumption that God can know eternally all possibilities, will be taken up in Chapter 3.[5]

It follows from the preceding analysis that God need never decide his response to our actions *after* we have performed them. Yet many philosophers and theologians have believed just the opposite. Origen wrote, "The Father himself is not impassible. If he is asked, he takes pity and experiences grief, he suffers something of love..." (Grant 1966: 30). Whether God "experiences grief" and "suffers something of love" will be taken up in Chapter 7, "Divine impassibility in feeling," but that he "takes pity," i.e., *does* something differently as a result of our request, can be appropriately treated here. Origen's sentiment that God takes pity in response to our request is captured more broadly in a statement from Hartshorne's *Creative Synthesis and Philosophic Method*: "God changes us by changing himself in response to our previous responses to him, and to this divine response to our response we subsequently respond" (277). It seems clear from this statement that, according to Hartshorne, God's actions are decided *after* our own actions and in response to them. Jung Lee sets forth the same position in *God Suffers For Us*:

The God whom we understand in Christ is certainly "not like that divinity of platonism who is unconcerned, and therefore unmoved," but "He alters his behavior in accordance with the changes in man." Thus, "God 'reacts' to the acts of men, and in that He 'reacts,' He changes". (40)

Shortly thereafter Lee notes that people's actions are not to be understood as causes of divine responses but as occasions of divine response – God thereby retaining his freedom. I assume that Hartshorne and Pike would accept this qualification. Still, the picture of divine action that Lee presents is one of God discovering at t_1 what a free creature does in its freedom at t_1 and subsequently deciding what to do in response. It also seems clear that Nelson Pike would contend that if God is a loving person, then this is the way we must picture his relation to the world.

Origen, Lee, and Pike, I believe, have not appreciated adequately the possibility that not only God's general objectives but also his specific decisions with regard to all possibilities can be part of his eternal will. If this can be the case, then it follows that anyone who holds the classical position that God knows eternally all possibilities should also hold that God can be loving in nature yet impassible in will because he can know independently of all actual situations all that he needs to know in order to make appropriate decisions relevant to every possible situation. Hence, there is never any good reason for God to wait until after an event (or even until it is occurring) in order to decide a response to it and to will accordingly; hence, there is no good reason why his will should be affected by what actually happens – even if he does not know eternally the choices of free agents. His will can be indexed to possibilities rather than actualities.

The preceding argument is not immediately relevant to Hartshorne because he believes that God cannot know future individuals and will never know all possibilities. Consequently, God, according to his conception, would be irresponsible to make irreversibly all of his decisions in advance of the relevant actualities because those actualities might disclose to God something that he did not know and which should have made a difference in how he responded. In Chapter 3 we will examine this position of Hartshorne's and why I reject it, but I believe I have already shown at the least that, because the classical position holds that there is no limitation on God's knowledge of possibilities, that position is not involved in self-contradiction or incoherence in claiming that God is both loving in nature and impassible in will.

But what do we do with Nelson Pike's claim that we ought not to think of God as immutable in will because, after all, he might want to change his mind, and, if he were immutable, he couldn't change his mind? We must reject it for reasons that are implicit in what has been said already.[6] I can think of no reason why God would ever want to change his mind, and several reasons why he would not want to do so. First, given eternal knowledge of all possibilities (henceforth "EKP"), God will never know anything more of relevance to the determination of his will than he has always known. Hence, he will never want to change his mind because he discovers something of relevance that he did not know earlier. There is, then, no reason why all of the intentions he will ever have could not have existed eternally. And, since it doesn't make sense to think of God as putting off until later what he could have done earlier, it seems reasonable to assume that all the intentions that God will ever have have always been existent. In brief, God's will has always been resolved with regard to every possibility, and because it is impossible that God could improve upon his decisions by the discovery of some hitherto unknown fact, it is unreasonable to believe that he might want to change his mind or would change his mind.

This is, of course, radically different from the human case. Sometimes we humans carefully plan what we will do at t_2 if p_1 does a_1 at t_1, but even so we may not follow through on our resolve because we forget to do so, or we succumb to moral weakness, or we discover that a_1 and its consequences were not what we thought they would be, or we discover that, though they were what we thought they would be, our reaction was not what we thought it would be. But none of these considerations would apply to God. He does not forget; he cannot be lured into betraying his resolve out of moral weakness (I_3), and because of his perfect self-knowledge and EKP he will never learn at any time anything about himself or anything else of relevance to making a decision for a later time. Finally, whereas change of resolve in a human case is virtuous when it is for the sake of a better resolution, a change in God's case could only indicate a defect in God because it would have to result from his being fickle or ignorant. My reasons for this claim are as follows. Either a change of resolve on God's part is for a better resolution or it is not. If it is for a better resolution, that indicates a defect in God's earlier resolution and therefore a defect in God's ability to formulate resolutions. If it is not a change for the better but a change for the worse, that indicates a defect in God's ability to stick by a good resolution. If the change is neither for better nor worse, but simply to a different resolution that is equal in value, that indicates fickleness in God – a changing of one's mind without good reason, and it might raise a question as to the trustworthiness of the promises of God.[7] My conclusion, then, is that, even if God can change his mind, there is no good reason to think he would do so. His resolves relate to all possible eventualities and cannot be improved upon.

IMPASSIBILITY AND ACTION

Is it the case that even if God's *decisions* for all time can be made eternally that still he must implement them at the right times and therefore must be passible to what is going on in the world so that he will know when to do what he has willed eternally? That is, even granted EKP, must not God be affected by actuality in order to know *when* to implement his decisions, even if he does not have to be affected by actuality in order to decide *what* to implement? I do not think so. Whether God is eternal or not, it is conceivable that his will could be not only decided eternally but also implemented eternally. Specifically, God's will could be that if p_1 does a_1 in c_1 (a certain set of circumstances), then e_1 (event$_1$) will occur; whereas if p_1 does a_2 in c_1, then e_2 will occur, and so on for every action that p_1 might perform in c_1.[8] But God should not be thought of as not willing e_1, e_2, *et al.*, until p_1 does a_1, or a_2, etc.; rather, he should be thought of as eternally willing a set of mutually exclusive possibilities the actualization of some of which is contingent upon human action.[9] Hence, God should not be thought of as implementing now this decision and now that. He should be conceived as eternally willing *and doing* everything that he ever wills and does.

Whether God is thought of as temporal or non-temporal, then, granted EKP we should not think of God as having to wait on a human action in order to decide his response or in order to know when to implement his eternal will in response to that particular action. Not only is God's decision eternally made for each action that I might perform at any time, but his will is eternally exercised with regard to each of my possibilities; to put this another way, his actions are eternally in place; or, again, he is eternally doing everything that he ever does. Hence, his actions are more properly called "*pre*sponses" than "*re*sponses."[10] God not only decides independently of our actions his response for each of our possible actions; he also wills independently each of those responses. Therefore, when we in our freedom actualize a possibility, God's "reaction" is and was eternally there. What comes after our action is not God's decision; it is what he has eternally willed given our action — no matter what that action might be.

Obscure as this position might seem at first, we are not without a human analogue. Consider a scientific genius who constructs a maze of a building — a little world, if you will — in which is implemented his will for a person whom he places therein. The person, whom we will call "the subject," is initially placed unconscious in an inner room that has four doors. Soon he wakes up and finds himself there. The scientist has willed that if the subject goes through door A he will slide down a chute into an aromatic room with four more doors; if instead of going through door A he goes through door B he will be forced by a slow but frightening beast to choose between two more doors; and so on. Perhaps I should add that in any room in which the subject refuses to choose, he will after a time be constrained to do so by a most unpleasant sound or odor, or else drop through a trap door. Obviously, no matter what the subject's choice, he subsequently experiences the will of the scientist — even though that will has been implemented in advance of the subject's choices.

The situation described is so far deistic but need not be. The scientist could accompany the subject through it all, providing companionship, clues, and counsel, though enjoying by various means protection from the anger or excessive dependence of the subject and from the physical impact of his various choices, knowing all along what the various stages and the ultimate outcomes of his choices will be, even though he does not know which choices the subject will make. If we extrapolate from the building to the world and from the scientist to God, it seems to me plausible that God could have constructed the world in such a way that, whatever we do in our freedom, our subsequent experience is always what he has eternally willed for us, and God no more need do anything *after* our choices in order to ensure that we experience what he has willed eternally than the scientist need do anything after the subject chooses door C rather than door A, B, or

D, in order to ensure that the subject experiences what the scientist has willed in advance.

Does this analogy break down if we press beyond the deistic mode to a theistic mode, i.e., from the scientist as mere observer to the scientist as companion? Yes, it does. If the scientist decides that he wants to accompany the subject, providing companionship at all times, explanations, encouragement, criticisms, and counsel at some times, the analogy fails because, even on the assumption that the scientist has not only pre-arranged the external environment of the subject so as to embody his (the scientist's) will, but has also decided in advance what his personal reaction will be to every possible action of the subject, the scientist will have to know *when* the subject is doing a certain act or feeling a certain way in order to know when to implement which of his predecisions regarding his *personal* responses to the subject, i.e., in order to know whether to encourage the subject, give him an explanation, criticize him, ignore him, or what. To be sure, the scientist can decide and embody in advance all of his *mediated* responses to the subject (that is, all of his responses that can be built into the environment) so that he does not have to make or implement those decisions after the subject's actions; but, even if we allow that he can *decide* in advance all of his personal reactions to the subject, what he cannot do is *embody* his personal reactions in advance (assuming, as we shall, that the scientist has always decided on two or more incompatible possible responses, each contingent on what the subject does). Consequently, the scientist must be passible to the subject in order to know whether and when to react personally to the subject in a predecided way. Apart from such passibility he would not know which of his decisions to implement when.

Is the same true for God? Must God be passible in knowledge in order to implement his will, even if his will has been resolved eternally? I do not think so. Indeed, even the scientist would not have to be passible in knowledge in order to have his will appropriately implemented were we to change his description in one respect. If the scientist were not a human but an extraordinary creature that was able to will that without change on his part he would be perceived by the human subject in any one of numerous ways contingent upon what the subject said or did, then, even though the scientist did not change anymore after the moment at which the subject awaked in the building, the subject would subsequently correctly perceive the scientist as encouraging him, criticizing him, ignoring him, etc., depending on what he the subject had to say or do and how the scientist had predecided his reactions to such sayings and doings. It seems conceivable, then, that such a creature would not have to be passible in order to know when to implement his predecisions about his personal responses to the subject. He would merely need to be there, and, no matter what the subject did, the subject would experience from moment to moment the mediated and unmediated will of the scientist without that will being passible with regard to content or implementation.

If we extrapolate from this extraordinary scientist to God, it seems that God could be eternally impassible in will and yet have his will implemented when it is appropriate, as he has eternally resolved it, without there being any change in himself. Understanding this point can be aided by considering the common belief that two people can experience God veridically in radically different ways at the same time; e.g., at one and the same time Pharaoh can experience the wrath of God and Moses the peace of God. This divine possibility does not work so well on the human level. If one witness said of a human that he was fulminating with wrath at t_1 and a second witness said that the same person was profoundly tranquil at t_1, we would say that it was impossible that both witnesses were correct. Why they could not both be correct seems to have something to do with our bodiedness. We are not capable of expressing wrath and tranquility at the same time, or of being wrathful and tranquil at the same time.

God is not bodied, however, and we commonly accept that he can relate to different people in different ways at the same time. But, if he is capable of being experienced in different ways by different people at the same time without there possibly being any change in him since the experiences are simultaneous, and, since the different people could not possibly be experiencing different parts of God at the same time (unlike the blind men feeling the elephant), why could not one person experience God in different ways at different times without there being any change over time in God's will or what he is doing? We should not think of God as having to readjust himself subsequent to c_1 in order to do what he has willed in response to c_1, as though he were a boxer slipping, parrying, and ducking a series of punches. God doesn't have to do anything after c_1 that he hasn't always been doing in order for me to experience subsequently his eternal will for me no matter what I in my freedom did in c_1. Hence, God can perform eternally and therefore simultaneously acts that are apprehended by temporal creatures as occurring at different points in time. As Aquinas might put it, God can will and affect changes without changing his will.[11]

A critic might make the following responses. "First, the fact that we cannot punish one person and comfort another simultaneously does not rule out the possibility that God can. If we had, for example, more arms and a second mouth that we could work independently, we, too, could simultaneously comfort one person and punish another." But that would miss my point, which is that God does not have or need parts in order to bring about simultaneously diverse experiences in different people, i.e.,

God does not accomplish these effects by disposing different parts of his body differently, as we would have to if we had the extra parts by which we could simultaneously relate to different people in different ways (which, by the way, we can do now to some extent, such as in protectively hugging one person with one arm while shoving another person away with the other arm). It is not the case, then, that God simultaneously communicates different messages to different people or causes different experiences in different people by disposing different parts of himself differently. God accomplishes all of these effects by mere willing.

To be sure, God could not simultaneously ignore a person and comfort him. The difference there is logical, not just physical. However, if my conception of God is correct, then God could simultaneously be resolved such that if Jones does a_1 he will feel ignored by God, whereas if he does a_2 he will feel comforted by him, without any change of will or action on God's part subsequent to Jones' action. "But," my critic might reply, "if at t_1 Jones veridically experiences God ignoring him, then at t_1 God is not comforting him. Similarly, if at t_2 Jones veridically experiences God as comforting him, then at t_2 God is not ignoring him. Now if God is ignoring (and not comforting) Jones at t_1 and comforting (and not ignoring) Jones at t_2, then there has been a change in God's actions, for the definition of a change in a subject is that the same proposition is both true and not true of it." My critic is certainly correct that a change must have taken place, but it does not follow that God has changed. Obviously Jones has changed, but whether God has changed is open to question. After all, just because the same pot of soup tastes wonderful today and awful tomorrow does not mean that the soup has changed. I may have got stomach flu meanwhile. Similarly, that I feel God's presence today rather than his profound absence may have nothing to do with a change in God and everything to do with a change in me. To be sure, God is causally responsible for the fact that Jones changes from feeling ignored by God to feeling comforted by God, and that I change from feeling God's absence to feeling his presence, but those changes could be due to the ways in which Jones and I have realigned ourselves with God.[12]

Let me summarize our progress to this point, and then we will explore more fully the nature of change and its bearing on how we should think about God.

God's love is immutable and his resolve is impassible. Nothing we can do or suffer at any point in time will change his love for us or his decisions about us. Hence, what we do or suffer will make no difference in what God wills or under what circumstances his will is enacted. He has always already decided in his love, wisdom and freedom what he will do for every possible free choice that we can make, and his decisions are implemented eternally. Consequently, what is subsequent to our action at t_1 is never God's response to our action but only our experience of God's eternal will for us as a result of what we have done at t_1. There is no change in God's will at t_1 or t_2 or between t_1 and t_2, nor should there be. The change is in us and our relationship to God; hence Aquinas is warranted in saying that God's relation to us is external as regards God's will, i.e., involves no change in God with regard to his will.[13] Indeed, what could or should be changed in God's will by what I actually do? I cannot change what he knows in advance *I might* do; therefore it is entirely conceivable that God could and would decide in advance and irrevocably how to respond to anything that I can do. We, too, can to some extent decide in advance a set of personal responses that are contingent upon what someone else does, but we cannot implement such responses in advance because of our corporal limitations. If our predecisions include anger if a certain person does one thing and affection if he does another, we cannot in advance of the situation be simultaneously angry and affectionate as we wait for that person to act, nor would such behavior on our part be appropriate. But God is not bodied and so he does not have to rearrange his body or facial expression when willing that we know his forgiveness and no longer his wrath; hence, there need be no change in God's will from t_1 to t_2 when we correctly go from feeling his wrath to feeling his forgiveness. The change is in us; that is, as a result of a change in us (repentance), we experience God's forgiveness at t_2 rather than his wrath, as at t_1, because he has eternally willed that if we did a_1 at t_1 we would experience his wrath and if we did a_2 at t_2 we would experience his forgiveness.

Contemporary discussion of the externality of God's relations to the world has in analytic philosophy been recast in terms of what Peter Geach calls "Cambridge change" (Geach 1969: 71–4, 99; 1972: 321–3). A Cambridge change takes place whenever an assertion about a thing changes from true to false, or vice versa. If "The window in my office is open" was true but now is false, then a change in the world has taken place. However, the fact that a Cambridge change has taken place, i.e., a mere change from a proposition being true to being false, does not enable us to infer that there has been a change in the thing about which the proposition is. As Anthony Kenny puts it, in agreement with Geach, the concept of Cambridge change "shows that not every change in the truth-value of a predication about an object is a genuine change in it" (Kenny 1979: 41). For example, if "Socrates is taller than Plato" is true now but false later, that does not enable us to infer that Socrates has changed. Perhaps he has remained the same height and Plato has grown. Further, "My shoes are the biggest shoes in the room" might change from true to false without my shoes changing in the least. A Cambridge change would be brought about if someone came into the room with larger shoes than mine. Hence, an assertion about a thing can change from true to false or false to true without there being the least change in the thing about which the assertion is. All the changes could be in the things to which the subject is explicitly or implicitly related. It may be, then, that no change in the world entails a change in God's will but that, rather, changes in the world, such as Creel now experiencing God's wrath and later God's forgiveness, turn upon changes in Creel and not in God.[14]

Given the understanding of impassibility that has been elaborated, it seems entirely possible for God to be impassible in nature and will, yet to love the world and to provide for its members in all of their uniqueness. Still, some people are concerned that the notion of an impassible God is an unappealing notion, and hence a religiously deficient notion. Recall, for example, Bertrand Brasnett's statement that "a very real and living idea of God" requires that we think of God as "functioning in time, changing his methods to meet varying needs..." (Brasnett 1928: 94). More recently Richard Swinburne has examined the kind of position that I have developed. He concludes that it is coherent, yet he rejects it because he judges that it fails to satisfy religious sentiment: "If God had thus fixed intentions 'from all eternity' he would be a very lifeless thing; not a person who reacts to men with sympathy or anger, pardon or chastening because he chooses to there and then." The biblical conception of God is of God "in continual interaction with men, moved by men as they speak to him, his action being often in no way decided in advance." Further, "Only a God who acts and chooses and loves and forgives is the God whom we wish to worship, and the pursuit of these activities, since they involve change of state, means being in time."[15]

In a slightly later book, *The Existence of God*, Swinburne takes up this theme again. First he says that a world entirely lawful, except for human choices, would be a world in which God "would never respond to men's sins as they committed them, their requests and acts of worship as they made them. And that would give our dealings with him a very impersonal quality" (238). He adds that God could, of course, eternally will special events and even miracles, so that the world would not be entirely lawful, even apart from human choices. But he laments that the occurrence of any such special event "would have been built into the world in advance."

God would not have been responding to the man's choice of a selfish path as he made it. God has the reason of friendship to seek living interaction with the men which he has made, conscious beings and free agents like himself. Hence one would expect him to intervene in the natural order occasionally in response to the human situation, especially in answer to request (i.e., prayer) for good things. (239)

Now let us evaluate these statements by Swinburne.[16]

Swinburne's fundamental point seems to be that to think of God as provident but non-reactive, i.e., as providing for our needs but antecedently to or independently of our actions, could not help but result in a notion of God as lifeless and impersonal. Several responses are in order. First, Swinburne is assuming that, when more than one interpretation of God is possible, we can reasonably assume that that interpretation is true which best satisfies our needs. For example, if it is possible for God to decide eternally his reactions to our behavior or to wait and decide them as or after we act, so as to engage in "living interaction" with us, then because the latter would be more religiously appealing, we can be confident that that is what God does. I do not believe this assumption is without merit. We should be able to make some inferences, at least at the level of plausibility, from the character of God to how he would relate to us. My disagreement is with Swinburne's assumption that humans cannot but feel that a volitionally impassible God would be alien. Generations of classical theists have not found God so conceived to be lifeless or impersonal or unresponsive or non-reactive. Nor am I troubled or put off by the notion of God having made eternally all of his decisions relative to me. I feel that, though God is volitionally impassible in relation to me, he is always aware of me, concerned about me, and has provided for me as carefully, thoughtfully, and lovingly as he would have had he had to wait until after I acted to do so. His volitional impassibility only makes me marvel all the more at how superior his abilities are to ours.

Another point of importance is that, if God can eternally decide and enact his decisions, as Swinburne allows, then it will be impossible to tell whether a feeling of the passing of God's wrath is something that God decided on and enacted only after our repentance or whether it was something that God decided and willed eternally and which we experienced as a result of our repenting rather than not repenting. I do not believe that the truth of this matter would be disclosed by a phenomenological analysis of religious experience. Rather, given that there is no universal human need in this respect, we must decide between these alternatives by inference from our concept of God, and it seems to me that, because, as Swinburne allows, God can have made his decisions and enacted his will eternally and because a devout religious life is possible on this assumption, as the classical tradition of theism testifies, and because the assumption of God's volitional impassibility is a more natural and simple assumption than its contradictory, we should prefer it.

Before leaving the question of the compatibility of my understanding of God with a personal relationship to him, let us examine some comments on this point by an American process philosopher, James Keller.[17] Keller points out that if God's actions are indexed to possibility rather than actuality, it follows that God's actions are never personalized to an actual individual. That is, God never makes a decision about you or me; his decisions are made relative to the possibility of you or me. Hence, in making his decision God was not responding to us – and doesn't that take the personal touch out of his decision? Doesn't God on this assumption become a mere force like gravity that impersonally causes heavy objects to fall on the surface of the earth and allows much lighter ones to float above it? Indeed, doesn't the Creel conception of God make it logically impossible ever to think of God as personally related to an actual individual?

Further, doesn't this conception mean that everything about the individual's relation to God depends on the individual rather than on God, given that God's will is settled eternally so that therefore what the individual experiences in relation to God always depends totally on what the individual does rather than on anything that God does? For example, if I repent and consequently experience God's forgiveness, it is not because God has responded to my repentance that I feel forgiveness; rather it is the case that by my repentance I have put myself in the stream of his forgiveness.

Finally, note that, even if God decides in advance or independently of my action how he will respond if I do a_1, in order for his response to be a genuine response there must be something that God starts to do after my act and because of it. Hence, if God is going to enter into personal interaction with us, then even if his decisions about us are eternal his responses to us cannot be.

These criticisms by Keller are sensitive, important ones that merit careful attention. Concerning the first one, Keller is correct that if God is volitionally impassible and has EKP but does not know future free acts, as I shall argue later, then God's decisions for actuality are not in response to actual individuals but are made independently of actuality. Still, if God's decision as to what he will do if an individual of my description does a_1 in circumstances c_1 is not made in response to the actual me, does that mean that I should feel personally slighted? Does that mean I should feel that God has not made his decisions about *me*, and that therefore he was not planning for or thinking about me after all, but merely about some possible entity? I see no logical constraint to feel this way, nor do I feel any emotional compulsion to do – which means, unless I have overlooked something, that my conception of God does not entail logically or necessitate causally the kind of negative reaction that Keller feels in response to what I have proposed.

Granted that God has EKP, he can make all decisions relevant to the existence and possible behavior of a creature such as I, should I come into existence. Obviously I do exist, but if my existence is contingent on the free decisions of other creatures, viz., my parents, then, if God does not know the future behavior of free creatures, then God did not know whether a creature of my description would come into existence or not. As far as God's providence was concerned that did not matter, though, because he, granted EKP, was able to make all the decisions relevant to a world in which I might come to pass, whether I came to pass or not and, if I did come to pass, no matter what decisions and actions I made and performed in my freedom. Such ability and decision on God's part does not bother me in the least. It only enhances my awe of the divine mode of being.

I agree that for me to feel that God has not simply provided for me as a possibility but is also aware of me as an actuality, it is necessary for me to believe that God is aware of what is coming to pass in the world and is seeing which of his contingent decisions is coming to pass and which are not, i.e., is seeing his will actualized in the world and in our lives as we make our decisions and act on them, but that kind of awareness is ensured under the doctrine of omniscience. Hence, God's decisions were not personalized to me but they were personalized to the possibility of me and could not possibly have been more thorough or caring had God waited until I became actual and active. I see no reason, then, to allow the doctrine of volitional impassibility to stand between me and a feeling of personal relationship with God, especially since it is part of a conception of God according to which God provides for me wisely and lovingly and observes at every moment how his will is being fulfilled in my life.

Keller's second point is that, according to volitional impassibility, the way God's will is being fulfilled in my life means that everything depends on me and nothing on him. If I repent, God doesn't forgive me; rather, I just put myself in the stream of his forgiveness rather than in the stream of his disapproval. My reply is that this metaphor of putting oneself in the stream of something is not entirely inapt, but it needs to be used cautiously. First, it is not the case that my experience is entirely up to me; whether I feel the surge of a vigorously flowing stream does not depend entirely on whether I place myself in it; it depends also on the fact that it is flowing vigorously rather than sluggishly or not at all, and that it is a stream of water rather than of lava or air, etc. Second, the stream of water cannot be compared to God as a source of experience because a stream of water cannot decide how it will affect someone who steps into it whereas God can decide how he will affect someone who repents in a certain way for a certain sin in certain circumstances. Whether God causes me to feel his forgiveness and how God causes me to feel his forgiveness, the texture of the experience, so to say, is something over which God has enormous latitude, whereas the stream has no latitude over whether I will experience it or how I will experience it if I step into it. If Keller says, "But once God's will has been made up, whatever he has decided is fixed and therefore when we repent it is like stepping into the stream which can have only one effect on us," I would demur by pointing out that God could have chosen to have a different effect on us whereas the stream could not have, so what we experience depends on what God has decided as well as on what we decide. Hence, on two counts, it is not the case that what we would experience in relation to a volitionally impassible God is entirely up to us.

Keller's third criticism is that a volitionally impassible God cannot truly respond to us and that, therefore, he cannot be personally related to us. This is basically the same as one of Swinburne's points taken up above, but it is such a difficult point that it merits further attention. First, though it follows from volitional impassibility that God does not make his decision after repentance or initiate his forgiving of me only after my repentance, it is only after my repentance that I begin to experience God's forgiveness, and I begin to experience it only because God has decided that I should, and my experiencing of it is an effect of God acting upon me. Hence, God has willed eternally that, should I repent for a certain sin in certain circumstances, I should consequently experience his forgiveness in a certain way. Then God experiences me come into being, commit that sin in those circumstances, repent of that sin, and then experience his forgiveness in a certain way because of what he has eternally willed and done. If Keller and Swinburne want to reserve "response" for only those actions the willing of which is initiated after the actions which occasion them, I have no objection, but I know of no good reason to hold that responses in this sense are a necessary condition of a personal relationship between God and creature. There can be mutual awareness, caring, deciding, and willing between beings without it being the case that these activities are initiated temporally by both participants in the relationship. Consequently, there is no good reason why such a relationship could not be genuinely personal. To be sure, given Keller's definition of "response," God may not be responding to my repentance, but it can still be the case that God has made a decision about the possibility of my repentance and is acting such that I will experience his will regarding that possibility should I actualize it. Before I repent God is doing all that he needs to do in order for me to experience his forgiveness should I repent. Hence, though I begin to feel God's forgiveness only after I repent, it need not be the case that that is so because God begins doing something different after I repent. His decision and action *vis à vis* my repentance could be eternal, i.e., not made and implemented at a certain point in time, but always made and implemented. Yes, then, because God's part of the interaction as to whether and how I should experience his forgiveness is eternally decided, it is now up to me whether and how I experience God's forgiveness. I cannot help but walk in the stream of his grace as eternally decided for me, but the bottom I walk on and the currents I feel are not an impersonal matter on God's part or mine.

As a final response to Swinburne, who emphasizes the importance of God's response to petitionary prayer, let us focus on the question as to whether petitionary prayer would be rendered meaningless by the volitional impassibility of God.[18]

In their *Development of Logic*, William and Martha Kneale say that "Statements, commands, requests, etc., are to be distinguished by their different functions in social life. The function of statements is mainly, though not solely, to convey information, that of commands and requests to induce people to do things, and so on" (53). Swinburne also thinks of petitionary prayer as a species of request, i.e., a request is an act aimed at inducing any person to do something, and a prayer is an act aimed at inducing God to do something. However, I would argue that petitionary prayer should not be thought of as a stimulus intended to induce or even, to use Jung Lee's weaker term, occasion a change in the party being addressed. Why? Because the party being addressed is always God, and God in his omniscience always knows what is good for us and in his love always wills what is good for us. For all possible situations he tenselessly knows and wills what is good for us, though we must take advantage in time of what he knows and wills. Hence, in petitionary prayer we should not think of ourselves as trying to *prevail* upon God; we should think of ourselves as trying to *avail* ourselves of his grace. Jesus' Gethsemane prayer seems paradigmatic of these points. It contains both heartfelt candor – "Father, take this cup from me" – and profound confidence in God's wisdom and love – "Yet thy will be done." By praying Jesus acted on the classical conviction that sometimes we must ask of God in order to receive; by concluding "Thy will be done," he expressed the classical conviction that God always already knows and wills what is good for us. Hence, prayer should not be conceived as an effort to influence God's will, as Hartshorne, Pike, and Swinburne would have it, but as an effort to avail ourselves of God's eternal providence for our welfare.

There is, then, nothing in the doctrine of volitional impassibility which requires that God be thought of as aloof, unresponsive, impersonal, or insensitive to the world. Given the understanding of God that has been elaborated, it is entirely possible for God to be impassible in will yet to love the world, to provide for its individuals, to relate to them in their uniqueness, and to make his presence to them keenly felt. Hence, the concept of God as immutable in love and impassible in will seems entirely adequate religiously and philosophically. Whether a conception of God as impassible not only in nature and will but also in knowledge and feeling would be philosophically and religiously adequate remains to be investigated. First, however, inasmuch as my defense of God's impassibility in will is based on the assumption that God knows all possibilities, I must provide a defense of that assumption, lest it and what I have based on it be dismissed out of hand.

3

Continuity, possibility, and omniscience

IT IS AN ASSUMPTION of classical theism that God knows not only the entire realm of actuality – past, present, and future – but that he also knows the entire realm of possibility in the sense of knowing all things that could have come to pass but will not, e.g., a certain shade of blue that will never become actual, or a certain member of a species of animal that will never exist.[1] Critics of classical theism have generally accepted without a blink God's knowledge of all possibilities and rushed on to dispute the claim to God's knowledge of the future. There is, however, a discerning philosopher who has challenged the claim that God knows all possibilities in the preceding sense. I speak of Professor Charles Hartshorne. To be sure, he holds that God is omniscient in the sense that he knows all actualities as actualities and all possibilities as possibilities, but he adds that possibilities are by nature vague and indeterminate to varying degrees so that, for example, God could not have known *that* shade of blue until it became actual; he could, at best, only have known of the possibility of new shades of blue, without knowing precisely what they would be like. The scope of this interpretation of possibility is enormous: it extends to the individual members of every species, to species themselves, and to possible worlds. Regarding the latter Hartshorne says, "Whatever possibilities there are God knows them. But there are, for me, no possibilities in the sense of Leibnizian possible worlds..."[2] Hence, not only individuals, but also species, genuses, and possible worlds exist only in a vague and indeterminate manner until they become actual.

If Hartshorne is correct, then obviously God's knowledge is much less extensive than traditional believers have thought, and, moreover, God's omniscience dictates that his knowledge will continually increase as more and more things become actual. A corollary of this point is that God's will could not be impassible and immutable because he would not be able to make his decisions about the world in advance of things actually occurring because one cannot knowledgeably and responsibly make decisions about one knows not what. Obviously, then, because of its attack upon the coherence of the traditional conception of God and current talk about possible worlds, Hartshorne's position is a formidable doctrine. I am convinced that, if his arguments for it are sound, then the jig is up for the classical conception of God and Leibnizian talk about possible worlds, such as we find in the writings of Saul Kripke, David Lewis, and Alvin Plantinga.

CHARLES PEIRCE ON CONTINUITY

Hartshorne's conclusions about God's knowledge of possibility appear to be based on Charles Peirce's analysis of continuity. There are discussions of continuity throughout the six volumes of *The Collected Papers of Peirce*, which were edited by Charles Hartshorne and Paul Weiss. Indeed, continuity is the central idea in Peirce's philosophy, whence he named his philosophy "synechism." Especially relevant to Hartshorne's conclusions are 1.163–72, 1.499, 3.563–70, and 6.164–213. In 1.165 and 3.569 we find keys to Peirce's understanding of continuity. In the former he says that "the idea of continuity involves the idea of infinity," and in the latter he says that a continuum is "something every part of which can be divided into any multitude of parts whatsoever." These points are elaborated in 6.170:

A true continuum is something whose possibilities of determination no multitude of individuals can exhaust. Thus, no collection of points placed upon a continuous line can fill the line so as to leave no room for others, although that collection had a point for every value towards which numbers, endlessly continued into the decimal places, could approximate; nor if it contained a point for every possible permutation of all such values.

It seems reasonably clear from the preceding passage that Peirce is defining, or at least describing, the nature of a continuum in terms of two claims, one positive and one negative. The positive claim is that a continuum is something which is divisible – the result of the division being of the type of the continuum divided, whether it be a line, an angle, a color spectrum, a pleasure spectrum, or something else. The negative claim is that a continuum is not exhaustively divisible into a finite number of results; between any two results, e.g., two points on a line or two shades on a continuum of red, it is possible in principle to derive an unlimitable number of additional points or shades of red. In brief, there are no atoms in a continuum (6.173).

This position of Peirce's on continuity, a position that I find persuasive, has a striking implication for our understanding of possibilities. If, following the terminology of W. E. Johnson, we speak of a continuum as a determinable and a point on the continuum as a determinate, it follows, according to Peirce, that determinable points, as they exist in a continuum, "are not individuals, distinct, each from all the rest" (3.568). The significance of this is that a possibility is not knowable in its distinctness until it becomes actual because before it becomes actual there is no "it" to be known. Before it becomes actual, at best we can only know of the possibility of something like it. Peirce develops this point in 6.185–7.

That which is possible is in so far *general* and, as general, it ceases to be individual. Hence, remembering that the word "potential" means indeterminate yet capable of determination in any special case, there may be a *potential* aggregate of all the possibilities that are consistent with certain general conditions; and this may be such that given any collection of distinct individuals whatsoever, out of that potential aggregate there may be actualized a more multitudinous collection than the given collection. Thus the potential aggregate is, with the strictest exactitude, greater in multitude than any possible multitude of individuals. But being a potential aggregate only, it does not contain any individuals at all. It only contains general conditions which *permit* the determination of individuals.   (6.185)

Clearly, then, neither human, angel, nor God can apprehend potentiality in the mode of an exhaustive set of individuals or, as Whitehead might put it, as a set of discrete eternal objects.

Peirce goes on to say that, though we can have only a vague idea of possible but unactualized individuals, it is not so with the classes of which those individuals would be members were they to become actual. Of the classes we can have a distinct idea. Consider, for example, the aggregate of whole numbers: "though the aggregate of whole numbers cannot be completely counted, that does not prevent our having a distinct idea of the multitude of all whole numbers. We have a conception of the entire collection of whole numbers. It is a *potential* collection, indeterminate yet determinable" (6.186; also 6.187). Similarly, of the potential aggregate of all abnumeral multitudes Peirce says, "This potential aggregate cannot be a multitude of distinct individuals any more than the aggregate of all the whole numbers can be completely counted. But it is a distinct general conception for all that – a conception of a potentiality" (6.187).

Peirce's final thrust in this series of statements is to warn that:

A potential collection, more multitudinous than any collection of distinct individuals can be, cannot be entirely vague. For the potentiality supposes that the individuals are determinable in every multitude. That is, they are determinable as distinct. But there cannot be a distinctive quality for each individual; for these qualities would form a collection too multitudinous for them to remain distinct.   (6.188)

Peirce's point seems to be that we can have a clear and distinct idea of the continuum or universal, e.g., length or redness, of which an actual individual is a part or an instance, but at best we can have only a vague and somewhat indeterminate idea of unactualized possibilities of a continuum. Why? Because potentiality can be grasped only in the form of continuity, and continuity is of the nature of infinity, and it is impossible in principle for us to know exhaustively the infinite individuals that can be actualized from a continuum.

Notice that in the preceding I said "impossible for *us* to know." Peirce does not explicitly draw the conclusion that it is also impossible for God to have such knowledge. Indeed, the spirit of several of his remarks seems contrary to such a conclusion – though they are not so explicit as one would like. See 2.227, 4.67, and 4.583. Whitehead does seem to have been explicit that God possesses such knowledge, as can be seen in his doctrine of eternal objects, and it is perhaps at this point that Hartshorne departs most sharply from Whitehead. It is possible, however, that Whitehead was wrong and that Peirce overlooked an important implication of his own position, so let us now look at Hartshorne's arguments for his claim that God can know potentiality only as vague and indeterminate.

HARTSHORNE ON GOD'S KNOWLEDGE OF POSSIBILITY

Hartshorne's position on continuity and possibility is set forth most fully in his early essay, "Santayana's Doctrine of Essence," and in his later chapter, "Abstraction: The Question of Nominalism." In both locations he cites Peirce extensively and summarizes Peirce's position on continuity as follows, using points on a line to illustrate his contention:

> ... continuity admits of any multitude, and since further a maximal multitude is impossible, and anything less than a maximal multitude of points on a line must omit something which could have been there, it follows that the continuum of possibilities cannot be any distinct set or multitude at all, but is rather something beyond multitude and definite variety, an inexhaustible *source of variety* rather than variety itself.
>
> (Hartshorne 1951: 166)

In *Creative Synthesis and Philosophic Method* Hartshorne makes it clear that for Peirce such continua were not restricted to mathematical or geometrical entities. "As Peirce held," he writes, "possible qualities of *feeling* form a continuum without definite parts" (65–6). These statements seem to me an accurate summary of Peirce's position on continuity and possibility, and I believe that position is correct. From this position Hartshorne derives the conclusion that, though God is always omniscient in the sense of knowing everything that can be known, still the scope or quantitative content of God's knowledge is continually increasing as new things come into actuality that could not have been known earlier because they did not exist in a manner in which they could have been known, viz., as actual, i.e., as precise and determinate. Let us look at numerous passages in which this conclusion is contained; later we will reconstruct Hartshorne's argument to this conclusion.

In his early opus, *Man's Vision of God*, Hartshorne wrote,

Everything which is in the least particular, such as "light blue," or "sour," we have no reason for regarding as eternal, not because there was or could ever be a time when blue was not blue, or when blue was green, but because there may have been a time when blue was the subject of no truth whatever, since no such item was included in the whole of reality, or in the content of omniscience. Not that it was then true that "blue is not included in reality," but that it is *now* true that the whole of what was then real failed to contain blue, since no color which then was real was what we now know as blue.

(245–6)

In a 1935 paper on Whitehead, Hartshorne expressed the preceding position using the color red as his illustration:

To argue that it must be eternally true that red is red and not blue, and that hence red itself must be eternal, is merely to beg the question. Of course it can never have been *false* that red is red, but if red is an emergent in the universe, then before this emergence it was neither true nor false that red was red – or anything else. For truth and falsity alike require ideas, and it is just the question whether an idea of red is or is not an eternal ingredient of the universe. The proposition *red is red* can never have had any but a positive truth-value; but if there was once a time when there was no such proposition, then at that time "it" could have had *no* truth-value, or any other property whatever, for there was no such it. Nor is there any criticism of Whitehead's work which has been more uniformly made even by sympathetic interpreters than this one of the unsatisfactoriness of the eternal objects.   (1972:32)

In a much more recent statement, Hartshorne voices similar sentiments:

I see no ground at all for supposing that, besides numbers or similarly abstract entities, including metaphysical categories, every quality of sensation or feeling that occurs in experience must have its eternal duplicate. Feeling as such, quality as such, yes, but not red, sweet, as determinate qualities identical with those we enjoy in experience. Feeling is a determinable of infinite range, not a vast sum of determinates.   (1970: 65–6)

Responding to criticism of the position set forth in the preceding passages, Hartshorne writes,

One objection to this view needs to be met at once. Against the idea of determinable characters it might be held that prior to determination of the determinable the determinations must have been there as possibilities, one for each determinate character that can ever arise. This may seem self-evident. It can, however, reasonably be denied, as follows. A determination, prior to coming into existence, was neither possible nor impossible, it was nothing, for there was no such "it," and only of what in some sense is can anything be predicated, even possibility or impossibility. *After* being constituted in existence, the "it" may then have the retrospective relation of absence from antecedent existence, but this relation is external to such existence.   (1951: 141)[3]

In other words, there is no eternal duplicate of any actuality which is identical with that actuality in every respect except that it lacks existence. That which becomes actual did not exist before, not even as a possibility (if what we mean by "a possibility" is something that has all the definiteness of an actuality except that it lacks the dimension of actual existence).

Consequently, as Alvin Plantinga argues in *The Nature of Necessity*, chapter 8, because we can properly make singular affirmations only about things that exist, we cannot properly say anything about something before it comes into existence. To be sure, of anything that exists it is true that it was possible for it to come into existence, but it does not follow that before it came into existence we could have meaningfully said that it was possible for it to come into existence.[4] Before it came into existence we could not have known precisely what we meant by speaking of "it"; we could not have been *referring* to "it" because it did not yet exist and therefore was not there to be referred to, and there could have been an indefinite number of things that would have satisfied any *description* that we might have given of "it."

By contrast, a completely specific possibility, one to which the Law of Excluded Middle applies in every respect, is actual.[5] Any other possibility is indeterminate to some extent and less than actual to that same extent. Hence, when anything becomes actual it is truly an emergent in the sense that *it* did not previously exist anywhere in reality – not even in the mind of God as a perfect copy lacking only actual existence.[6]

This position is restated in Hartshorne's more recent work, in which he reaffirms his unity with Peirce and his departure from Whitehead, who in *Science and the Modern Man* speaks of color as something that "haunts time like a spirit."

My view here is the Peircean one, obscure and difficult as it may be, that all specific qualities, i.e., those of which there can be negative instances in experience, are emergent, and that only the metaphysical universals are eternal, something like Peirce's Firstness, Secondness, Thirdness. I do not believe that a determinate colour is something haunting reality from all eternity, as it were, begging for instantiation, nor that God primordially envisages a complete set of such qualities.   (1970: 59)

A few pages later Hartshorne says regarding the creation of a painting,

The advance possibilities for a painting are only relatively definite. The pigments may already exist; the human senses are largely fixed. Thus the painter knows roughly what he can do. But that he can do just *this* which he subsequently does, not even deity can know until it is done. The "this" of an actuality simply has no advance status, modal or otherwise. Creativity does not map the details of its future actions, even as possible.
(65)

In recent correspondence, December 16, 1980, Hartshorne put his point this way:

What you or I now are is from the standpoint of eternity nonexistent. Not that we were impossible from that standpoint, but that "we" as individuals were not being in all. I reject the idea of *merely possible individuals*. All individuals are actual. God knows the actual as actual, the possible, all of it, as possible, and this means as more or less indefinite. Just before my Mother conceived me I was a somewhat definite possibility, and known to God as such, but before the human species there was no possibility (nor yet an impossibility) corresponding to Charles Hartshorne. Tomorrow's possibility is more definite today than it was a year ago, not only for us but for God.

Yet more light was shed on Hartshorne's understanding of possibility when he said in a paper delivered on March 7, 1981, to the Society for Philosophy of Religion,

... a large class of important modern philosophers reject the idea of eternal, and eternally knowable, possibilities except in extremely abstract forms such as mathematical possibilities, infinitely less particular than the fullness of concrete reality. As Peirce and Bergson vividly saw, actualization is particularization. Becoming is creation, production of new definiteness, not of exact duplicates of definiteness already and eternally in being.[7]

Later in the same response Hartshorne said, "The issue is not as to whether God knows all possibilities. I hold that the divine knowledge is all-inclusive, knowing actualities as actualities and possibilities as possibilities." "But," he adds in a postscript to his letter, as though continuing the preceding remark, "what some people call possibilities are not real at all but only mere words." Therefore they cannot be known by God or anyone else except as mere words.

Now let me present a summary of what I understand Hartshorne's argument to be. No two individuals on a continuum can be immediately close; therefore there can be an indefinite number of other individuals between every pair of discrete individuals on a continuum. From this it follows that it is impossible in principle for a continuum to be known exhaustively by means of a collection of individuals that constitute it; even an infinite collection of individuals would be inadequate because in between any two of them there could be an infinite number of others. Hence, no matter how many possibilities on a continuum one may be familiar with from their actualization, there are always even more of which one is ignorant, except perhaps in a vague and indeterminate way. Hence, even God in his omniscience cannot know all possible individuals, at least not as a set of discrete individuals. Rather, God must know unactualized possible individuals as contained in a continuum; but to know possible individuals as contained in a continuum is necessarily not to know them as determinate and discrete but as indeterminate and vague, and therefore it is not to know them as individuals. Hence, God, as we, must wait upon creativity to find out what is possible because we can only find out from the actual what is determinately possible. Prior to the actualization of possibility, i.e., the specific determination of possibility that creativity brings about from the infinitude of possibilities, we can only make guesses more or less approximate, depending on the range of our experience, from what is and has been actual to what is possible, e.g., from these shades of blue to the possibility of another shade of blue somehow between them.[8]

Part of the significance of the position that determinate qualities are emergent is that they could not have been known ahead of time in their determinateness. This means that God, as well as we, is continually increasing in knowledge as new shapes, colors, textures, creatures, etc., come to be, and it would seem to mean that sometimes God, as well as we, is completely surprised by what occurs, as when a new color (as distinguished from a new shade of the same color) occurs, or, even more dramatically, as when the perception of color occurs for the very first time. The latter would be an instance in which the first member of a species or genus becomes actual. Presumably Hartshorne would defend the idea that God, too, would be surprised upon such an occasion because, even though he might already be familiar with the genus, knowledge of the genus does not imply knowledge of its species, even as knowledge of a species does not imply knowledge of all the individuals that will belong to the species. Hartshorne makes this point with regard to individuals and species in the following statement:

To understand "whiteness," and to know all the things that ever have been or will be white, are two things different in principle. This is, it can be claimed, the very meaning of universality, without which we should have no rational knowledge. It is the definition of the universal that it does not involve all its instances.   (1951: 155)

With regard to the relation between species and genus Hartshorne says, "The ultimate eternal logos, the real essence of existence as such, includes all the generic factors necessary to knowledge, such as relation, time, plurality, number, quality, and the generic interrelations of these." But he adds that he does not "see any reason for supposing that such 'essences' as redness must be involved distinctly in the generic ideas" (1951: 164). Hartshorne summarizes these points and relates them to God in the following passage from *Man's Vision of God:*

it is the very nature of the universal that one can know the genus without knowing all the species, or any of them with perfect distinctness, and certainly without knowing the individual natures which the genus makes possible. Not even God sees the individual natures as items in the generic, for it is a contradiction to make the common property imply the differences, past and future alike, thus destroying temporal distinctions.

(133)

In brief, God knows eternally the genuses and species of which he is the instantiation, but all else he must learn at the window of creativity. Clearly, then, his knowledge cannot be wholly eternal, immutable, or impassible. Even with regard to what is possible in the way of worlds, God knows only "indeterminate possibilities for worlds, nothing more" (1970: 127).

In conclusion, if Hartshorne's analysis is correct, the classical conception of God's knowledge must be recognized as incoherent, and Leibnizian talk about possible words must be recognized as babble. Referring to the Leibnizian notion of "the completely defined possible world," described in what Plantinga calls "a world book," Hartshorne says, "there are, for me, no possibilities in the sense of Leibnizian possible worlds"; rather a possible world is merely the notion of "vague directions for further determination."[9]

AN ALTERNATIVE TO HARTSHORNE

The preceding sections on Peirce and Hartshorne have been purely expository, but my ultimate concern is philosophical. Hence, I turn now to evaluation of these positions. The core of Peirce's continuity thesis is that a continuum is infinitely divisible and therefore cannot be comprehended by apprehension of a set of discrete individuals, no matter how large the set. The core of Hartshorne's thesis on possibility is that it is impossible in principle for anyone, even an omniscient being, to have eternal knowledge of all possibilities by knowing possibilities independently of actualities. Apparently Hartshorne holds this position because he believes it is implied by Peirce's continuity thesis. I believe he is wrong in this belief – though this is certainly a difficult issue and his position a thoughtful one. My position is that Peirce's continuity thesis is correct and that there is a position on possibility that is compatible with Peirce's continuity thesis yet makes plausible how God can know all possibilities in the traditional sense. In order to argue successfully for this position against Hartshorne's thesis on possibility it seems clear that one must make plausible the idea that God's knowledge of possibilities is in some relevant sense exhaustive in spite of Peirce's continuity thesis. I believe this can be done as follows.

We are all familiar with the fact that we can take two sticks of equal length that are hinged at one end only and rotate them from a fully closed position to a fully open position, i.e., from an angle of 0° to an angle of 180°. If we close the sticks again, add an elastic band to the unhinged ends of the sticks, and then open them again from 0° to 180°, we will in the process have circumscribed the angularity of every possible isosceles triangle. I submit that, when we realize this, we will have understood what a Euclidean isosceles triangle is because we will have comprehended it as a continuum of possibilities. By moving the sticks from closed-in-line to open-in-line we exhaust the number of isosceles triangles that those sticks can make. There were an infinite number of points through which we passed and at which we could have stopped which would have constituted an isosceles triangle had we stopped. Further, there were no additional stopping places; we didn't miss a single point at which an additional triangle could have been generated. The same point could be illustrated by thinking in terms of screwing a crescent wrench from shut to open or of turning a rheostat from off to maximum.

To be sure, in generating our triangles we did not actually stop at an infinite number of places along the way. Moreover, it would be impossible for us or God to stop at every point along the way because such points are in principle inexhaustible. Even if God has been generating isosceles triangles of different angularities every moment for the whole of his existence and therefore has generated an infinite set of such triangles by now, he cannot have generated all possible discrete isosceles triangles (even on the assumption that the length of the equal sides is being held even) because, even if God generates an infinitely large set of such triangles, there is always possible an even larger such infinite set. Clearly, then, though a continuum is something from which an infinite number of individuals can be analyzed (abstracted/decided/identified/generated), a continuum could never be constructed by putting together any number of individuals or particulars. Indeed, part of the significance of a continuum is that it allows for inexhaustible creativity; even God cannot exhaust the richness of a continuum. Neither, however, can God be exhausted by a continuum. Part of the significance of his omnipotence is that he is able everlastingly and unrestrictedly to act according to the inexhaustible resources of limitless continuity. Presumably he is the only individual able to do so.

The significance of the preceding analysis is that, in understanding the isosceles triangle as a continuum of possibilities, we know all there is to be known about the possible relations among the angles of isosceles triangles. No isosceles triangle can henceforth come into existence the angularity of which could surprise us. For any isosceles triangle that ever becomes actual, we already know, and not merely in a vague and indeterminate sense, that its angularity is possible. Moreover, we can generalize from isosceles triangularity to triangularity in general and draw the same conclusion. No geometer should ever be surprised by a new triangle into saying, "I didn't know such a combination of angles was possible!" Hence, to understand the triangle as a continuum is to know independently of specific, actual triangles the possibility of all triangles that ever become actual subsequent to that understanding. If an individual's understanding of this is eternal, then, of course, to that individual no triangle that ever becomes actual will be unfamiliar. Whether such understanding could be eternal is an issue we will address later.

Meanwhile let us ask whether the fact that a continuum cannot consist of discrete individuals means that it must be impossible for God to know all possible individuals in advance of their becoming actual. The answer must be "yes" and "no". "Yes" for two reasons. First, as we have seen already, it is logically impossible for anyone to know as discrete all individuals that can possibly be excised from a continuum. Even if one extracts an infinite set of such individuals, there is always a yet larger set possible. Hence, an exhaustively infinite set of individuals could not have been known by now or ever be known, even in the mind of God. The second reason for saying that God cannot know *even one possible individual*, much less all possible individuals, in advance of its becoming actual is that a thing cannot be known as actual before it becomes actual. This is a point that Hartshorne's writings have helped me understand and with which I now concur. If that very triangle there, for example, somehow existed in the world but in a mode imperceptible to anyone but God until t_1, then it did not become actual at t_1; it merely became humanly perceptible at t_1. God knew it as actual before t_1 because it was actual before t_1. However, if the triangle was not actual before t_1 and became actual only at t_1, then even God did not know it as actual before t_1.

If one objects, "But the object existed in the mind of God before it existed in actuality, and therefore God knew it before it became actual," I would disagree as follows. An object that exists in the mind of God, or for that matter in a human mind, but not in the world cannot be identical with an object in the world. An object which is "merely in the mind," as in imagination or conception, rather than perception, cannot be identical with an object in the world even if the object in the mind is *corresponded to* or *succeeded by* an object which is indiscernible from it in all respects except that it is actual. At most such objects could be qualitatively, structurally, and contextually (each in its own realm) indiscernible, but not identical *simpliciter*.[10] Hence, Hartshorne is correct that we should not confuse imagination and possibility with one another. The distinction between the actual and the possible is of quite another order from the distinction between the perceived and the imagined (1941: 224–5). "Potentiality" refers to that quality of the existent that enables it to possess as actual a property that it does not now possess.

Strictly speaking, images in the mind are not themselves potentialities – though they may and frequently do allude to the potentialities of existents. Hence, when the potentialities of an existent are actualized in such a way that they are indiscernible from something that we had in mind, it is not the case that what we had in mind has taken on actuality; it would be closer to the truth to say that actuality has taken on what we had in mind. If by "the potential has become actual" we mean that the very thing we had in mind has taken on actuality, then that is not true; rather, something has become actual that corresponds qualitatively and structurally to what we had in mind and fulfills the intentionality of what we had in mind by being actual rather than imaginary. Hence, the imaginary is not transformed into the actual, or the abstract into the concrete, by being moved over from the one realm to the other or by being infused with a third dimension, or some such thing. Only the concrete is transformed into something concrete that resembles or is partially identical to or fulfills the imaginary. Potentialities for concreteness – and here I believe Hartshorne and I are in agreement – are inherent only in the concrete.

But, if Hartshorne and I are correct that an actual object cannot be known as actual before it becomes actual, does that mean that Hartshorne is correct that therefore God will learn from the process of actualization things about possibility that he did not already know? I do not think so. To return to our example, God did not know that triangle there as an individual before it became actual, but he knew about the possibility of it because he eternally knows the triangularity continuum of which all actual triangles are instantiations. Hence, from no number of actual triangles will God learn what triangles it is possible for there to be. There is more, of course, to an actual triangle than the relations of its angles. It will have size and perhaps color, but I do not see these facts as implying that God will, after all, learn something about possibility from the actuality of individuals. Individuals are determinate in the sense of cutting at specific points the continua to which they correspond or in which they participate. A particular triangle at a moment is exactly this shape, that color, such and such a size, and so on. I see no good reason to say that, though God knows perfectly the continuum of triangularity, he does not know perfectly the continua of size and color, or, for that matter, feeling and all other types of possibility.[11] Hence, it seems reasonable to believe that God can have known eternally the possibility of a triangle, i.e., a complex actuality, that cuts the continua of size, shape, and color at just those points. To be sure, as Hartshorne insists, to know a possibility is not to know an actuality; however, I am arguing, to know a possibility thoroughly is to know exactly what an actuality will be like that instantiates that possibility. In each case of the emergence of a possibility into actuality, just because it is impossible to know all tokens of the type by means of a finite or even an infinite set of tokens, it does not follow that God cannot by knowing the type know the range of possibilities that any actuality of that type must instantiate.[12]

Such knowledge on God's part would be impossible, of course, if knowledge of a possibility is always knowledge of a range of possibilities – and Hartshorne seems to believe that that is all we can mean when we talk about possibility, viz., something general, vague, and indeterminate. But that belief is in part, I think, the result of his choice of metaphor, viz., touch, for selection of a quality. He points out correctly that we cannot select a single shade of red by touching a spectrum of such shades. Touch necessarily has breadth, and breadth necessarily spans an infinite number of shades on a spectrum. But what if we slice the continuum instead of touching it? Then — assuming that the continuum is homogeneous in shade when looked at from its end — we will have got ourselves a single, determinate shade of red, and, if one knew the continuum thoroughly, I see no reason to think that one would ever be surprised by any shade of it that might ever become actual.

Consider another analogy, viz., shades of red being generated electronically in a small disc, the hue being controlled by a knob so that if you turn the knob one way the hue gets richer in a continuous fashion, and if you turn it the other way the hue gets thinner in a continuous fashion. You can stop the process at any point and the resulting hue is always distributed homogeneously across the disc. In this way it seems that, by generating a temporal continuum of hues, we avoid the problem of having to touch a spatial continuum of hues. Still, the two characteristics of continuous change of hue and no change of hue would be combined in a spectral rod, and so, I suggest, the idea of slicing such a rod to obtain a determinate hue is the one that best reveals how possibilities might be known as determinate.

To summarize, Hartshorne claims that when anything becomes actual, qualities emerge which even God could not know independently of their actualization. But, if I am right about how and what God knows in knowing the realms of possibility, there is no reason to think that he would not know in advance of every actualization of an individual every property and relation that any individual might instantiate. This is possible because God knows possibilities in the mode of continua, and to know a continuum perfectly, as God would, is to know exhaustively and simultaneously an infinite range of possibilities of a certain type — shape, size, color, number, feeling, etc. In knowing a continuum and knowing that it can be decided at any point, one knows all the possibilities that can be instantiated by any individual that will (or could) ever exemplify the universal of which that continuum is the fulfillment.[13] In line with this position I believe that the expression "the realm of essence" is most meaningfully applied to universals and their combinations understood as continua. To know the realm of essence is to know the range of logical possibilities, i.e., of simple qualities and relations and their possible combinations.

To know such combinations, however, is not to know an individual as actual before it becomes actual; an individual becomes knowable as actual only upon becoming actual. Hence, we should distinguish between possible individuals and the possibility of individuals. For reasons given earlier, what God knows eternally cannot include all possible individuals as discrete from one another. But, prior to the emergence of any individual, God will know the possibility of that individual by virtue of knowing the continua to which any actual individual must correspond (or instantiate/ actualize/participate in). Consequently, God will not learn from an emergent anything new about what is possible, and, further, it makes sense to speak of God being aware of a continuum of possible worlds and being able in advance of the creation of any of those worlds to decide his specific will for the creatures therein.

We must, then, beware of an ambiguity in, "God cannot know x before x becomes actual." Taken as meaning, "God cannot know x as actual when x is not actual," it is analytically true and acknowledges Hartshorne's point that no one can know an object as actual before it is actual. Taken as meaning, "When x becomes actual God will learn something about possibility that he did not know before," it is false because of God's exhaustive knowledge of the continua that any object must exemplify, and it acknowledges the classical point that God learns nothing from the flow of events that he would need to know in order to decide his will in general or in specific.

Does the position that I have been developing make a mockery of creativity? Hartshorne has lamented frequently that the doctrine of possible individuals does just that. He says, for example, "If all the 'forms of definiteness,' each perfectly definite in itself, are eternally given to God, it is not altogether clear to me what actualization accomplishes" (1972: 95). I am sympathetic to this complaint and believe that my position, which speaks of the possibility of individuals rather than of possible individuals, maintains the emergent nature of the products of human creativity. The frontispiece that William Blake drew for his *The Marriage of Heaven and Hell* never existed before Blake drew it. To be sure, God knew of the possibility of it before Blake drew it, but God did not know it as actual until it was drawn. Nor was its coming into existence a mere sleight of perception whereby God, who had seen it all along, whisked away a perceptual handkerchief, thereby causing others, including Blake, to suddenly begin seeing it in the 1790s; nor should it be thought that until that point it had been in another realm and known there by God so that Blake's artistic strokes were not of the nature of creativity but rather of the nature of rubbing away a patina beneath which lay the already existent drawing – an illusion causing Blake and others to think that he was creating it rather than merely uncovering it.[14] To the contrary, Blake brought into actuality for the first time something the possibility of which God knew eternally, but which neither God nor anyone else knew as actual until Blake created it. God knew eternally the possibility of that individual, but he did not know eternally that individual as a possibility.

However, is it coherent to claim that God's knowledge of *possibilia* does not increase? Before responding, let me explain why Hartshorne believes it must increase. To say that God is omniscient is, in the broadest sense, to say that he knows everything. Most philosophical disputes over omniscience have to do with the scope of "everything." Does it include the future, for example? Hartshorne would say that whatever else omniscience might include, it must include knowledge of everything that can be known at the present moment, and that would include everything that is actual and has been actual. From this it follows that a being would be omniscient even if the future is not knowable as long as it knows all the present and the past. Further, if it is in principle impossible to know a specific shade of color that has not yet occurred, then it would not count against God's omniscience if he did not know it before it became actual – though it would, of course, count against his omniscience if he did not know it as soon as it did become actual and remember it perfectly ever thereafter. Hence, given the Hartshornean assumption that there is no knowledge of specific possibilities apart from actualities, it follows that because God is by nature omniscient, his knowledge of possibilities will increase as novel actualities emerge (and, as we saw earlier, according to Hartshorne every actuality is novel).

The epistemological position from which Hartshorne's theological position is drawn appears to be contained in the following passages. In *Whitehead's Philosophy* he writes, "I can indeed know what the thing known would be though I myself did not know or feel it; but I cannot possibly know what it would be were it now unknown and unfelt; any more than I can know what an existent Platonic form would be were there nothing concrete to embody it" (12). This is, Hartshorne adds, the Aristotelian principle that "the universal can have being only as it is concretized somehow." Whether or not this was Aristotle's position, it does seem to be Hartshorne's position that what Brand Blanshard calls a "specific universal," e.g., this shade of red, cannot be known by man or God apart from the actual.[15] Before it becomes actual, it simply is not available to be known – though, of course, as soon as it does become actual, God knows it and remembers it perfectly ever thereafter. This position is reaffirmed in *Man's Vision of God*:

There seems but one way to know a quality, and that is to feel it. There is nothing in it to think, if by thought is meant relating; for a simply quality is not a relationship, but the term without which relations would not be possible, as the complex presupposes the simple. God must equally know qualities and relations, and how he could know a quality except by having it as a feeling-tone, a quality of his experience itself, we have not the faintest clue in experience.   (223)

God, then, can know a particular quality only by feeling it; but only that which is actual can be felt, and not all possible qualities can be discretely actual simultaneously; therefore God must wait upon the temporal process of actualization to gain knowledge of qualities that have not yet come to pass.

The classical theist might react to the preceding argument by insisting that it must be possible for God to know possibilities apart from actualities because he is omniscient and therefore knows all things. That, of course, would beg the question. The debate is not whether God knows all things but whether "all things" can range coherently over unrealized possibilities in such a way that God will learn nothing about them from actuality. Hence, the only promising way to proceed, it seems to me, is to attempt to show that the idea of God knowing possibilities that have not been actualized is a coherent notion. That, of course, is what I have been trying to do by explaining how God's knowledge of possibilities should be understood as subsumed within his knowledge of continua.[16]

Let me try to develop my position further by claiming that I know there can be shades of blue other than those I have seen. Moreover, I claim, this knowledge is not merely formal, i.e., a warranted induction based on experiences of having seen new shades of blue emerge between shades with which I was already familiar. Give me two shades of blue that I can discriminate perceptually and I will mix or imagine another one in between them. Hartshorne might reply along the line of John Morreall's analysis by saying, "Yes, but there was an infinite number of possible shades in between the two you started with; therefore you did not know for certain which shade you would wind up with when you mixed your paints or exerted your imagination." That, I agree, is true. However, if I were more mentally agile, why could I not imagine a spectrum of blue beginning with the one shade I was given and ending with the other?

It seems commonly conceded since Hume, and correctly I believe, that we are capable of imagining a single shade of blue in between two others that are given to us. Why not a spectrum in addition to a single shade – even as we can imagine a spectrum of isosceles triangles in between one with a vertex angle of 60° and another of 90°. I see no reason to rule this out as a possibility. Moreover, if the generation of such a spectrum by imagination seems a coherent possibility for us, certainly it also is for God. Further, I see no reason to rule out the possibility that God could "imagine" the entire spectrum of shades of blue inasmuch as it seems reasonable to assume that he knows the factors that go into making shades of blue, as distinguished from other colors, just as we know the factors that go into making a Euclidean triangle.

What Hartshorne objects is that (1) you can imagine a spectrum of blue only by virtue of having already seen some actual shades of blue – from which it follows that God, too, must wait upon actualization of at least two shades of blue before he can imagine such a spectrum, and (2) the shades of blue in your mind are not actual; they are imaginary. Regarding (1) it seems true that in order to grasp a continuum one would have to do so immediately or mediately. A continuum given immediately would have to be perceived or imagined. The latter is ordinarily the result of imaginative generalization from two or more instances of a spectrum, so let's examine the perceptually immediate possibility first. That possibility would depend upon there having actualized somewhere in reality a spectrum, of blue, for example. I can think of no reason, however, to believe that there is necessarily an actual spectrum of blue in the world, so it would be *ad hoc* to assume that there is and always has been; hence, it would seem that God, as we, must wait upon the emergence of an actual spectrum or at least upon two or more instances of blue (from which he can make an imaginative generalization) before he can apprehend the blue spectrum.[17] Hence it seems that either Hartshorne is correct that we should think of God as learning about possibilities from actualities, or we must make it plausible that God can immediately and eternally know all possibilities apart from becoming. I would like to argue for such knowledge on God's part from the combination of his omniscience and his omnipotence.

The concept of omnipotence is by no means a limpid one, but roughly it means that God can bring about anything that is not self-contradictory. Because it is not self-contradictory for God to create an object of any particular shade of blue, it follows that he can create an object of any shade of blue, whether he functions as direct efficient cause (the classical tradition) or necessary contributory cause (the neo-classical tradition). From his omniscience it follows that he knows himself perfectly, and from his perfect self-knowledge it follows that he knows perfectly well everything that he can bring about, whether as sole creator or co-creator. Therefore he knows all qualities and relations independently of becoming because actualization of them is within his power and he knows himself, and therefore his power, perfectly.[18]

Hartshorne might object at this point that God has perfect knowledge of his powers only in a generic sense, e.g. prior to the emergence of a novel shade of blue, he knew that he could bring about *some* shade of blue, but he could not have known that he would bring about that very shade of blue there.[19] Such a response, it seems to me, leads to serious difficulties.[20] First, it is implausible enough that, according to Hartshorne, God doesn't know exactly what he is up to when he is trying to bring about a hitherto unactualized shade of blue, but the problem becomes even more serious when we realize that, presumably, once upon a time there was no blue, so then God didn't know that he could create blue or how to do it; worse yet, presumably once upon a time there was no color in the universe so that God did not know what color was, or that or how he could create it – and why would this not be true of shape as well?

Hartshorne insists, to be sure, that God must always be creating a universe, but even so I see no reason to think that a universe necessarily includes shape or color, and Hartshorne himself states that "by going back far enough into the past one could (with sufficient knowledge) come to a stage at which whatever definite specificity you wish to point to was not yet in being, and was in its specificity neither possible nor impossible, though some less definite possibility was established by what had happened up till then" (1970: 68). The significance of the preceding statement seems to be that there is no past limit to God's ignorance of possibility. To be sure, in the process conception of God he has always been creating and aware of a world; therefore he always has an infinite amount of knowledge of the past, the present, and their possibilities. Given what Hartshorne says on 1970: 68, however, God's ever infinite knowledge becomes thinner and thinner as it regresses into the past because there is less and less that God knows. By analogy consider that there are an infinite number of decimal places between zero and any positive number; nonetheless, the real difference between zero and a positive number depends on the size of the number and not on the fact that there are an infinite number of decimal places between it and zero. Consider for example the difference between 1,000,000 and zero, 500,000 and zero, 250,000 and zero, and so on, infinitely diminishing the larger number by dividing it in half. No matter how small the quotient becomes, there will always be an infinite number of decimal places between it and zero, yet clearly that fact does not diminish the significance of the enormous difference between a googol over one and one over a googol. Similarly, the fact that on Hartshorne's principles God's knowledge must ever be infinite does not diminish the significant difference that should obtain between his knowledge now and his knowledge a googol of years ago.[21]

It follows from Hartshorne's conception of God, then, that the farther we project into the past, the more ignorant we must suppose God to have been, so that we must think of him as asymptotically approaching complete ignorance of possibility. Hence, in Hartshorne's conception of God we must accept as a fact that once upon a time God was very, very ignorant; otherwise we must stipulate an arbitrary floor to God's knowledge in order to preclude the trivializing regress of God's knowledge that is implied by Hartshorne's position. The first move results in an unworthy conception of the divine being; the second move is indefensibly *ad hoc*. The alternative that I am proposing is in its own ways "obscure and difficult," as Hartshorne concedes of his own position (1970: 59), but these characteristics as contained in my position, which is basically the classical position, strike me as none other than the kind of obscurity and difficulty that we should expect to encounter when we try to understand the divine mode of knowledge.[22]

Second, there appears to be an implication of Hartshorne's position that cancels out the significance of God's regressive ignorance and favours my position. Since God has always existed and, according to Hartshorne, has always been creative, at any point in time he will have always already had an opportunity to learn an infinite number of things, and no matter how far back we go – a million years, a trillion years, a googol of years – God will have always already existed an infinite number of years and learned an infinite number of things. Moreover, I have been able to think of no reason to exclude the possibility that no matter how far back we might go in divine history, it will always already be the case that God has learned all that could be significantly learned, i.e., has learned all that he needs to know in order to make good decisions about all possible future situations. Personally, I see no significant difference between such "learned" knowledge and eternal knowledge of all possibilities; it is always possessed and always adequate.

To be sure, there would always be some new shade of blue or some new angularity of triangle showing up in actuality (I am proceeding on Hartshorne's assumptions here), but given all that God would already know, there would be no reason why these novel experiences of blue and angularity should be significant for his decision-making, anymore than the fact that there are shades of green and triangularities that I have not encountered means that I cannot make good decisions in advance about how I shall respond (in home decorating or industrial calculations, for example). Hartshorne might object, "But how could you ever know that there was nothing significant for decision-making left for God to learn?" I would reply, "I couldn't know this, but neither could you know that there is some such something left to learn. Moreover, if it is possible for God to know eternally everything of significance, then we should think that he does because to know eternally everything of significance is greater than not to do so, and by nature God possesses the maximum of any positive attribute that applies to him."

To summarize, Hartshorne's assumptions about God imply that he grows asymptotically ignorant as he recedes into the past, but they do not imply that God's ignorance is ever significant as regards his decision-making for the future. Hence, given the assumption that the maximum of an attribute that can be attributed to God ought to be attributed to God, Hartshorne, because of his own assumptions, ought to think of God as always knowing all that he needs to know in order to make indefeasible and exhaustive decisions about the future. We should, then, never think of God as significantly ignorant, i.e., as having to wait on actuality in order to be able to make a knowledgeable decision. I do not see how Hartshorne could discredit this conclusion by showing or even making plausible that at any point in time every *kind* of thing that will ever happen could not have already happened and thereby provided God with adequate knowledge to make all decisions about the future. The fact that things occur that are radically new in *our* experience is of no significance for Hartshorne, of course, because God may well be familiar with nearly identical things from the remote past or remote regions of the universe. Hence, even granted Hartshorne's claim about the inherent vagueness of potentiality, he cannot rule out the possibility that God is never significantly ignorant and therefore knows eternally every possible quality and relation of significance. To defend the point a bit differently, at every moment in the divine past there will have always been time enough for every kind of thing to have happened that will ever happen, and therefore there will have always been time enough for God to know everything significant that there is to be known, and therefore it would never have been the case that God needed to wait on actuality in order to discover something that he needed to know in order to make a decision about the future.

Leaving aside what Hartshorne ought to think because of his own principles, let's now look at another problem with his position. Specifically, it follows from Hartshorne's dual claims that God is a necessary contributory cause to everything that becomes and that God is ignorant of much that can become, that he is also ignorant of much of what he can do. Hence, it is implicit in Hartshorne's position that there are always things that God could bring about but of which he is ignorant as to the fact that they could exist, that he could bring them about and, therefore, of how to bring them about. To be sure, Hartshorne could respond that God would know *that* he could and *how* he could bring about things similar to those that he was already familiar with from actuality, but it is surely a corollary of his position that the less similar a possibility is to anything that has ever come about, the less clearly God would know that he could bring it about or how to do so.

There is here, it seems to me, a serious question as to how God knows *what* he can bring about and *how* to bring about anything that has not yet existed. Does he use trial and error? Does he thrash about and accidentally discover what is possible and how to cause it? Does he systematically vary his will, like a chemist conducting a series of experiments in which only the quantity of an agent is varied while all other factors remain the same? And given the process conviction that God's influence on the world is limited to persuasion, how could God knowledgeably lure into existence a something he knows not what?[23] Hence, either God would be restricted to trying to bring about new things identical to those that had happened before, or he would have to aim at bringing about he knew not quite what. Surely this is a less exalted conception of the knowledge and power of God than is the classical conception. If it is the best we can do within the limits of reason, then so be it. I have been arguing that something more is intelligible.

The preceding problem is even worse than it appears at first because Hartshorne holds that no quality can be duplicated identically; each instance of a quality is uniquely affected by its history and relations, and no two instances of quality can have the same history and relations. This position is expressed partially in Hartshorne's comments that:

> ... the qualities of things are as particular and unique as the things. When we think that two objects have or can have the same hue of color, we are thinking in terms of approximation; the idea that the two hues are ever exactly the same is either a sheer assumption or it presupposes as its verification an absoluteness of qualitative comparison which itself is a sheer assumption, controverted by much significant evidence.
>
> (1972: 33)

He goes on to say, "the same essence can be in different things; but only if by essence we mean an entity which in itself, and not merely as we see it, is vague."

In *Creative Synthesis and Philosophic Method* Hartshorne writes,

> ... the precise qualities of particulars are themselves particular and unrepeatable. Only abstract, more or less generalized traits are repeatable. I am here differing from Santayana as well as Whitehead. Something very like this blue can occur over and over, but not precisely *this* blue. Particular qualities in their absolute definiteness are irreducibly relational and historical. The illusion to the contrary comes from forgetting that inability to detect a difference is not the same as ability to detect absolute similarity. If we were divine, it would be otherwise. But I assume that God knows all non-abstract or wholly determinate qualities of particulars to be unrepeatable. (64)

In other words, two extant qualities may be qualitatively indiscernible to human perception, but they never are to divine perception, which sees things as they are in themselves. Now, if this is true, then God never quite knows what he is doing, i.e., what he wants to do or what he will get as a result of his actions. It is impossible for God to know how to bring about anything with precision because, no matter what he does, the result will be different, in ways that could not have been anticipated, from everything else that has ever existed or been known.

The preceding position does not seem to fit with thought or experience. Regarding experience, given the incredible degree of precision that we humans have achieved by means of technology, we should, at the very least, be staggered by the kind of precision that divine intention could achieve in the world, yet I see no recognition of this point in Hartshorne's writings. Because absolute precision is conceivable, I see no reason to rule out the possibility that God could achieve such, as by creating two qualitatively identical patches of red. Hartshorne might object that our empirical experience is that, whenever we examine two seemingly identical patches of red under close scrutiny, we almost always discover them to be qualitatively discernible. He might further object that even the appearance of qualitative homogeneity in one patch of red is always the result of a kind of perceptual averaging over myriad occasions of red that are not identical in shade. But, I would ask, if the perceptual result, i.e., the redness as experienced by a perceiver, is an average, then why could not two perceptual averages be identical even though there are no qualitatively identical particles in either patch, even as two arithmetic averages can be identical though none of the numbers contributive to the two averages are the same? Isn't it conceivable that God could know two perceptual averages as the same while knowing the constituent occasions to be qualitatively different? I do not see how we can rule out this possibility.

Further, what about the qualitative relations among actual occasions themselves, those smallest units of reality?[24] Hartshorne might accept the conclusion of the preceding paragraph but add that his claim was directed not at how things appear to us but how they appear to God, who sees things as they are in themselves. I would respond that to accept the conclusion of the preceding paragraph is to accept that God could apprehend qualities identical in two or more of us – results of perceptual averagings on our part though they be – and that should be enough to establish the possibility of identical qualities.

Now let's pursue another point; namely, we can conceive that God might experience two actual occasions as being qualitatively identical. Hartshorne might say, "But we can conceive of that only in abstraction from the histories and relations of those actual occasions." I would disagree. It seems to me that Hartshorne is presenting here an empirical thesis as though it were a metaphysical thesis, i.e., is presenting a thesis that might be true but does not have to be as though it had to be. Why could not different histories and sets of relations result in identical qualities, even as different sets of numbers can result in identical averages? To address the problem more directly from Hartshorne's point of view, why could not two actual occasions be presented with overlapping ranges of possibilities? And if they could be presented with overlapping ranges of qualitative possibilities (even by only one unit of overlap), why could they not happen to choose to actualize identical qualities? I simply do not understand the strength of Hartshorne's conviction that qualities are like drone bees, forever retired after just one use. I can imagine arguing that God has chosen to prevent identical recurrence of any quality; indeed, Hartshorne could make a good empirical argument for that thesis; but I see no good reason to say that God can neither prevent nor bring about identical recurrence of any quality because such a thing is impossible in itself.

To return to the problems that result from taking Hartshorne's position, consider that God would not only not be able to make or lure into existence two identical colors; he would never know in advance just what color he would get. The most that God or anyone can do in creative activity, according to Hartshorne, is to shoot in a promising direction, chosen on past experience, and hope for the best: "As causes we never know just what we are causing" (1970: 127). God, according to Hartshorne, is no exception to this principle. Further, the less similar one's circumstances and actions are to one's earlier circumstances and actions, the less confident one can be of what will result from one's actions. Hence, the more God's present circumstances and actions differ from his earlier acts and circumstances, the more surprised, even startled, perhaps unpleasantly, he is likely to be by what results. "Oh my God!" I can imagine him saying, "I didn't know *that* would be the outcome!" Will this tend to make God exceedingly cautious, varying his actions by only miniscule amounts so as to minimize the risk of getting significantly unpleasant results? Or will the spirit with which God proceeds to act vary with the kind of results he has been getting most recently?

Finally, perhaps most radically, it follows from the unrepeatability of God's actions and the inherent vagueness of potentiality that God never knows in advance what *he* will do until he finds himself doing it. Presumably at times he surprises himself not only by what he brings about, but also by what he wills. In the face of such striking results, I sometimes wonder whether Professor Hartshorne is a startlingly profound philosopher or a philosophical puck. Whichever, he is wonderfully provocative, and I prefer him to his anti-metaphysical counterpart, David Hume, so let us proceed to a fourth problem in his position.

Hartshorne is emphatic that God has power, as do all individuals, and presumably he holds that one of the things that God knows eternally is that he has power. But, if what God knows eternally is merely that he has power, without specific knowledge of what his power can bring about, it seems an instance of empty knowledge, i.e., of knowledge that is not knowledge. It amounts to God knowing eternally that he can effect something but without knowing anything that he can effect. To be sure, he always knows what he *has* effected, but none of that, according to Hartshorne, can be repeated, and unactualized possibilities can be known, at best, only vaguely. It follows that God never knows clearly what he can do, though he knows he can do something. Such, I submit, is at best an obscure notion and at worst a meaningless one.

If I am correct, then either God must have innate knowledge of at least one effect that his power can bring about or he must learn that he has such power. If God has learned that he has such power, then – because nothing can surpass God in knowledge – it was not by means of someone telling him about it; therefore he must have learned of his power accidentally or • intentionally. It would not make sense to hold that he learned of it intentionally since before he knew of it he would have had no reason to believe that it existed, and without a reason to believe that it existed, he would not have been able to investigate the possibility intentionally, since we can seek intentionally only things of which we have some knowledge, whether direct or indirect. Hence, God must have learned of his power unintentionally, i.e., accidentally. But how might that have come about? Presumably he didn't have a muscle twitch that caused some effect in the world that he subsequently came to understand himself as causally responsible for. Equally, it would not appear that he came by his knowledge by doing something comparable to pushing buttons or pulling strings or proposing ideals and noticing consequences. Why would he have pushed or pulled or proposed in the first place since he did not yet know that he had power? It appears, then, that it is indefensible to hold that God learned that he has power, and it is also indefensible to hold that God could know he had power without knowing at least some of what he has power to do. Consequently, we must hold that God's knowledge of his power and at least some of its range is innate (or, perhaps better, "immediate"). But, if God must immediately and eternally know at least some of what he, as a being of power, can bring about, it would be arbitrary to say, "Well, he eternally knows he can bring about that shade of red or that pitch of sound." Why that one rather than this one? Criticism of this *ad hoc* response leads to the conclusion that he must know all possibilities eternally and know them as continua, not as individuals, for reasons set forth earlier.[25]

To summarize, God must have eternal knowledge of his power and such knowledge must be abstract, i.e., not dependent upon any specific thing that he has brought about. Such knowledge would be *empty* (and therefore no knowledge at all) if it included nothing specific, and it would be *arbitrary* if it included eternal knowledge of only the power to bring about this shade of red or that pitch of sound (which knowledge would violate Hartshorne's claim that all knowledge of possibility is vague and indeterminate – and surely he would not argue that God has such knowledge of his power because some specific shade of red, or some other specific quality, exists eternally). Hence, in saying that in knowing himself God knows he has power, and in knowing he has power he knows what he can do, we should not mean merely that he knows that he can do something, but not what; nor should we mean that he knows he can do anything, but without knowing specifically anything that he can do. Rather, we should mean that he knows eternally and exhaustively all that he can do.

Another problem in Hartshorne's position has to do with the relation of imagination to perception, and the implication of that relation for memory. David Hume accepted, in spite of the anomaly that it created for him, that given two shades of blue, a human could imagine a third shade in between them without having perceived that shade before. Surely Hartshorne would allow as much. But, if he does, shouldn't he also allow that given God's unlimited powers of thought, he would be able to fill out the whole spectrum, so that any shade of blue that he henceforth perceives in the world, he will have already been familiar with? Hartshorne might reply, "But the color as seen in imagination is itself an emergent. When we ask a human to imagine a shade of blue that he has never seen or imagined before, he does not know what shade it will be before he actually imagines it, and neither does God. Hence, the fact that we can image new shades of color independently of perception does not imply that they are not emergents, i.e., does not imply that they could have been known before they emerged. Qualities emerge in imagination as well as in perception." Regarding humans I agree with this point because our knowledge of color has a temporal beginning. But what about God? Can we not at least conceive of God being eternally aware of (or "conceptually prehending," as Whitehead might say) the blue spectrum?

Recall my earlier argument that no matter what time we choose in the past, no matter how far back, it was preceded by an even longer period, indeed, an infinite temporal period, during which God could have apprehended all shades of blue as a continuum (either by means of immediate imaginary knowledge of such a continuum or by having seen instances of blue and filled in the rest by an act of imagination or conception). Perhaps Hartshorne would reply that, given his radical principle of uniqueness, viz., every instance of a quality is qualitatively unique, it follows that a quality apprehended in imagination, even God's imagination, would not be qualitatively identical with a quality apprehended by perception. (God would know this directly by seeing a qualitative difference; we, because of the limitations of our senses, must, according to Hartshorne, acquire this knowledge through reason.) Hence, a perceived quality cannot be identical with any part of a qualitative continuum in imagination because different factors go into generating a perceived quality and an imagined quality. Hence, no matter how extensive or ancient God's powers of imagination, no quality he ever imagines can be identical with a quality that he discovers in the world.

Perhaps the most pernicious corollary of Hartshorne's principle of radical qualitative uniqueness has to do with God's memory. According to Hartshorne, God is a society of actual occasions, i.e., smallest units of reality, that come into being and subsequently perish just like the actual occasions that constitute all other complex individuals. This means, together with Hartshorne's principle of radical qualitative uniqueness, that the series of actual occasions that are identical with God's memory of an instance of blue in the world would have to be not only numerically differ-ent but also qualitatively different from the occasions of blue that God originally encountered in the world. The significance of this, given that the successive occasion of God's memory of the original perception cannot be qualitatively identical with the original perception, is that God can never remember anything exactly as it was.

It also follows from Hartshorne's dual principles of qualitative unique-ness and social divinity that God's memory of something must – because no two occasions can be qualitatively identical – become more and more unlike that of which it is a memory as time passes.[26] From all this follows that, even immediately after a person dies, God will not remember that person perfectly. Presumably immediately after the person's death God's memory of the person will be very like the person, but, as we saw earlier, God's memory must be continually changing because no two actual occa-sions can be qualitatively identical. Hence, an actual occasion of memory cannot be qualitatively identical with an actual occasion of perception, so one is confronted with puzzles: just how different is it initially? is there some minimal difference in the features of successive occasions? is there a range of possible initial differences? if so, what, if anything, determines the initial difference?

The problem gets worse as time passes. The memory of an event may be nearly identical to the event immediately after it occurs, but what about a million years later? a googol of years later? Hartshorne finds a great deal of value in the belief that though we will not survive death subjectively we will be everlastingly remembered and cherished by God. He writes in 'The God of Religion and the God of Philosophy,'

I deeply honour that ancient people who, almost alone in the world, could accept their status as neither divine nor immortal. But, implicitly, at least, they were assured of a kind of immortality from this alone, that God would everlastingly know and love them *just as they were* in their earthly careers. For there cannot be a counterpart to forgetting in God.

(157, emphasis mine)

But now it appears that Hartshorne's principles imply that, though God will remember us, he *cannot* remember us as we really are and, to make things worse, his memory of us must ever slide down a slippery slope of deviation from the truth. We appear to be left with nothing more than a causal relationship which could eventually result in memories so distorted or remote from the original as to be grossly misleading.

This problem does not by itself, so far as I can see, require that Hartshorne abandon his principle of divine dual transcendence; but, if he is going to protect his conviction that God will remember us perfectly forever, then it does seem to require that he allow that it is possible for a quality to be repeated across the gap from perception to memory and identically over time.[27] This might be done by agreeing with Whitehead either that qualitative identity of distinct entities is possible or that God is a single actual entity and not a society of successive occasions.[28] There may be good reasons for adopting both of these positions of Whitehead's, but either by itself seems adequate to provide for perfect memory on God's part. If God is a society of successive occasions, he will nonetheless be able to remember us perfectly if different actual occasions can be qualitatively and structurally identical. Similarly, if God is a single everlasting actual occasion, he will be able to remember us perfectly whether Hartshorne's principle of qualitative uniqueness is true or not because our features will be indelibly and immutably impressed upon him who is a single, enduring occasion that experiences flawlessly and remembers everlastingly without loss or distortion.

To summarize, as Hartshorne's principles now stand, they entail that God cannot remember anything perfectly and that his memory must get worse and worse as time passes. Triggered by these implications are such questions as the following. Does God realize that he is not remembering us correctly? If not, he is not worthy of the name "God," given its dominant meaning in philosophical and religious contexts. If he does realize that he is not remembering correctly, then he must remember us correctly, since he could only know that one memory was not correct if he had another memory of the same thing that was veridical. But then he would have to have misremembered in at least one case – which is impossible for God, as Hartshorne himself testifies. And we should ask, "If God misremembers and also remembers correctly, how could he know which memory is veridical given the fact that in order to resolve the problem he would have no higher authority to appeal to than himself?" If we try to get around this problem by suggesting in Hartshornean language that God has only a "vague and indeterminate" awareness that his memories are gradually becoming faded and distorted, mustn't we then think of him as increasingly distressed and frustrated at the loss of precious memories?

Finally we come to the point at which I believe Hartshorne and I are farthest apart. He holds, as we saw earlier, that to know a genus, e.g., "animal," is not to know thereby the species thereof, e.g., "dog," and to know the species, e.g., "dog," is not to know future members of that species. I, by contrast, hold that to know the genus perfectly is to know all its possible species, and to know the species perfectly is to know the possibility of all its individual members. In what sense do I mean this? As can be inferred from earlier arguments, I do not mean that to know a species perfectly is to know all its possible members as discrete from one another. That, I agree, is impossible. Rather, it is to know a continuum of which any specific individual would be an instantiation, and therefore it is to know independently of actuality the possibility of every individual that will ever be actual.

I certainly agree with Hartshorne, however, that to know a species is not to know thereby the members of it that will become actual. To hold that it did would violate two metaphysical principles that I hold in common with Hartshorne: (1) an individual cannot be known as actual until it is actual, and (2) the future will of a free finite agent cannot be known for certain in advance, not even by the agent himself, much less by anyone else.[29] If, however, one knows the limits within which triangles must exist and the method of their generation, then, I believe, one knows the possibility of every triangle that will ever exist. Consequently, when the conditions that can eventuate in an actual triangle do eventuate in an actual triangle, one who has the preceding knowledge will never before have seen that triangle, but there will be no surprises in it for him. The same point, I believe, can be defended with regard to all other qualities, relations, and complexes thereof.

Humans, to be sure, do not understand genuses and species with the kind of mastery and clarity of which I have been speaking. Perhaps we do understand some species in this mode, species such as triangularity, and to a lesser extent colors, though here there is great variation among us. Gifted geometers show with illustrations that they are able to imagine moving, three-dimensional linear continua that boggle the mind of the layman, and I believe the same is true of gifted artists with regard to color. At the same time, I certainly feel that I am only touching an idea rather than grasping it – perhaps, even more accurately, merely pointing to an idea dimly seen rather than touching it – but the kinds of difficulty I see here strike me as the kinds we should expect to encounter as finite, corporeal beings attempting to understand the divine mode of knowledge.

As a corollary to my position, I would like to suggest that the higher one rises in the continuum of intelligence, the more clearly and extensively one understands possibility in terms of continua. This claim applies to ontogeny as well as phylogeny. In terms of ontogeny, the more perfectly an individual, such as a human, understands a genus or a species, the more clearly and extensively he understands it as a continuum, and the more clearly and extensively he understands it as a continuum, the more clearly and extensively he understands the possibilities that are inherent within it. In terms of phylogeny, a type of being who is capable of understanding perfectly all genuses and species will understand all the possibilities that are inherent in reality. I do not believe humans are capable of enjoying such understanding of the entire realm of possibility, but I know of no reason to think that God has not always enjoyed it.

Assuming this conception of God's knowledge of possibilities, we turn now to an elaboration of the concept of possibility in relation to divine creativity. From this elaboration will come the framework within which I will expand my position regarding God's knowledge of possibility and address the question of the possibility or impassibility of God's knowledge of the past, present, and future.[30]

4

God, plenum, world

ACCORDING TO MOST THEISTS, God created the world *ex nihilo*, i.e., out of nothing. This is to say that God did not act *upon* anything in creating the world; his willing the world was the sole and sufficient cause of the world beginning to exist. This doctrine of creation was not arrived at easily; it was the outcome of considerable controversy in the early church. It seemed to the fathers of the church a necessary doctrine to protect their faith that because God is supremely perfect: (1) he is distinct from the world, (2) his existence does not depend upon the world, (3) the existence of the world depends on him, (4) there is nothing that can coerce or even influence his will, (5) there is nothing that can limit or even resist his will, (6) there is no ultimate dualism or pluralism in reality, and (7) the world can never descend below the possibility of redemption by God. More generally the motive behind the doctrine of creation *ex nihilo* seems to be to protect the idea that God must be thought of as able to perform any creative or redemptive act that is logically consistent. He must, for example, be able to create a material world that is good, and, should it become corrupted by the free actions of its inhabitants, he must be able to redeem it.

Heterodox theists as well as orthodox ones defend creation *ex nihilo* (henceforth CEN). Paul Tillich writes, "God finds nothing 'given' to him which influences him in his creativity or which resists his creative *telos*. The doctrine of *creatio ex nihilo* is Christianity's protection against any type of ultimate dualism" (1967: 253). Peter Bertocci is not averse to an ultimate dualism, but nonetheless he defends CEN: "By saying that God created 'out of nothing,' we are simply denying (a) that he made it out of something, and (b) that the creation is to be identified with him" (1951: 451). Also, "All that is not God depends for its existence upon God – this is the fundamental thought in the doctrine of creation" (1951: 450). Elsewhere he writes in defense of CEN, "If there are two or three ultimate, co-eternal Beings, is it not completely incomprehensible that they should be so complementary? Why should they find that they can interact in a way that does make this kind of orderly world possible?" (1969: 200). That is, any attempt to explain the relations between two or more ultimately independent beings would have to be *ad hoc* and therefore philosophically unsatisfactory.

I agree that the preceding characteristics of God must be protected because God is by definition a supremely perfect being. I also agree that the concept of CEN would protect those characteristics. However, I do not agree that the concept of CEN is coherent. Neither do I believe that CEN is entailed by the concept of God. I believe the fullness of the notion of God can be maintained by means of another theory of divine creation that I will explain after I explain my reasons for rejecting CEN.[1]

My rejection of CEN is predicated on my understanding of creativity. To create is to actualize a possibility, i.e., to make actual what was not actual but only possible. As Aquinas and Hartshorne agree, there is no possibility apart from actuality. Possibilities are possibilities of actualities. From nothing nothing becomes.

CEN is, of course, not based on the assumption that the world has come from absolutely nothing; it holds that the world has come from God, who has always existed, and who, therefore, ensures that the principle *ex nihilo nihil fit* is not violated. In Bertocci's words,

> ... *creatio ex nihilo* does not actually mean that God took "nothing" and made something out of it. The theist would agree that "from nothing" nothing can come. Neither God nor man can do what is not even thinkable, make nothing become something! But creation out of nothing does not mean that God "took nothing and made something out of it." "Out of" nothing, nothing comes, to be sure. But the personalist does not start with "nothing." He starts with God and says that this Person (far from being nothing himself) is the Creator-Ground of all.
>
> In a word, to say that God creates is to say that beings now exist *that did not exist before*. Finite beings are not made "out of God" or "out of some co-eternal being." They are made, produced, created. There is nothing contradictory in saying that a Creator brings into being what was non-existent without the act of creation; to create means just that! (1969: 202)

It seems to me, however, that this kind of reasoning does not escape conflict with the principle *ex nihilo nihil fit*.

Possibilities are always possibilities of something, i.e., are resident in something in the sense that the something has the capacity of becoming, i.e., being actualized into or evincing the x under consideration. Theism rejects the idea that such possibilities are resident in God because that would imply pantheism, i.e., that God becomes what is created and that, therefore, the world is God. But if the possibilities of creation are not resident in God, they must be resident in something external to God or be resident in nothing. Nothing, however, cannot have a possibility resident in it; if it could, it would not be nothing; it would be something. Therefore CEN implies either pantheism (God creates out of nothing other than himself) or absurdity (God creates out of nothing, not even himself).

The illusion of the adequacy of CEN has perhaps resulted from a failure to see the triadic nature of a free intentional act of creation. Such an act essentially involves (1) a possible free willing, (2) a possibility inherent in a given, and (3) actualization of (2) by means of actualization of (1). (1) is not actualized by anything; it is a basic action.[2] Tradition has understood correctly that if x is logically self-consistent and there is no logical inconsistency in God causing x, then necessarily, if God wills x, x will come to pass. Hence, when the agent is God, actualization of (1) entails the fulfillment of (2) when (2) is the fulfillment of what God wills. With finite agents, however, actualization of (1) does not entail the fulfillment of (2) because the fulfillment of human volition is always contingent on factors over which the agent does not have complete control. It has apparently been inferred from this discrepancy between the divine and the human case that God's will would be effective even if there were nothing existing independently of God's will containing possibilities for God to actualize. However, the fact that God's willing is necessarily effective does not entail that we can logically dispense with the necessity of something other than God, a something the possibilities of which are actualized by the willing of God.[3] The church's instinct has been right in rejecting such a something because all the previous ways of conceptualizing it resulted in limitations upon God. But the resort to CEN is also unsatisfactory.

Because actualities and possibilities are exhaustive of reality, a possibility must be a possibility of an actuality, of another possibility, or of nothing. Regarding the last alternative, we have seen that nothing can have no potentiality to be actualized. If, for example, there had ever been absolutely nothing in reality, then, because it is incomprehensible that something could be actualized from nothing by nothing, it is incomprehensible that there could ever have subsequently been anything. But there is something; therefore there must never have been absolutely nothing.

A critic might respond, "But I can imagine there being absolutely nothing, and then there being something." The challenge, however, is not to *imagine* blankness followed by something; I agree that we can all do that. The challenge is to *understand* how there once could have been absolutely nothing in reality yet that state have been followed by the occurrence of something. To imagine nothing followed by something is not the same as to understand the possibility of such a thing. In the former the existence of at least the imaginer is assumed, whereas in the latter case it is stipulated that absolutely nothing exists, not even the imaginer. In the latter case, it seems to me, we must give precedence to conception over imagination and conclude that, though we can imagine absolute emptiness followed by something, we understand that such a thing could not happen because it would involve a contradiction, viz., that nothing have no potentiality and yet have some potentiality.

I have argued above that either God must create out of himself, which implies pantheism, or out of nothing, which implies absurdity, or out of something other than himself. This last alternative has been rejected by mainstream theism because, however it was conceived, it always led to unacceptable limitations upon God. I would like to propose a variation that, I believe, avoids such limitations and the logical absurdities of CEN. Let's begin by expositing more thoroughly the concept of an unactualized possibility.

The concept of an unactualized possibility is a triadic concept involving three notions: (1) that which can be but is not, (2) that out of which (1) can be actualized, and (3) that by means of which (1) can be actualized from (2). Assumed here are the following principles: (A) potentiality must exist in something; (B) only that which is actual can actualize a potentiality; (C) potentialities are not causally efficacious. (C) implies that a potentiality cannot actualize itself; it must be actualized by something other than itself. If it could actualize itself, it would not be a potentiality but an actuality; but if it were an actuality and not a potentiality, it would not have need to be actualized; indeed, it could not become actualized because it would already be actual. Hence, the concept of becoming is relational and requires an actualizer in addition to something that bears potentiality.

Because the concept of potentiality requires that there be something in which the potentiality inheres, the notion of a possibility that inheres in nothing is meaningless, as is the notion of a possibility for which there is absolutely no possible actualizer. Hence, to speak of a mere but genuine possibility is to speak of something that could be but is not.[4]

Because possibility is a relational concept, when we speak of the possibility of something we may be speaking of it in any of three senses. When we say "x is possible," we may mean first that it is possible relative to itself, i.e., that its concept is meaningful and not self-contradictory. Second, we might mean that there exists, or could exist, something out of which it could be actualized. Third, we might mean that there exists something that could function as the efficient cause of that possibility becoming actual. In order for something to be possible in sense 2, it must be possible in sense 1; in order for something to be possible in sense 3, it must be possible in sense 2.

It follows from the preceding analysis that the simplest and completest world in which becoming is possible would be one in which there were two distinct things: one which embodied the full range of logical possibilities, or passive potentiality, and the other, active potentiality, which embodied the ability to actualize or provide the necessary conditions for the actualization of the full range of logical possibilities. That is, there must be one thing that embodies the entire range of passive potentiality and another that embodies the entire range of active potentiality. The former would be purely passive in the sense that it would be entirely dependent upon the latter for actualization of its potentialities, and the latter would be purely active in the sense that it is entirely independent with regard to which potentialities it can and does actualize. These points will be pursued at more length, but for now I would like to cease speaking of these two "things" in abstraction.

The idea of an individual that is omnipotent pure activity fits perfectly well with the theist conception of God. Indeed, I believe that individual is identical with God. Though I will not defend here this identity, it is certainly the case that according to theism God can create, i.e., can actualize possibilities. Just as certainly this is a correct belief because it is greater to be able to create than not to be able to create. Further, it is greater to be able to actualize or provide the necessary conditions for actualization of the full range of possibilities than not to be able to do so; therefore we should think of God as omnipotent. As we saw earlier, however, in order for God to actualize possibilities that are not inherent to himself – actualizing his will to, e.g., create the earth, is inherent to himself, but the earth is not a possibility that lies in any sense within him – there must be something that is the repository, so to say, of those possibilities. I will call this repository of all possibilities not inherent to God "the plenum."[5]

The plenum is distinct from God but is not created by him. The plenum must be distinct from God, given our rejection of pantheism and CEN, but it is not and could not be created by God because it is the passive ground of his omnipotence. Apart from it God would not be omnipotent because he would have nothing upon which to exercise his power; therefore apart from it he could not be God; therefore apart from it there would be no God. Hence, as well as not being able to create the plenum, God could not destroy it because in destroying it he would destroy himself – but he exists necessarily and therefore cannot perish or be destroyed, not even by himself.

To put this point another way, it would be indefensible to hold that God creates a condition of his own omnipotence. Before he created it, he would not be omnipotent and therefore would not be God; but nothing can become God. Therefore, either the plenum is eternal and uncreated, along with God, or there is no God. Hence, the existence of God entails the existence of something other than God, something that passively contains the full range of logical possibilities, viz., the plenum.[6]

Lest the notion of the existence of God depending on the existence of something distinct from himself seem too outrageous, consider now that the existence of the plenum is contingent upon the existence of God. The plenum is the dwelling-place of all possibilities, and, as we have seen, nothing is a possibility in the full-bodied sense apart from something or someone that is capable of actualizing it. But only God is an adequate efficient cause of the possibilities of the plenum. Hence, apart from God there is no plenum.[7] A possibility that cannot be actualized is not a possibility, and an all inclusive set of possibilities that cannot be actualized is not a plenum. Hence, the theist should say not, "In the beginning was God," but, "In the beginning was God and the plenum," because neither could exist without the other. The power of God would not exist apart from something to exercise it on, and the plenum would not exist apart from something that could actualize its possibilities, as can God.[8]

In the last several paragraphs we have been examining the distinctness of God and the plenum; now we shall focus on their unity. I have been persuaded by Spinoza that there can be only one real infinite, or, as some would say, only one real absolute. It is impossible that there could be anything in existence in addition to a real infinite. Moreover, it seems clear that a real infinite would have to include the possibility of becoming because it would include an exhaustive plenitude of possibilities many of which could not be actualized simultaneously and which, therefore, would have to be actualizable subsequently to one another or they would not be real possibilities.[9] Consequently, the real infinite or absolute must have both an active and a passive side by means of which becoming can occur. The passive side must be an infinite reservoir of possibilities and the active side must be omnipotent in relation to those possibilities. These two sides of the absolute are God and the plenum.[10]

It follows that insofar as arguments for the existence of God succeed, they do not prove the existence of God only, but of God and the plenum, i.e., of the absolute. If, for example, the ontological argument succeeds, then the absolute is that the necessary existence of which it proves.[11] The absolute, however, is not something in addition to God. It is not above God or superior to God. It is not a GOD above God. It should not be deified by capitalization. The absolute is simply God and the plenum in their mutual dependence, a dependence which puts no limitations on God but is a necessary condition of the reality of God.[12]

I have denied that God could create the plenum. Let me pursue that point. If God were to create the plenum, that would be equivalent to him creating the possibility of his having creative possibilities. Alvin Plantinga may be touching on this point in his *Does God Have A Nature?* There he states, "Perhaps there's no such thing as the color red; it still won't be up to God whether it's possible that there be red things" (86).[13] My point, and perhaps Plantinga's, is that, if there is no God, then it is certainly not up to God whether it is possible that there be red things, and, if there is a God, it still will not be up to God whether it is possible that there be red things. What is basically possible for God is not contingent upon his will. God is not sovereign over the range of his power. His sovereignty is over the exercise of it. God is necessarily an omnipotent being. He could not be otherwise. Consequently, it is necessarily the case that, if there is a God, then red things are possible. To put the point more generally, God cannot create the possibility of his having basic possibilities that he would not have had had he not created them. All the basic possibilities that he has, he has by nature, and those possibilities include, unilaterally or cooperatively, actualization of the entire range of the plenum, beyond which there are no further possibilities.

Note that, according to my understanding of these matters, in creation by volition there are two potentialities that are actualized. On the one hand the creator actualizes a potentiality of his will, i.e., there is a potentiality of himself that he actualizes. On the other hand he actualizes a potentiality of something other than himself. For illustration of this distinction, consider a person who wakes after an accident, does not know that his lower extremities have been paralyzed, and wills to move his left leg. When he does so he succeeds in actualizing a potentiality of his will, viz., willing his leg to move, but he does not succeed in actualizing a potentiality of his leg, viz., movement of it (let's assume that the relevant muscles, tendons, etc., are functional so that the leg would flex if electrical stimulation was applied appropriately). A difference between God and ourselves, of course, is that, because God is omnipotent, his will is a sufficient cause of whatever he wills insofar as it is not contingent upon the concurrence of another free will. But the fact that what God wills must occur in such a case does not mean that we can dispense with the notion of the plenum and conclude that God creates *ex nihilo*. Failure to note the distinction between actualization of a potentiality of one's will and actualization by means of one's will of a potentiality that is not a potentiality of one's will might lead one to think mistakenly that nothing more is needed for divine creation than an appropriate act of divine will.

Soon I will show how I believe the spirit, though not the letter, of CEN can be redeemed within my position, but for now I reiterate that God by means of his will actualizes potentialities that are not potentialities of his will, and I add the caveat that surely by means of his will God does not actualize his will. If he had to actualize his will by means of his will, he would be caught in an infinite regress from which there would be no return.[14] To be sure, a potentiality of his will is actualized *in* his willing, but *by* his willing is actualized a potentiality of that which is not his will, viz., the plenum.

What kind of a reality is the plenum? I find it difficult to say. If it exists, it exists necessarily, not contingently, but it does not exist as an individual or as a thing. Rather, it is the passive possibility of there being an individual other than God — God being the only individual that exists necessarily. The plenum must be actual in some sense, but not in the sense that it was once potential or could have been. This means it will be a different type of actuality from the things that are actualized from it. Its reality consists of it being determinable, not determinate, whereas the reality of the things that are actualized from it consists of their being determinate as well as determinable. The plenum is not this or that; it is the passive possibility of this or that.

At least part of the difficulty of saying what the plenum is is due to the fact that the concept of the plenum is a limiting concept and therefore refers to something beyond ordinary experience. To say that it is a limiting concept is not to say that it limits God but that it stands for something beyond which thought in principle cannot go. It stands for the ultimate "material cause" of all contingent being. I am not comfortable here with the term "material," but I have made it clear that I agree with Aristotle that becoming requires something out of which a contingent individual, property, or relation can emerge. The pantheist says that the material cause of contingent existence is God; the traditional theist says that there is no material cause of contingent individuals. In this chapter I have rejected the former position without argument and criticized the latter position. It seems to me that reason requires that there be a "material" cause of all contingent existence. That cause, I submit, is the plenum, even as the will of God is the efficient cause of all contingent existence.[15]

It might be helpful to point out that "plenum" is not a natural kind term as I use it. It does not refer to a specific kind of stuff, as does "gold," for example. If it did, I would be doing science, not metaphysics; I would be presuming to say what kind of stuff all contingent beings are made of. But that is not what I am saying; I am saying merely that there must be something out of which all contingent things are brought into existence.

The term "matter," by contrast, is used sometimes as a natural kind term, i.e., to refer to whatever all physical things are made of.[16] If there *is* one kind of stuff of which all physical objects are made, then the term "matter" has a referent. But whether there is such a stuff is something to be established by scientists, not assumed by philosophers. Even if there is such a stuff, there is no reason to believe that it exists necessarily. Rather, it can and should, if it exists, be thought of as having been actualized from the plenum. Hence, the concept of matter as the physical stuff of which all physical objects are constituted is not a basic notion. Further, it seems to me that the value of the natural kind concept of matter has been considerably depreciated by developments in science and philosophy. Science has disclosed many different physical substances, from chemicals and metals to submicroscopic particles, but it has shown no sign of being on the verge of discovering *one* kind of stuff out of which all physical things are constituted, nor is the viability of science dependent on the assumption that there is such a stuff. One might reply that science has found its version of matter in mass/energy, but that would be a mistake. The concepts of mass and energy operate in physics not as substance terms but as measurement terms that presuppose something to be measured. Hence, when "matter" is used as a natural kind term, we should not expect it to do the work of "plenum," the metaphysical term that stands for the plenum.[17]

Some of Aquinas' descriptions of prime matter make it sound very much like my plenum. He says, for example, "prime matter is infinite in its potentiality" (1975: I.43.6). But presumably it is infinite in its potentiality for the becoming of material creatures only; hence, I would not want to identify the plenum with prime matter because the plenum must be the source of every type of contingent being. If it is possible for there to be contingent entities or properties other than material ones, such as spiritual or mental ones, the plenum must be the source of their existence too. Further, Aquinas understands matter as something limited: "Every matter is limited to some particular species by the form with which it is endowed" (1975: II.16.3). Also, "there is no one matter which is in potentiality to universal being" (1975: II.16.9). In order to complete the concept of God, however, we need the concept of something that is not limited to some particular species and that is in potentiality to every possible species of contingent being, including material beings. The concept of the plenum is just such a concept. Hence, it is not identical with the concept of pure or prime matter, but it is, I believe, just what we need to make sense of the illimitability of divine creation.

Now I would like to show that, though CEN should be rejected in its literal form, its spirit can be retained within the doctrine of the plenum. In creating from the plenum, God does create *ex nihilo* in the sense that what he creates he does not create from antecedent individuals or matter. In the beginning, metaphysically speaking, there were no individuals other than God and there was no stuff lying around in the platonic or Thomistic senses of matter. Hence, I agree almost entirely with E. L. Mascall when he says that in divine creation, "There is no emission of substance, no medium between God and the world, nothing but the omnipotent fiat by which the creatures receive their very existence together with their natures" (1949: 146). Creation from the plenum does not involve emission of substance from God nor manipulation of a pre-existent substance. It requires only an act of will on God's part. Perhaps the plenum is a medium in Mascall's sense, but, if it is, it is not so in any sense that detracts from the power of God. The plenum is not a medium through which God must go to get at the world or to act upon the world, nor is it in a literal sense a substance which can be shaped into a world, like a lump of clay that can be shaped into a sphere.

Moreover, because the plenum is logically predeterminate, i.e., does not by its nature contain any determinations, it is not something that would register upon our senses.[18] Hence, it is nothing that we can know by perception. Indeed, the *idea* of the plenum is a limiting notion for, *inter alia*, something that is beyond our apprehension. Obviously, then, creation from the plenum would seem to us like creation from nothing.

In order for us humans to create, we must begin with something that is sufficiently definite to be apprehended by our senses and then transformed by some physical or mental manipulation. Human creativity seems restricted to acting upon a determinate given (as in bending a wire) or rearranging determinate givens (as in arranging flowers), or in combining two or more determinate givens (as in mixing paints or chemicals or musical notes). To start with something absolutely formless, as God does with the plenum, seems like starting with nothing, like willing something into existence from nothing, but it isn't. It is to actualize by mere willing a potentiality of something that is infinitely receptive to infinite power. Such power is God's alone, and God alone can cause the original existence of individuals, i.e., can make individuals "stand out" from the plenum. Hence, I agree with Aquinas and Mascall that "to create (that is, to give *existence*) belongs to God alone..." (1949: 72), but I do not believe that this point entails CEN.[19]

Richard Swinburne sees clearly that God must not be restricted to creating from pre-existing matter, but he does not see that this does not entail CEN. Consider the following statement from *The Coherence of Theism*:

Creating the universe *e nihilo* (not, that is, out of any pre-existing matter) would be a basic action of God. Human beings do not have the power to bring matter into existence (given that we construe "matter" in a wide sense which includes energy). It is, however, fairly easy to picture what it would be like for them to have such a power. If I could just by so choosing produce a sixth finger or a new ink-well (not made out of pre-existing matter) I would have the power to bring matter into existence. Others could see that I had this power by asking me to perform the acts in question. (139)

Swinburne reiterates this point in *The Existence of God*:

Some of the acts attributed by the theist to God are acts of creating *e nihilo* (i.e. not out of pre-existing matter); others are acts of moving, or changing the characteristics of, existing things. Creating matter *e nihilo* is not something which men are able to do, but it is easy enough to conceive of their doing it. I could just find myself able as easily to make appear before me an ink-well or to make a sixth finger grow, as I am at present able to move my hand. Various tests (e.g. sealing off the room and keeping its contents carefully weighed) could show that the ink-well or finger were not made of existing matter. Creating *e nihilo* is a perfectly conceivable basic act. (48)

Careful analysis of these statements shows that either they do not entail CEN or they call for a redefinition of CEN that presupposes the plenum.

I agree with Swinburne that we need not and should not think of God as creating out of pre-existing matter, for reasons given earlier. I also agree with Swinburne that creation by God should be thought of as a basic act, i.e., as an act that is immediate and direct, not contingent upon first performing some other act (1977: 102–3). God wills and his will is done. Swinburne might rejoin with a subsequent definition: "a basic action is something which an agent just does, does not do by doing anything else" (1977: 132). His objection, based on the last phrase, might be that, according to my conception of God, God does not create immediately and directly; he creates by acting on the plenum, and therefore his action is not basic. Such a rejoinder would be mistaken, however, because it fails to acknowledge that God does not, according to my conception, first act upon the plenum in order to create matter and then by means of a second act create a material object, say a planet, from that matter. Rather, God's action is direct and immediate. He wills the existence of a planet and it is immediately actualized from the plenum. Hence, God does not create the planet by first doing something else. As Genesis puts it simply and eloquently, "God said 'Let there be light,' and there was light."

Even if Swinburne were persuaded that divine creation from the plenum is a properly basic act, he might object that there is no need for my concept of the plenum. If, as he puts it, he had the power to produce a new ink-well merely by willing it, and we made certain that nothing entered the room during his act of creation and that nothing in the room was transformed into the ink-well, we would all agree that he had created the ink-well out of nothing. If an observer exclaims idiomatically, "He created that ink-well out of thin air!" Swinburne should object, "But I didn't! We have measured the quantity of air in the room and it has remained constant!" Still, for the following reasons that does not settle the issue.

Swinburne is presuming to answer a metaphysical question with an empirical procedure. Sealing off the room and measuring its contents would be appropriate to determining whether the ink-well had been formed out of something physical that was already in the room, or that entered the room after the experiment had begun. If this were done and we could not detect anything out of which the ink-well might have been created, then we would be warranted in saying that Swinburne created the ink-well out of nothing, i.e., out of nothing physical. But that procedure and its results are irrelevant to the question as to whether creation out of absolutely nothing makes sense, i.e., is conceptually coherent. Swinburne simply does not engage that question so far as I have detected. Rather, he takes it for granted that, because we can imagine something coming into existence without being created out of something else physical, therefore there are no conceptual problems in the notion of creation *ex nihilo*. I have said already why I believe there are. Further, if the rationalists have taught us anything it is that metaphysics must be conducted by means of concepts, not images.

In conclusion, if all Swinburne means by saying that God can create an individual *ex nihilo* is that he can create an individual by means of a basic act and without the use of pre-existent matter, then I agree with him that God can create *ex nihilo*. That is, we can save the notion of creation *ex nihilo* by agreeing that "nihilo" is not meant to be totally unqualified, that to create "from nothing material" is to create "from something non-material." But he may mean something more.

Now let us see how a similar qualification applies to a valuable analysis of CEN by Peter Geach. In the maiden article of *Sophia: A Journal for Discussion in Philosophical Theology*, Geach provided the following analysis of divine creation:

"God brought it about that x is A" may be construed as

"(I) God brought it about that (Ex) (x is an A)"
"(II) (Ex) (God brought it about that x is an A)"
(II) implies that God makes into an A some entity presupposed to his action; but (I) does not; and we express the supposition of God's creating an A by conjoining (I) with the negation of (II), for some suitable interpretation of "A." For example:

> God brought it about that (Ex) (x is a human soul in body b); and for no x did God bring it about that x is a human soul in body b

expresses the supposition that God created a human soul in b, and did not cause some entity presupposed to his action to be the soul of the body b.   (1962: 6)

This analysis by Geach is compatible with Aquinas' claims that (1) that which is created (in the Thomistic sense of that term) does not undergo change, i.e., *it* is not passive to divine action in the moment of its creating because before that moment it did not exist, and (2) that in the act of creation there is no real relation of God to a creature, i.e., God does not create one individual by acting on another individual antecedent to it. "There is just one A," Geach writes in elaboration of this point, "and God brought it about that (Ex) (x is an A); and for no x did God bring it about that x is an A; and c is an A." The creative act is expressed by the first three conjuncts, none of which mentions c, and the third of which denies that c was made from any individual.

This is a valuable and illuminating analysis that is compatible with the plenum and works perfectly well as long as we restrict the reference of "x" to actual individuals, such as hydrogen or clay or gold or dogs, etc. If its scope is extended to the plenum, we fall into the conceptual difficulties of classical CEN. In another publication from the same period Geach uses an analogy that breaks down in an instructive way. Speaking of how we are to understand what it means to say that God "made" the world, he illustrates the value of contrasting senses of that term.

> For example, in one respect the use of the word when applied to God is more like "the minstrel made music" than "the blacksmith made a shoe"; for the shoe is made out of pre-existing material, and, once made, goes on existing independently of the smith; whereas the minstrel did not make the music out of pre-existing material, and the music stops if he stops making it, and similarly God did not make the world out of anything pre-existing, and its continued existence depends upon his activity.   (1961: 110)

Geach's choice of examples is wonderfully illuminating, but his development of the minstrel analogy is misleading. To be sure, the minstrel did not make his music out of pre-existing sounds, but the fact that his music was not generated from pre-existing sounds does not mean that it was made from absolutely nothing; rather, it was made, for example, by acting upon a lute. Similarly, that the world was not generated from pre-existing matter does not mean that it was generated from absolutely nothing. The value of Geach's examples is in pointing out the radical emergence and contingency of finite existence. They do not suggest that creation from nothing is intelligible – unless "thing" in "nothing" is used to refer only to that which is determinate.

If "thing" is used to refer only to that which is determinate, then in creating from the plenum God creates from no thing. He creates from something "without form and void," but from something *absolutely* without form and void. If the plenum possessed form by nature, then the world could not be created from it because the plenum would always already constitute a world. In that case God could not create a world from the plenum; he could only transform the plenum from being one type of world to another. As Geach points out in reference to matter, "the world cannot have been made out of pre-existing material; for that material would itself already have been *in* the world" (1961: 110). To be sure, Genesis 1:2 describes the earth as without form and void immediately after God created it, but surely it is to be thought of as having been only relatively so, that is, as compared to the way the earth was when the author wrote. If the earth that God originally created had been absolutely void and without form, God's act of creation would have accomplished nothing; it would have created only the possibility of creating something further; but, as we have seen, God cannot create the possibility of his having possibilities, and he does not need to create matter so that he can then create physical entities. He can just directly create physical entities. Hence, in creating the earth God created something that was without form and void as compared to the way it was in the time of the author or in our time, but it was not absolutely without form and void. That distinction belongs to the plenum alone.[20]

In summary, to create is to act upon the given so as to cause some of its possibilities that are not actual to become actual. The plenum is the given to God and to God alone. For the rest of us the given is what God gives us by his acts of creation. Hence, God alone can create from the plenum. All others must actualize the possibilities of determinate actualities. This, I believe, honors the truth in the Thomist emphasis on the radical difference between divine creation and human creativity, but without falling into incoherence.

Finally, in expositing and defending my claim that the spirit but not the letter of CEN can be redeemed, let us return to the passage by the personalist philosopher Peter Bertocci quoted above on p. 65. Bertocci writes:

> ... *creatio ex nihilo* does not actually mean that God took "nothing" and made something out of it. The theist would agree that "from nothing" nothing can come. Neither God nor man can do what is not even thinkable, make nothing become something! But creation out of nothing does not mean that God "took nothing and made something out of it." "Out of" nothing, nothing comes, to be sure. But the personalist does not start with "nothing." He starts with God and says that this Person (far from being nothing himself) is the Creator-Ground of all.   (1969: 202)

It seems to be that this passage is a valiant but unsuccessful effort by Bertocci to vindicate what he acknowledges to be a difficult doctrine. He agrees emphatically that nothing can come from nothing and that no one, not even God, can make nothing become something. But then he says that God creates something out of nothing. He tries to vindicate this by pointing out that "the personalist does not start with 'nothing'. He starts with God..." That is true but beside the point. The point is that, according to Bertocci and others, God starts with nothing. If God starts with nothing, then either we reify nothing or we do not. If we reify it, we are making something out of nothing, and that is absurd. If we do not reify it, then we are saying that God can make something come from nothing, which according to Bertocci's professed principles is also absurd.

Bertocci goes on to say in the same passage:

> In a word, to say that God creates is to say that beings now exist *that did not exist before*. Finite beings are not made "out of God" or "out of some co-eternal being." They are made, produced, created. There is nothing contradictory in saying that a Creator brings into being what was non-existent without the act of creation; to create means just that!   (1969: 202)

All of this, it seems to me, Bertocci can have by means of the doctrine of the plenum without the difficulties of CEN. Creation from the plenum does not mean that finite beings are made out of God or out of a co-eternal being – at least if the latter expression means an inchoate stuff that must be manipulated. Further, finite beings produced from the plenum by God are non-existent prior to his creative act of will. Prior to creation they do not pierce reality or stand out from the plenum except as possibilities inherent to the plenum and known as such by God. In brief, God remains the sole active ground of all contingent existents, of all things that stand out from the primordial formlessness of the plenum.

It should now be clear that the plenum sets no limit on God. Let us examine this point over against two statements by Mascall. Early in *Existence and Analogy* he writes,

The ancient world had no lack of natural theology . . . But they never wholly managed to overcome the tension between transcendence and creation. Their philosophy always tended to fall into two irreconcilable parts. Sometimes they had a transcendent being whose activity was confined to the contemplation of himself, sometimes they had a divine artificer who was limited by the recalcitrance of the material upon which he had to work; in neither case was the world in its totality the product of his creative act.

(15)

The doctrine of the plenum has none of these faults. It allows God to retain his transcendence, yet to be immanent in the world. It does not require that he be confined to contemplation of himself; indeed, it requires that he know something other than himself, viz., the plenum. Further, it in no way implies that God will be "limited by the recalcitrance of the material" upon which he works. The plenum is perfectly responsive to his will. Finally, the world in its totality is the product of God's creative act. Nothing about the world was actual in the plenum prior to the creation of the world. In its every respect it was brought into existence by God.

Much later in *Existence and Analogy* Mascall states that, according to the cosmological approach to God,

In its unqualified assertion that God is self-existent and that every other being depends entirely upon him, it leaves no room for any semi-divine intermediaries between God and the world. No system of hierarchically graded aeons cascading down in a series of steadily diminishing divinity, no *Nous* or World-Soul neither fully divine nor yet exactly finite, no Arian Logos near enough to God to be able to make a world and yet far enough from God to demean himself to so lowly a work, nothing whatever to bridge the gulf between Being that is self-existent and being that is altogether dependent, except the sheer omnipotent fiat of God himself.

(124)

This is an expression of classical theist sentiment. I believe it is correct, but I do not believe it requires CEN. The doctrine of the plenum allows that God is self-existent; he certainly was not created by the plenum, and the only reason he would not exist if the plenum did not exist is that apart from the plenum it would be impossible for a being to possess omnipotent creative capacity. Further, the plenum does not require semi-divine intermediaries between God and the world. The causal efficacy of God's will upon the plenum must be immediate. If it were not, then God would be powerless because he has no parts or appendages by which he could indirectly exert his will upon the plenum – nor is there reason to think that the plenum would be susceptible to an indirect mode of influence. God's will is immediately effective on the plenum or it is not effective at all. But it must be effective; therefore it must be immediately effective. It follows that everything other than God that exists, that is a definite individual, that stands out from the indefiniteness of mere possibility, is ultimately dependent upon the will of God for its actuality.

There is, then, no where, no time, and no way in which the plenum resists, escapes, prevents, or limits God's will. It is perfectly and immediately receptive to his will. The concept of the plenum provides no ground whatsoever for the idea that there is in reality an ultimate active power other than God. God remains the sole Lord of becoming – bringing about or permitting all that ever becomes or exists contingently. Further, the plenum does not even influence God's will, much less coerce it; it does not put any type of pressure upon God to make the decisions that he makes. There is no initiative in the plenum. It is completely indifferent as to which of its possibilities God actualizes. Further, though it is the case that if God exists then necessarily the plenum exists, no specific possibility of the plenum is ever necessarily actual. The plenum does not constrain God to do anything in particular and it does not prevent him from doing anything that it is logically possible for him to do.

In brief, the doctrine of the plenum, together with the doctrine of God, provides an intelligible theory of possibility, actuality, and creation that enables us to avoid the difficulties of CEN without compromising God's freedom or omnipotence. Inasmuch as the plenum sets no limits to what God can do, and does not constrain what he does do, God's actions are decided freely on the basis of his wisdom and goodness. Hence, theists can reject CEN, affirm the plenum, and still declare with the elders beheld by St John: "Worthy art thou, our Lord and God, to receive glory and honor and power, for thou didst create all things, and by thy will they existed and were created" (Revelation 4:11).

5

Divine impassibility in knowledge

KNOWLEDGE is either of possibility or actuality. There seems to be no third alternative. Earlier I argued that God always knows the entire range of possibility. I would like to expand that claim now and focus later on God's knowledge of actuality.

From the claim that God's knowledge of possibility is necessarily exhaustive and everlasting, it follows that it is also impassible. God can never forget a possibility and, because a new one can never emerge, he can never learn of such. But what is the foundation of God's knowledge of possibilities? Aquinas argues that God knows all possibilities by virtue of knowing his own power.

> God necessarily knows things other than Himself. For it is manifest that He perfectly understands Himself; otherwise His being would not be perfect... Now if anything is perfectly known, it follows of necessity that its power is perfectly known. But the power of anything can be perfectly known only by knowing to what that power extends. Since, therefore, the divine power extends to other things by the very fact that it is the first effective cause of all things... God must necessarily know things other than Himself.

Aquinas adds shortly after the preceding that

> ... whatever effects pre-exist in God, as in the first cause, must be in His act of understanding, and they must be there in an intelligible way: for everything which is in another is in it according to the mode of that in which it is.[1]

Necessarily, then, God always knows himself perfectly, and therefore he knows his power perfectly. Because his power extends to all possibilities, either directly or indirectly, therefore by knowing his power he knows everything that is possible.

For reasons that can be inferred from my critique of CEN, I do not believe that Aquinas' position is as good as we can do. Given that CEN is impossible, obviously God cannot know the realm of possibilities merely by means of knowledge of his power. Why not? Because apart from the plenum his power would be null. Possibilities must have a passive base as well as an active effectualizer. Apart from something bearing potentialities that God could actualize, God would have no power. But of course a being without power would not be God, so that apart from the plenum, i.e., the passive base of all contingent possibilities, there could be no divine power and therefore no divine knowledge of possibilities that could be actualized by divine power.

It seems to me more plausible to say that God knows in the plenum all non-divine possibilities. The plenum is the primordial object in which God, as subject, sees all contingent possibilities, somewhat as a sculptress sees possibilities in a piece of marble. By contrast to the sculptress, though, God knows directly, exhaustively, and always all the possibilities of the plenum.

By contrast to this position, Plato, on one interpretation, spoke of a realm of forms of which God has knowledge and of a realm of matter independent of the realm of forms. As a result of this division Plato was obliged to explain how the forms could be imposed on the realm of matter. I agree with Aristotle that Plato was not very successful in this. It does not make sense to speak of forms apart from that of which they are possibilities – in Plato's case, matter. If the forms are known by themselves apart from matter, then they are not known as possibilities. They are known as a kind of actuality. If they are known as possibilities of something, which seems to me what should be the case, then they are not known independently of that something. To be sure, the distinction between form and substance is still viable, but to know the forms as distinct is not to know them as existing independently, and that seems to have been Plato's mistake, viz., to think of the Realm of Ideas and the Realm of Matter as existentially independent of one another, capable of being brought somehow, we know not how, into relation by creative efficacy.

Aquinas followed in the platonic tradition because, although he rejected the position that matter is uncreated and that the forms exist independently of God, he retained the platonic idea that the forms do not depend on matter (or in my case the plenum) for meaningful existence. Plato's solution led to an impassable dualism; Aquinas' solution led to CEN. I think we can do better by postulating a plenum the possibilities of which are known and capable of actualization by God. God cannot know these possibilities in his mind apart from the plenum because apart from the plenum they are not possibilities. It is by knowing the plenum and his power in relation to it that God knows all possibilities. Apart from his knowledge of the plenum God could not know his power over contingency because he would know nothing the possibilities of which he could actualize. Conversely, apart from knowledge of his power God could not know the plenum as the ultimate repository of all possibilities because something cannot be known as a possibility apart from knowledge of something that can actualize it.

Notice that God could not know himself apart from the plenum because he could not exist apart from the plenum. Necessarily, then, in knowing himself he knows the plenum, and in knowing the plenum he knows himself. But let us try to imagine a being that had all the characteristics of God that could possibly be had if there were no plenum. Assuming that such a being could know itself, it would not know itself as having power because it would not know anything over which it could exercise power because there would be no such thing. Here we have Aristotle's God eternally thinking itself, oblivious to potentiality or contingent actuality because there is none. If such a being knew itself to be omnipotent, it would know that it could do anything that could be done, but because there would be nothing that could be done, it would not know anything that it could do. Hence, its knowledge in this respect would be empty, merely formal, if not meaningless. The plenum is the presupposition of meaningful divine power, and therefore also of meaningful divine knowledge of omnipotence.

Does this position imply that God's knowledge of possibility is passible? No. To be sure, it implies that God's knowledge of possibility is dependent, viz., on the plenum, but, whereas passibility implies dependency, dependency does not imply passibility. Passibility is vulnerability to change induced by something distinct from that in which the change takes place. We have seen that God's knowledge of possibilities cannot be changed. Hence, God's knowledge of possibility is dependent but immutable and therefore impassible.

If we make an important distinction, however, we discover that there is a respect in which God's knowledge of possibility is not only dependent but also passible. In the preceding paragraphs of this section I have been writing about God's knowledge of *abstract possibilities*, i.e., possibilities that could ever be actualized, without regard for when or where or by whom or whether they will in fact be actualized. When we turn to God's knowledge of *concrete possibilities*, i.e., of the possibilities of existents, we discover that God's knowledge is passible as well as dependent. To be sure, such knowledge remains impassible in its comprehensiveness, i.e., nothing can change the fact that God always knows all the possibilities that are ever available to any individual. But at a specific moment in time an individual may have possibilities that it did not have earlier. God's knowledge that the individual *now* has those possibilities whereas earlier it did not have them implies that God's knowledge of the possibilities of existence is passible, i.e., changes as the possibilities of the individual change. Once upon a time, for example, God knew that it was not possible for me to go for a swim; now he knows that it is possible for me to do so. Hence, his knowledge of what is possible for me now has been changed by a change in my abilities.

We should note two types of concrete possibility: immediate and mediate. The immediate possibilities of an individual are those possibilities that the individual is presently capable of actualizing (given the supporting conditions necessary). The mediate possibilities of an individual are those possibilities that the individual is capable of becoming able to actualize. Doing computerized data analysis using SPSS, for example, is for me a mediate possibility but not an immediate one. I do not know how to do it, but I am capable of learning to do it. Flying by flapping my arms, however, is not a concrete possibility for me, at least not on planet Earth with current natural laws. Of every existent, then, God knows its immediate possibilities, its mediate possibilities, and thereby also what falls outside its parameters of possibility. God immediately and exhaustively sees these possibilities in existents, but he does not eternally or always see them in the existent because the existent does not always have them – though any possibility that any creature ever has immediately or mediately, God will have known eternally as an abstract possibility.

An important epistemological point here is that we humans come to know a determinable, like color, only by encountering instances of it. We cannot have knowledge of possibility apart from the flow of temporal actualization. Actualized possibilities, whether perceived or imagined, seem to be the saliences from which we generate the concept of a continuum of possibilities, i.e., universals. For example, we give meaning to "red" by identifying two instances of red somewhat removed from one another (perhaps one tending toward black and the other toward white) and saying, "I mean by 'red' those two colors and all the others that stand in a continuum between them."[2] God in order to know a determinable, like color, need not encounter one of its determinates in a world. He immediately and ever knows each determinable as a continuum of possibilities, and he has that knowledge by virtue of his grasp of the plenum. We know of the plenum mediately through transcendental reasoning about particular actualizations of it. God knows the plenum immediately through intuition of its possibilities.

I am, then, in agreement with the spirit of Aquinas' claim that "God necessarily knows things other than Himself." In making this statement Aquinas was presumably reacting to the Aristotelian position that God is oblivious to all things other than himself, and therefore – assuming that pantheism is not true, i.e., that the world is other than God – could not be the intentional creator of the world. Aquinas attempted to escape from Aristotle's conclusion that a perfect being would know only itself by arguing that a perfect being would have power, and would know that it had power, and therefore would know that to which its power extended, and therefore would know something other than itself.

Aquinas' reasoning in this regard is brilliant, but I believe it fails to take him all the way to his goal. Let me give two reasons. First, because of Aquinas' doctrine of CEN, his argument does not lead to God knowing things other than himself. It leads only to God knowing himself, since to know one's power in the absence of anything upon which to exercise it is, if meaningful at all, not to know something other than oneself (surely Aquinas would not violate the divine simplicity by saying that in knowing his power God knows something other than himself, as though God's power were something other than himself). Second, surely Aquinas would not say that the ideas God has of what can be created are not part of God — from which it follows that in knowing these ideas God is not knowing something other than himself. It follows from Aquinas' position that God necessarily knows something other than himself if and only if he necessarily creates something, which would, of course, be other than himself. But according to Aquinas God does not necessarily create. It follows that Aquinas' effort to vindicate the principle, "God necessarily knows things other than himself," fails.[3]

I agree, however, that that principle should be vindicated — otherwise it is incomprehensible how God could be the intentional creator and sustainer of the world. The way to proceed is by giving up the doctrine of CEN for the doctrine of the plenum. Yes, God necessarily knows something other than himself, viz., the plenum. Moreover, as Aquinas says, "the power of anything can be perfectly known only by knowing to what that power extends." In knowing the plenum God knows that to which his power extends and over which it holds unqualified sway. In knowing the plenum he knows that which is the substantial womb of all possibilities, and in knowing his omnipotence he knows that he is the Lord of the plenum.

In addition to vindicating the principle that God necessarily knows something other than himself, the doctrine of the plenum has salutary results regarding pantheism and human freedom. There is a pantheistic flavor to Aquinas' position that "effects pre-exist in God." Without the plenum Aquinas cannot help taking this position, or at least implying it, nor can he avoid its pantheistic implications if CEN is impossible. Acceptance of the plenum, however, enables one to clarify that effects pre-exist in God as efficient and final cause, not as material and formal cause. God is the efficient and final cause of the existence of the world, but the plenum is that the potentialities of which are actualized according to divine will.

Regarding human freedom, the plenum provides for its existence a foundation that is independent of divine creation, but without basing the actualization of human freedom on anything other than the will of God. This helps enable us to respond to a legitimate complaint against classical theism, a complaint that has been nicely articulated by Lewis Ford: "God could exercise all creativity," Ford writes, "but then whatever he creates could only be an extension of himself, like the objects of our imagination" (1977: 187). That is, if we are analogous to figments of human imagination, then it is difficult indeed to understand how we could have any subjective freedom. Every aspect of us would be generated by God. But if the substantial ground of our being is independent of God, though we are actualized by him, it seems more plausible that God could cause us to exist as creatures whose existence is not independent of his will but whose freedom, within limits, is. We will return to this topic in Chapter 10.

Having found in Aquinas a truth in need of a better justification, viz., "God necessarily knows things other than Himself," I find another in Whitehead. I agree with Whitehead that God should be thought of as "the unlimited conceptual realization of the absolute wealth of potentiality" (1957: 521). But Whitehead goes on, it seems, to say that the eternal objects of which God has unlimited conceptualization are known independently of actuality, as in Plato's system, and are known in unconscious fashion until they become relevant to becoming.[4] It seems to me that Whitehead has Plato's problem of impassibility between the world and eternal objects because the eternal objects are primordially known unto themselves and not as potentialities of something real. Indeed, Whitehead affirms a dichotomy between conceptual feeling and physical feeling. I am sympathetic to the distinction, but, if it is not based of the plenum, it seems to fall apart. Yes, it is meaningful to say that God "feels," "intuits," "knows," "prehends" actual individuals. Both their actuality and their potentialities are prehended by him. But the potentialities are prehended in the actuality and/or the plenum, and not apart from them. I am not willing to adopt the process position that God *physically* prehends all actualities, since God is not physical and perhaps not all actualities are physical (certainly it would seem to be a category mistake to say that the plenum is physical), but nonetheless the process position seems to me to be correct in insisting that God's knowledge of possibility is dependent on his knowledge, feeling, or prehension of something distinct from himself. The plenum is objectified in God as the realm of all non-divine possibilities; the world is objectified in God as the actualization of some of those possibilities. God's "unlimited conceptual realization of the absolute wealth of potentiality" is the result of the objectification in God of the plenum. Moreover, we should consider God's prehension of these possibilities to be conscious. Otherwise we must assume the existence of some mechanism that, according to Lewis Ford, ensures that God is conscious only of those possibilities that are relevant to the situation at hand, keeping all others at the unconscious level. Such a mechanism strikes me as awkward and *ad hoc.* It seems more fitting of the perfection and simplicity of God that he should not only be in touch with all basic possibilities, but always be aware of them.

There is another notion in Aquinas, Hume and Whitehead with which I agree and to which I would like to relate my notion of the plenum. Aquinas states that "Nothing is in the intellect that was not first in the senses" (1964: 1a.84.6–8). Hume states that "all our simple ideas in their first appearance are deriv'd from simple impressions, which are correspondent to them, and which they exactly represent" (*A Treatise of Human Nature* I, I, i). Whitehead, purporting to be in agreement with Hume, states that "all conceptual feelings are derived from physical feelings" (1957: III, 3, ii). The truth to which I believe these statements point is that knowledge of the possibilities of something requires that one be passive to that something – that one be impressed by it and 'prehend' it. I believe this is true even in the case of God. God is passive with respect to knowledge of the plenum (which is the something in which he apprehends all possibilities), but his knowledge of the possibilities of the plenum is immutable. If God's knowledge of pure possibilities (his 'conceptual feelings') were not based on his awareness ('prehension') of something in which those possibilities are inherent, then (given the incoherence of CEN) he would not know qualities and relations as possibilities for actualization; he would know them merely as actualities in his awareness.[5]

To summarize, God's knowledge of abstract possibilities is dependent but exhaustive, everlasting, and impassible, following from his perfect apprehension of the plenum, which is the reality of all contingent possibilities. God's prehension of the infinite realm of abstract possibilities is not a prehension of the possibilities of nothing, or merely of his own power, but of his power in relation to that to which those possibilities are inherent. By contrast, God's knowledge of concrete possibilities, i.e., the possibilities of actual individuals, is dependent and exhaustive, but temporal and passible, i.e., God's knowledge of the possibilities of an actual individual changes along with changes in those possibilities. Hence, God now knows me to have now some possibilities that I did not have earlier and to lack some others that I did have. The double "now" is used advisedly. An eternalist would want to leave out the first "now" because it indicates that God's knowledge of actuality is passible. Soon I shall argue that it is.

GOD'S KNOWLEDGE OF THE PAST

Is God's knowledge of the past impassible, i.e., not subject to change by external factors? Again we must answer "yes and no." God always knows everything that has occurred but no longer is occurring, and he always knows those things perfectly, not vaguely, mistakenly, or incompletely. Moreover, what is past cannot cease to be past, so God's knowledge cannot be changed by things ceasing to be past. Hence, that God knows the past exhaustively and perfectly is immutable and therefore impassible. However, the content of the past changes, i.e., the past gains content as the present changes, since every change in the present (that which is actual) means that something that was the case is no longer the case. Consequently, God's knowledge of what is past must change as things pass from being the case to no longer being the case, and hence God's knowledge of the past must be passible, i.e., subject to change by what occurs in the present. When that which is occurring ceases to occur, God's knowledge of the past is expanded and thereby changed. Hence, God's knowledge of the past is perfect and exhaustive in form but it is dependent and passible in content because it is affected by changes in the present.

GOD'S KNOWLEDGE OF THE PRESENT

God's knowledge of the present parallels his knowledge of the past. God's knowledge of the present is perfect and exhaustive, but it is dependent on what is (God does not know what is apart from what is) and what is contingently is subject to change. Therefore God's knowledge of what is contingently must be mutable, and not only mutable but passible, i.e., subject to change by what is actual and distinct from God. These points are perhaps most persuasive when change is related to the modes of time, and especially the present.[6]

I believe that Nicholas Wolterstorff is correct that the present should be understood as the pivotal temporal mode (Wolterstorff 1982: 77–8). The present is inclusive of that which is actual; the past is inclusive of that which was actual but no longer is; the future is inclusive of that which is not actual but will be. Note that these temporal modes are dependent upon the distinction between actuality and non-actuality. We only create problems for ourselves when we reify time in any mode. Time is not itself a thing; it is a notion abstracted from the durance of objects and it can be initially abstracted by us only from objects the durance of which involves change. The present is a function of those things that are actual; the past is a function of those things that were actual but no longer are; the future is a function of those things that have never been actual but will be. Such notions as simultaneity, before and after can be explained in terms of the preceding distinctions; such questions as, "What time is it?", "When did it occur?", and "How much time did it take?", will obviously have relative answers depending on the events and processes to which one chooses to anchor one's chronometer.

God knows what is actual now not only by virtue of knowing what his will is for now but also by "seeing" that what he has always willed is now actual, whereas before it was not. I believe this implies that God's knowledge of the present changes as circumstances in the present change. Peter Geach says, "God sees creatures *as* changing and *as* being in different states at different times, because that is the way things are and God sees things as they are" (1969: 93), but then Geach adds that God is unchangeable. I believe these statements are incompatible. That God sees things as they are is unnegotiable, and a changing thing can be known as changing only by a knower whose awareness follows along with it. Therefore the awareness of the knower must be passible to the changing object. This seems true of God as well as of all other knowers.

One might object that at best this would be true only of God's knowledge of changes in free agents because in all other cases God will by knowing his will know independently of things what will happen. However, whether changes in the present are brought about by God's will or by the will of his creatures is irrelevant to whether he must be passible to changing things in order to know them as changing. The epistemic principle is the same whatever the source of change: a changing thing can be known as changing only by a knower whose awareness changes along with it. Consequently, even if God has always known the future exhaustively so that he has always known that in the summer of 2000 I will make a trip to Austria, still his knowledge of what I am doing must be passible because what I will do is not alterable but what I am doing certainly is. Hence, even if his knowledge of what I *will* do is impassible, his knowledge of what I *am* doing must be passible, i.e., subject to influence by what I am doing.[7]

GOD'S KNOWLEDGE OF THE FUTURE

I have already argued that God knows perfectly the past and the present, but does he also know the future, i.e., does he know all that will come to pass? To be sure, insofar as God knows all abstract possibilities, he knows everything that will come to pass, but does he know those possibilities that will be actualized *as* possibilities-that-will-be-actualized *or* only as possibilities-that-could-be-actualized? It follows from the position that I took in Chapter 1 that God always knows those possibilities that will come to pass insofar as he is the sole free agent for their actualization. But what about those possibilities that are contingent upon the choices of other free agents – agents who are, to be sure, dependent upon the divine will for their existence, but who are, nonetheless, free in the libertarian sense of being able to actualize a possibility or not actualize it, and whether they do or not is entirely up to them, i.e., their decision is not determined or completely caused by anything external to them or internal to them? Let us examine three influential positions according to which God's knowledge of the future includes such knowledge, indeed, is inclusively perfect and therefore impassible: (1) divine foreknowledge, (2) divine eternality, (3) divine middle knowledge. All three positions assume that because God is omniscient, he must know the future exhaustively, i.e., he must know not only what can be but what specifically will be.

Jonathan Edwards, a prominent proponent of divine foreknowledge, inferred from divine omniscience that no creature is free in the libertarian sense. His reasoning went as follows.[8] There are only two ways to know a thing: the direct way and the indirect way. Something is known directly when it is immediately present to the knower. I, for example, know that I now have the perception of myself typing rather than playing the piano. But can the future be known in this direct way? Obviously not – not even by God. Why? Because, as we have seen, the future is that which is not yet, and that which is not yet cannot be present to be known directly. Hence, God can no more know the future as actual than he can know the present as not actual, or the past as changeable.

But can the future be known indirectly, i.e., by means of something other than itself – mediately rather than immediately? According to Edwards the answer is "yes." Whenever what will occur is predetermined by what is occurring, we can know the future by knowing the present and its causal effects. Indirect knowledge, then, depends upon determinism. It follows that, inasmuch as God is omniscient, therefore God knows the future exhaustively. The future is determined in every respect, and, inasmuch as there is nothing for the future to be determined by other than the will of God, it follows that the future is determined in every respect by the will of God. Hence, Edwards concluded that, because God must know the future but cannot know it directly, he must foreknow it, i.e., know it indirectly, and therefore it must be completely determined by his will, and so there is no freedom of human will.

Some have thought that a "possible worlds" approach to divine knowledge could be used to show the compatibility of divine foreknowledge with human free will. Luis de Molina of the sixteenth century termed this kind of knowledge "middle knowledge" (*scientia media*).[9] Middle knowledge stands between knowledge of what *could* happen (my "EKP") and knowledge of what *will* happen (Aquinas' "knowledge of vision"). It is knowledge of what *would* happen. If God has middle knowledge, God knows not only all that I *can* do; he knows also all that I *would* do if I were a certain way in certain circumstances and confronted with certain alternatives. Hence, God knows what I do in every possible world in which

I exist. By contrast to Jonathan Edwards' version of foreknowledge, middle knowledge does not mean that God knows what I will do in the actual world merely by knowing his will. God's knowledge of what I will do in the actual world is dependent on his knowledge of what I do in the possible world of which the actual world is an instantiation, and God's knowledge of what I do in that possible world is determined by what I do, and not by what he wills. Hence, God's knowledge of what I do in each possible world in which I act freely is determined by my decision; my decision is not determined by his knowledge; indeed, nothing determines my decision; it is a basic act. However, by knowing which possible world is the actual world, God foreknows my actions without violating my freedom.

This ingenious theory attempts to reconcile divine omniscience and human freedom by showing that God's omniscience must cover all possible worlds and that the actual world must be among those worlds and therefore be known by God. The flaw in this theory is its assumption that God can know which possible world is the actual world. At first it seems that surely God must know which possible world is the actual world, but further analysis shows why he cannot, at least when the actual world includes free creatures. The notion of middle knowledge begs the question as to whether God knows the-future-actions-of-free-agents (henceforth called "future contingents") by assuming that, because God must have knowledge of all possible worlds, he must therefore know what free agents will do in the actual world, which is, of course, an actualization of one of the possible worlds, all of which he knows.

This unwarranted inference arises, I believe, from a failure to distinguish two modalities of knowledge of possible worlds. The first modality consists of knowledge of all logically possible worlds, i.e., all worlds that are self-consistent or internally coherent. The second modality consists of knowledge of all creatable worlds, i.e., all worlds that would come to pass were they willed by God. Obviously the scope of the second set of possible worlds might be equal to but could not exceed the scope of the first set. Not so obviously, but just as surely, the scope of the second set could be narrower than that of the first set. It is possible, for example, that, though free creatures are capable of not sinning (so that for every possible free creature there is at least one logically possible world in which it does not sin), it is nonetheless a fact that, no matter which possible world God actualized, there would be no actual world in which any free creature did not sin. In such a case God would know that there was no possible world that he could create in which free creatures did not sin.[10] How can there be a logically possible world that God cannot create? Because what happens in a world in which there is a free creature depends in part on that free creature. God cannot unilaterally create a world in which free creatures freely refrain from sinning. Whether they sin or not is up to them; if they will sin in every possible world that is made actual, then God cannot actualize a possible world in which they will not sin even though there could be such a world if free creatures so chose.

If we follow out the logic of the Molinist position, I believe it becomes clear that God cannot have mode 2 knowledge of worlds in which there are free creatures. Consider Alfred Freddoso's picture of what it would be like if God had such knowledge. It would mean, Freddoso points out, that because Katie is a free agent, God would know one possible world in which Katie will wash her car at T, and another possible world which is the very same as the first possible world up to T except that at T Katie does not wash her car. This illuminates nicely part of what is implied by free agency, viz., that all things being the same up to T, Katie could have acted otherwise at T than she did in fact act. But contrary to what Freddoso suggests, this device provides no reason at all for thinking that God could unilaterally institute the one world rather than the other and thereby foreknow what Katie will do at T by knowing which possible world the actual world is.[11]

Free creatures participate with God in creating the world, i.e., in determining which possible world the actual world becomes — not in the sense of bringing it into existence in the first place, of course, but in the sense of deciding freely some of its possibilities rather than others once it has been brought into existence. Hence, with regard to worlds in which there are free creatures, God's knowledge is limited to mode 1, i.e., to what *can* come to pass. He sets the limits to the possibilities for free creatures in the actual world, but he does not foreknow which of those possibilities they will actualize. Whether this is the world in which Katie washes her car at T or the world in which she does not wash her car at T is up to Katie, not God. That is what it means for God to have created her as a free agent, viz., that he made her a co-creator in determining this world. When God creates a world with free agents in it, he is logically limited to presenting them with alternatives in that world; but whether that world becomes a world in which Katie freely washes her car at T or does not is up to Katie, and the issue is not resolved until T.

God, then, has given free creatures the capacity and responsibility to participate with him in creating this world, and not even God knows in advance which possible world we will bring into actuality. Consequently, God must be passible in relation to change in the world in order to know whether this is the possible world in which Katie freely washes her car at T or not. To be sure, God does know eternally the parameters within which our choices will take place, and the consequences that will flow from our various possible actions, but the full actuality of the world is a joint product of the decisions and actions of God and free creatures. Which possible world the actual world is is still being decided – but the only decisions left to be made are those by us. Because they are free they cannot be foreknown by God knowing his will or possible worlds.

Still, there is something in the notion of God that haunts us with the conviction that in his omniscience God must know the future, including free creaturely actions. Let us look at a third type of attempt to vindicate this conviction. Eternalists insist that humans are free and that God knows what we will do in our freedom, but they deny that God *fore*knows future contingents, i.e., knows them by means of knowing something else. Their strategy for avoiding the dilemma of human freedom versus omniscience is to attempt to break the horn which says that God cannot know the future directly.[12] The most impressive recent attempt to do this is by Eleonore Stump and Norman Kretzmann. In their article, 'Eternity' (429–58), they explain, illustrate, defend, and apply the position that God is eternal.[13] God's eternality, i.e., his "complete possession all at once of illimitable life," means *inter alia*, that the entire content of time, including the future, is timelessly present to God. Clearly this position cuts across Edwards' argument that God cannot know the future directly. Indeed, Stump and Kretzmann say explicitly, "It cannot be that an eternal entity has a vision of Nixon's death before it occurs; in that case an eternal event would be earlier than a temporal event. Instead, the actual occasion of Nixon's dying is present to an eternal entity" (442). Later the authors state that "the only way in which an eternal entity can be aware of any temporal event is to be aware of it as it is actually happening. And from the eternal viewpoint every temporal event is actually happening." Hence God does not *fore*know the future. The future, the present, and the past are ever present to God. By contrast, "There is no single temporal viewpoint; even when the temporal present is taken to be absolute, the temporal viewpoint that is correctly designated as *now* is incessantly changing" (457). The authors disclaim that their position implies "that the future pre-exists somehow, so that it can be inspected by an entity that is outside time" (442). It does not, however, seem to me that their defense of this disclaimer is successful if it is true that change is not illusory.

I have no doubt that Jonathan Edwards would have given up any belief for the glory of God, but he does appear to have preferred to work things out in such a way that his position did not nullify the reality of change. If he had given up that belief, he could have agreed readily enough with eternalists that God knows the future directly. That is, if the experience of perceiving or undergoing becoming is an illusion peculiar to creatures, then there are no future events, i.e., no events that are not now actual but will be; hence the seeming non-existence of future events is an illusion; everything that we ever experience as coming into being or passing out of being is something that God knows as always happening. Hence, what we call the future is timelessly present to God but only gradually revealed to us. As Plato suggested, time is related to eternity as sequential vision of something is related to instantaneous vision of it; time is the moving peephole through which we see partially and successively the panorama of which God is timelessly aware.

An eternalist might defend her position against the preceding charge by arguing that, just because things are not changing in God's awareness, it does not follow that change is an illusion. To be sure, relative to God things are not changing; he knows them all as actual. Relative to earthly creatures, however, things are changing – really changing. That is to say, relative to us some things have not yet come to pass, but relative to God all things that will ever come to pass have always come to pass.

Stump and Kretzmann defend this distinction by alluding to the relativization of the concept of simultaneity in modern physics. According to this reconceptualization of simultaneity,

> ... there is no privileged observer (or reference frame) such that with respect to it we can determine whether the two events are *really* simultaneous; simultaneity is irreducibly relative to observers and their reference frames, and so is time itself. Consequently, it would be a mistake to think that there is one single uniform mode of existence that can be referred to in specifying 'at once' in (G) [Simultaneity = existence or occurrence at once (i.e., together)] in order to derive a definition of temporal simultaneity.   (438)

The point seems to be that, as simultaneity is relative to the observer, so that the same two events can be simultaneous to one observer yet without contradiction non-simultaneous to another observer, so one and the same reality can be future (and therefore non-actual) with respect to one observer (such as a human) and yet without contradiction be present (and therefore actual) with respect to another observer (such as God) if the modes of being of the two observers are appropriately different. The key notion here seems to be that there is no privileged observer. Whether two events are simultaneous or not *really* depends on the observer, i.e., the reference frame from which the judgment is made, and whether one and the same event is actual or not depends on the mode of being of the observer, i.e., whether the observer is eternal or temporal.

To the preceding argument I would like to object first that the analogue is not relevant. It treats a metaphysical problem as though it were epistemological. Two events that are simultaneous could affect the same perceiver at the same time or different times. Two events that are not simultaneous could affect the same perceiver at different times or the same time. That P_1 observed E_1 and E_2 simultaneously does not mean that E_1

and E_2 occurred simultaneously. The former says only that two perceptions occurred simultaneously; it does not entail that the two events which
caused the perceptions occurred simultaneously – as we can now illustrate
dramatically by reference to simultaneous perceptions of stars, some of
which exploded thousands of years apart.

What makes two events simultaneous is not that they are perceived
simultaneously but that they occur simultaneously. Moreover, I believe
that we have a perfectly good and simple notion of simultaneity. Simultaneity is not a triadic relation, as can be seen from the fact that we can
conceive of a simultaneity relation in a world in which there are only two
objects. However, introducing a third object is a valuable way of explicat-
ing the notion of simultaneity by pointing out some of its implications. For
example, assuming that light always travels at the same speed, if E_1 and E_2
are simultaneously occurring, motionless sources of light and there is a
motionless object exactly midway between them, then it will take light
from those events exactly the same amount of time to reach the closest
respective surfaces of that object, and those two surfaces will be struck
simultaneously by the light emitted from E_1 and E_2. However, it is not
necessary for there to be an intermediating object or any third object for E_1
and E_2 to occur simultaneously (a similar analysis can be applied to the
simultaneous duration of objects).

It seems, then, that the notion of simultaneity is not meaningless apart
from an observer, i.e., a third party, but in order to explicate it we may turn
to its implications for a third party. The fullest explication, I suspect,
arises from application of the calculus, whereby it can be deduced from the
relative rates of motion of two objects and an observer, plus their distances
and angles from one another, and the speed of the medium of transmission
(e.g., light or sound), whether two objects that were not perceived as
occurring simultaneously nonetheless occurred simultaneously or whether
two objects that were perceived as occurring simultaneously did not in fact
occur simultaneously. One could also extrapolate whether two events that
did not occur simultaneously would nonetheless be perceived simultaneously by O_1 and whether two events that did occur simultaneously would
nonetheless be perceived by O_1 as not occurring simultaneously. Hence, if
we relativize simultaneity to an observer, then there is no vantage point
from which absolute judgments of simultaneity can be made – or, to put
the point another way, every vantage point becomes an absolute vantage
point so that two events can occur both simultaneously and non-
simultaneously at the same time. But then the simultaneity being spoken of
is the simultaneity of perceptions and not the simultaneity of the events
causing the perceptions.

I do not mean to suggest that we should return to a pre-Einsteinian notion of simultaneity in science. A creaturely attempt to judge whether two events have occurred simultaneously can be made only from a specific frame of reference within the world – a world the whole of which we cannot take into account. Hence, there are good reasons to say that humans cannot determine absolute simultaneity and therefore should understand that they can perform only relativistic ascertainments of simultaneity. For these reasons Einstein as a scientist appropriately abandoned the metaphysical aspects of simultaneity to focus on its epistemological aspects as a phenomenon of human perception and cognition. Humans cannot judge whether two events occur simultaneously relative to one another but only relative to the effects of the events upon an observer, thereby allowing that the same two events could occur simultaneously to one observer and non-simultaneously to another. Stump and Kretzmann are correct, then, that there is no privileged reference frame from which humans can determine that two events are simultaneous *simpliciter* to one another – but that does not mean that there is no possible frame of reference from which such knowledge could be had.[14]

Further, the use of the simultaneity example seems disanalogous because, in the problem that the analogy is supposed to illuminate, the question is not whether the same *two* events could occur simultaneously to one observer but not to another, but whether one and the same event, such as Nixon dying, could be simultaneously in the present of one being and in the future of another. If the answer to the second question is "yes," it follows that one and the same event can be simultaneously actual and not actual (hence the simultaneity here has to do not with the occurrence of two events but with the occurrence of one and the same event in two modes of existence). The Stump/Kretzmann solution is that the question, "Is x actual?", cannot be answered until it is expanded to include the prepositional phrase, "to whom?", and then it can be answered variously depending on the mode of being of the one on behalf of whom the question is asked. If the one on behalf of whom the question is asked is eternal, then the answer (assuming that we are considering something that, humanly speaking, does not yet exist but will) is always "yes." If the one on behalf of whom the question is being asked is temporal, then the answer is "no" – revealing that the question can be simultaneously answered "yes" and "no" without contradiction.

Isn't it the case, though, that God must be affirmed as a privileged observer – that if he holds something to be true, it is true? that if he holds something to be good, it is good? that if he is aware of something as actual, then it is actual? I have been unable to escape this intuitive conviction in spite of impressive counter-arguments by Stump/Kretzmann. God does not know the past as actual any more than he knows the future as actual.

To be sure, we can say that he knows the past as vividly as he did when it was actual, but that is not to know the past as actual. It is to know it with the clarity and completeness with which the actual is divinely known. But, because that which is not actual cannot be known as actual, it follows that, if the future is known as actual by God, then because God cannot be mistaken our belief that the future lies before us must be false, and the occurrence of change must be an illusion. Time becomes the platonic peephole through which we observe things that God knows to have been always in existence. We thereby come to the mistaken impression that things occur sequentially when in fact, as God knows, they exist simultaneously. In brief, either a thing is changing or it is not. If God does not know it as changing but we know it as changing, then one of us is mistaken, and it surely is not God. Therefore if eternalism is true, then experience of change is an illusion.

If my contention that eternalism implies that change is an illusion is correct, one might want to reject eternalism simply on the ground that this implication is intuitively absurd. I do not believe, however, that we are limited to an intuitive rejection of eternalism. I believe, as does Peter Geach, that it can be proved that change is no illusion and that, therefore, eternalism is false.[15] To be sure, it might, as phenomenalists claim, always be an illusion on my part that my perceptions of change are being caused by changing objects that exist externally to me and independently of me, as realists would have it. Perhaps when I believe I am perceiving it is always the case that I am hallucinating or being subjected to divine or demonic mind control. But even so there cannot have been an illusion in my experience of undergoing subjective change, whether in mental imagery, thoughts, or feelings. I understand that an evil demon or God almighty could make me believe I was perceiving an external object undergo change when in fact I was not, but I do not believe it is possible for change to be not taking place in any mode when I experience change.

Notice that eternalism must hold not only that God knows as actual, and therefore unchanging, that which is external to me, but also that God knows my experience, my future subjectivity, as actual and therefore unchanging. But I know that my experience is changing, i.e., is passing from potential to actual, from one state to another, and therefore I know that God does not know my future subjective states as actual, and thereby I know also that eternalism is false, since it implies that God knows my subjective states as actual when they are not actual. It is impossible that he could, and it is a fact that my subjective states have passed from non-actual to actual. Therefore eternalism is false. As Geach puts it, "A man can no more 'only think' he has changing impressions of the world than he can 'only think' he is unhappy" (1972b: 305). The experience of temporal succession cannot be an illusion because "the so-called illusion of successiveness is already a real succession of experiences: just as misery cannot be an illusion, because to be under the illusion of misery would be real misery" (1969: 92).

Perhaps I cannot know that there are existing independently of me objects undergoing the changes that I seem to perceive, but I can know directly (as Edwards might put it) that changes are taking place in my thinking, feeling, believing, or imaging. Inasmuch as these changes are coming into being only now, God could not have known them as actual earlier. (An eternalist would, of course, say that God *didn't* know them as actual *earlier*. Eternal knowledge has no temporal relations to anything. But that only dodges the issue at hand, viz., whether it is possible for a thing to be known as actual by God when it has not yet become actual in the world.) Even if I were an eternalist and went so far as to say that my thinking, feeling, or imaging was not changing and never did, i.e., that all that I ever think, feel, or image I have always been thinking, feeling, or imaging, still, it seems to me, it would have to be conceded that the content of my awareness of what I have always thought, felt, and imaged, is changing, so that God cannot know in advance as actual what I will be aware of as my thoughts, feelings, or images. As Anthony Kenny has put it, "changeless awareness of a changing world" is not possible (1979: 48). Hence, God must be passible in his knowledge of the future.

It follows, then, that God can know the future, but only insofar as it can be known indirectly, that is to say, insofar as it is determined solely by his will. This means that any knowledge that God has of the future is impassible because, as we saw earlier, his will is impassible. This also means that if humans are free, God cannot know their future free choices because the only things about the future that can be known are things that are necessary in themselves or depend entirely on the will of God. This is to say more than that God does not know future free choices as actual before they become actual. That is also true of future actualities that are wholly determined by God's will. God knows which of the possibilities that are entirely dependent upon his own will will become actual; but he does not know which of the possibilities of free creatures will become actual.

Geach seems to be developing the opposite position with his God-as-chess-master analogy (1972a: 325; 1977: 58). If so, he is adequately refuted by Anthony Kenny: "When a Grand Master plays a novice he may foresee every possible move, but he does not foresee which moves will actually be made: even if the game goes no further than Fool's Mate there are many different pairs of opening moves the Fool can make" (1979: 59).[16] This does not mean that God is therefore always in something of a muddle until a creature makes a decision. Geach's analogy of God-as-chess-master illustrates this nicely with regard to a situation in which the alternatives are disjunctive, viz., the chess game. But, as we have seen, it is meaningful and reasonable to believe that, because God knows by means of continua and not by means of disjuncts what each individual can do, God has always provided for whatever a free agent might do. There are no disjuncts between which we can choose an alternative that will catch God unprepared.

Even insofar as the future is to be totally determined by God's will, i.e., will not be influenced by another free will, God in knowing the future does not know that which is actual; what he knows is what will come to pass; he does not know *that* which will come to pass; he does not know the future as actual until it comes to pass, and then, of course, it is not future, it is present. Prior to that he knows only the possibility and the certainty of it coming to pass (insofar as we are speaking only of things that are to be determined totally by the will of God).

Hence, God has no knowledge of the future by vision, no *scientia visionis* as Aquinas puts it. Perhaps the notion that "possible individuals" stands for "individuals" resulted from people's efforts to make sense of God's knowledge of the future by vision. One could have reasoned, "Because God knows the future by vision, he must know something that is not actual in the world. Hence, God must know each object before it becomes actual in the world. That is, he must eternally know each object as identical to itself in every respect except that of actuality." I have argued already that this kind of thinking is mistaken. It seems more correct to say that God knows not the object itself, minus only the one quality of actuality – as though a possibility were an actuality minus the actuality – but, rather, knows the possibility and inevitability that there will come to pass an individual that fulfills a certain description or cuts certain continua at certain points. An actual individual does not spring into existence by virtue of its counterpart in the realm of possibility having actuality laminated to it or suffused into it. There are no such counterpart individuals in the plenum before or after the emergence of individuals. Here Hartshorne seems to be correct that there are no individuals apart from actuality and determinateness. God does not see individuals in the plenum; he sees in the plenum the possibility of individuals. God does not see possible individuals in actualities; he sees in actualities the possibility of further actualities.

To summarize, God always knows exhaustively what the future can be, and he always knows what it will be insofar as it is completely determined by his will. Moreover, he always knows what his will will be no matter what other free agents finally decide and do. However, insofar as what he wills is alternatives for free creatures to choose between or among, God does not know which of the alternatives will come to pass. What he knows is that each agent must choose within the parameters set by its powers and circumstances.

It follows from this analysis that free creatures have some degree of control over what God will know. Hence, as was pointed out earlier, God's knowledge exceeds his power inasmuch as he can know the possibility of things, e.g., "Jane freely refraining from lying," that he cannot make happen. God cannot make a free creature do x freely — though, of course, he can and must make it *possible* for a creature to do x freely. Hence, God's knowledge exceeds his power, but nothing necessary, inexorable, possible, past, or present escapes his knowledge. Nothing escapes his knowledge that is knowable now or everlastingly; hence, nothing escapes his knowledge but the future free decisions of his creatures and, therefore, which of their alternatives will be implemented. It follows that free creatures have some degree of control over what God will know in the present. I, for example, can cause God to know me as finishing this paragraph before or after I eat lunch today.

Peter Geach has been emphatic that "any 'rethinking' of God's change-lessness... can lead only to an alien and incoherent view of the Divine" (1972a: 322; also 1969: 105; and 1961: 110–14 and 119). Geach's concern seems to be that, if God is changed by the changes that he institutes, then he must be thought of as part of the world rather than transcending it and, if he is only part of the world, then he can create it *ex nihilo* neither in the Thomistic sense nor in the qualified sense that I accepted earlier, and he must be thought of as just part of the system of causes in the world rather than as the cause of the system. In Geach's own words, "if God is changed by the changes of creatures, then God will only be one more ingredient in that aggregate of changeable beings which we call the world, and will not be the Maker of the World" (1972a: 322; also 1961: 114). I am sympathetic to much of what I believe motivated Geach to make these statements. I, too, have argued that God's nature, will, and knowledge of basic possibilities must be immutable. However, to insist that God has "changeless awareness of a changing world," as Kenny puts it, is to build incoherence into the concept of God. Allowing possibility in God's knowledge of change entails no inappropriate limitation of God's nature, will, or knowledge of possibilities. Though it does follow that we should think of God as part of the absolute, i.e., as part of the whole constituted by God, plenum, and world, it does not follow that we should think of God as part of the world.

It follows from the above that God's knowledge of the inexorable future, i.e., the future as entirely dependent upon his will, is impassible; however, he has no knowledge of the contingent future, i.e., the future as contingent on the decisions of free creatures. It also follows that, because God has no knowledge, either passible or impassible, of the contingent future, that his knowledge of the present must be passible where the behaviour of free creatures is involved. That is, the free creature within limits determines what God knows her to be doing. When the free creature makes a choice she causes God to know what he did not know and could not have known before, viz., what the creature would do in its freedom at a certain time. God does not know in advance what a free creature specifically will do because what she will do is not actual or determined until the moment of her choice. Hence, God's knowledge of what is becoming actual, i.e., is happening in the present, is affected by the decisions of free creatures. What God will know is to some extent dependent upon and under the control of free agents, but, as we have seen, this does not imply that God must wait upon the decisions of free creatures in order to decide or implement his response.

In conclusion, I believe that the above solution gets around both the problem of foreknowledge and the problem of eternality. It gets around the problem of eternality by protecting the reality of change and avoiding the obscurity of the Stump/Kretzmann explanation of the relation of eternity to time. It gets around the determinism implied by foreknowledge by holding that God does not and cannot have foreknowledge of future contingents. It neutralizes objections to the resultant lack of knowledge on God's part by showing that (1) God always knows all abstract and concrete possibilities, (2) individuals cannot be known as actual in advance of their being actual, (3) future creaturely free actions are in themselves unknowable, and (4) because of (1) God does not need to know the contingent future in order to determine and implement his will in an appropriate way.

Parenthetically, my position removes what was an important motive for Aquinas' adoption of the position of divine eternality. Aquinas points out in *The Disputed Questions on Truth* that some people "have said that God does not know future contingents. This opinion," he objects, "cannot stand, for it would eliminate providence over human affairs, which are contingent" (q.2, a.12). Providence over human affairs would, of course, be no problem for God were human affairs entirely determined by his will. But they are not, and so, Thomas thought, God must know what we will do in order to formulate a response to it, but the freedom of our doing can be preserved only if God's knowing of it is in the mode of present observation, not foreknowledge. Hence, Thomas concluded, the future must be *present* to God.

We have seen the difficulties with this doctrine, and Thomas overlooked the fact that, if God knows all possibilities, then he can exercise providence over human affairs just as completely and adequately as he could if the future were present to him. Hence, the dilemma "Either God cannot exercise providence or humans are not free" is, as Aquinas saw, a false dilemma, but it is not false for the reason he thought. He thought it false because he believed that eternalism allowed him to break both horns. We have seen that eternalism itself is a broken reed, but we can still defeat the dilemma by means of EKP. To be sure, this means that God cannot, as C. S. Lewis would have it, adjust the past in response to what he knows future contingents will be, as in saving my son from drowning at t_1 because he knows that at t_5 when I find out about the boating accident I will pray that my son not have drowned, but this divine inability is not a loss that could have been prevented, and, because the future remains within the confines of God's goodness, wisdom, and power, it does not imply a flaw or deficiency in his providence (Lewis 1947: 185–6; Geach 1969: 90).

Perhaps the following aside is appropriate here. If process thinkers are correct that necessarily every individual enjoys some degree of freedom, i.e., an individual is by nature free, so that God cannot create an individual without freedom anymore than he can create a triangle without sides, that simply means that God never has knowledge of the future behavior of any individual other than himself. If this is true, then God does not know what any creature will do in the future. Even this extreme situation, however, would create no difficulty for God as regards his own decision-making and actions. Because of his knowledge of possibility his will can be and presumably is eternally decided as regards anything any creature might decide to do.[17]

Eternalism does not presuppose the necessary freedom of every individual, but it was introduced into Boethius' *Consolation of Philosophy* in order to redeem the doctrine of human freedom from those who thought it incompatible with divine omniscience. Under analysis it seems to me that eternalism itself is not compatible with human freedom. Consider that, if God knows what I will do in the future because he eternally knows me as doing it, then, if he knows me as doing it, I must be doing it and I must have always been doing it. But if I am doing it and have always been doing it, then there was never an opportunity for me to have done otherwise; but, if I never had an opportunity to do otherwise, then I was never free to do otherwise. That is, eternalism implies that I have always been making all the choices that I ever make. Hence, there was never an opportunity to do otherwise. But, if there is never an opportunity to do otherwise, then it is never the case that I am free to do otherwise. Therefore, if eternalism is true, then human behavior is not free.[18]

6

God, time, and eternity

I HAVE REJECTED the doctrine that God knows the future as actual, that what to us is future is present to God. Therefore I also reject the doctrine that God is eternal in the Boethian sense. Still, I feel closer to the classical position on this issue than I do to the process position, so I would like to state more fully my intuitions on God, time, and eternity and then propose what I believe to be an advance upon the Boethian conception of eternality.

For three reasons it would not make sense to say that God is temporal. First, God does not change with respect to any of the determinations that are his by nature, e.g., his existence, essence, knowledge of absolute potentiality, or will. (In Chapter 7 I will address the issue of God's bliss.) Second, none of these aspects of God has or could have a beginning or end. Third, the duration of none of these aspects of God can be meaningfully measured. These points do not mean, however, that temporal assertions cannot be made meaningfully of God.

The last sentence needs elaboration, and elaboration of it requires that I propose a definition of time. Foolhardy as it might seem to make such a proposal, and, as sympathetic as I am to Augustine's lament about the difficulty of saying what time is, I venture the following. Time is the order or medium of sequential duration. That which exists in time is something the existence of which is contingent and the duration of which is therefore sequential. Temporality is the mode of duration enjoyed by anything the existence of which is contingent. Contingent existence is necessarily successive existence because, even if a contingent existent has always existed and never changed, still its existence is being continually renewed, sustained, received from moment to moment.

Perhaps I can add some clarity to my position by contrasting it to that of G. H. von Wright in his *Time, Change, and Contradiction*. There von Wright says that "duration is, after all, a notion secondary to that of temporal succession..." (17) But that seems backward. Duration – or, perhaps better, "durancy" – is the property of lasting or enduring that any existing thing must have, else it would not be an existing thing. Hence, it is by virtue of having the property of duration that a thing might have the further property of temporal succession.

Von Wright also argues that time cannot pass without change. Here I believe that Sydney Shoemaker is correct. Time can pass without change. Though Shoemaker's article, 'Time Without Change,' was contrary to my convictions when I first read it, I now agree with his point and believe it is implicit in Aristotle's observation that time can measure rest as well as motion and change. To be sure, the *passage* of time could not be measured if nothing were changing; in order for the extent of duration to be measured, there must be change in the instrument of measurement even if there is no change in that which is measured. If, for example, we imagine a world in which nothing is changing but a single clock, I assume we would agree that time was passing in that world and that its passage could be measured by means of the clock. If the clock, too, were stopped, would it be correct to say that time had stopped in that world? I do not think so. The *measurement* of time would have become impossible because of the absence of a working measuring device. But, because the world's duration would be received from God and enjoyed successively, even though the length of its duration could not be measured because of the absence of a usable instrument of measure, still it would be a kind of thing the duration of which it would be meaningful to measure, i.e., to time (using "time" as a verb). In brief, the concept of time is meaningless apart from the concept of contingent duration and the conceivability of the measurement of successiveness.

Also relevant to this point is Aquinas' analysis of temporality. He begins by pointing out that any being whose existence has a beginning or an end is temporal. He adds that any being that undergoes a change is temporal. With less clarity but no less confidence he adds that any being that is changeable, even though it does not change, is temporal. With all of this I agree, and, because the modality of the last qualification includes the earlier ones, it seems to me that we can simplify Aquinas' position as follows: any changeable being is a temporal being, i.e., exists in the order of successive duration. If a being has a beginning or an end or undergoes a change, that demonstrates that it is temporal, but these are not necessary conditions of temporality. An entity could be without beginning, end, or change, and yet be temporal, rather than atemporal, because its existence and characteristics were contingent upon and therefore subject to change by God. Moreover, as pointed out earlier, it would enjoy its existence successively from God. Hence, even though it did not change, time would be passing relative to it, and so time would pass in a world of unchanging creatures.

God, by contrast, does not enjoy his existence successively. To be sure, God enjoys duration, as does anything existent, but his duration is not received or renewed or sustained. His nature is such that he simply is. He is not only unchanging in this respect; he is unchangeable – and that, as Aquinas saw, makes a categorical difference between God and creatures. All existents other than God could have not existed. Moreover, all existents other than God are continually dependent on the will of God for their continued existence. God's existence, by contrast, is not received from beyond himself; nor does he receive it from himself. He simply is. His duration is necessary, not contingent, and therefore it is atemporal rather than temporal; i.e., God exists outside the order of contingent existence and successive duration. His mode of duration is eternality, not temporality, eternality being a mode of existence in which duration is enjoyed atemporally.[1]

Plotinus has said some particularly illuminating things on these topics. In the *Enneads*, III.7.6., he wrote:

... the conception of Eternity demands something which is in its nature complete without sequence; it is not satisfied by something measured out to any remoter time or even by something limitless, but, in its limitless reach, still having the progression of futurity: it requires something immediately possessed of the due fullness of Being, something whose Being does not depend upon any quantity (such as installments of time) but subsists before all quantity.

I can think of no other passage in which time and eternity have been distinguished so brilliantly. That which is eternal is by nature complete without succession or development. This mode of existence is not satisfied by anything the existence of which can be measured out to a remoter time (thereby revealing successiveness in its existence) or by anything that is limitless in some respect but characterized by progression in time, i.e., which can be characterized by installments of existence proceeding into the future. That which is eternal must simply be, must be necessarily, completely and immediately possessed of the fullness of its being. On the assumption that there can be only one eternal being, it follows that all other individuals exist by virtue of receiving installments of sequential duration from the one individual who is eternal. Hence, the life of every individual other than God necessarily has a past, present, and future, no matter how brief the segment of time it may occupy. By contrast, as Philo says, "in eternity there is no past nor future, but only present existence" (Philo 1930: sec. 277.32). Because God is unchanging, unchangeable, and in no respect dependent on anything as he is in himself, it would be a category mistake to speak of a past or future within his life, or to say that he "grows older" as time passes (that is a notion applicable only to individuals whose mode of existence is that of temporal duration). In no respect can God's life be described as involving sequence or successiveness; as Plotinus puts it, God is "instantaneously entire, complete, at no point broken into period or part" (III.7.3). Plotinus goes on to say of eternity that "all its content is in immediate concentration as at one point; nothing in it ever knows development"; it is "Life in repose, unchanging, self-identical, always endlessly complete..." (III.7.3 and 11). There is, however, an important qualification to be made here, a qualification that will not be acceptable to Boethians. We will look at it closely after noting something that God's eternality does not imply.

That God is eternal, and therefore exists outside of time, i.e., outside the order of successive duration, does not imply that no temporal statement can be applied meaningfully and truly to God. For example, if I say on the assumption that there is a God, "God existed at the time that I was born, and therefore he has now existed at least 44 years," I believe I speak truly. Further, there are a number of open-ended statements of this sort that can be made of God meaningfully and correctly: "God has existed longer than the Rock of Gibraltar"; "God will exist longer than planet Earth"; "God is older than the oldest living human"; and so on.

Such statements would be false and misleading if they were taken to mean or imply that exhaustive temporal measurements can be made of God's existence. To be sure, as the numbers in the set of whole numbers can be counted, so the duration of God can be measured, but the duration of God can no more be measured exhaustively than the numbers in the set of whole numbers can be counted exhaustively. God's aseity means that his duration cannot possibly be measured exhaustively; his aseity means that he simply is. With regard to his existence there is no change within him, and because his duration is not received, it is not distributed into before and after. Therefore any effort to measure his duration exhaustively would be a category mistake, and to say that his duration is infinite is not to give its measure but to assert the inapplicability of measure to it in itself.

Statements about God involving temporal indicators would also be misleading and false if they were taken to imply that there was, could be, or could have been a time at which God did not exist. Once we understand that God exists necessarily, we should realize that he exists at the same time as or while anything else exists or happens. Hence, the durancy of God enables us to make simultaneity or duration statements about the existence of God in relation to the world without implying that God's existence is temporal. To say that God existed at the time that I was born is merely to say that God enjoyed duration at the moment that I came into existence; to say that God has now existed 44 years longer than he had when I was born is not to say that God exists in the order of time; it is to say that God has enjoyed duration the entire while of my existence from birth to now.

Perhaps I can make my position clearer by reference to a debate between Delmas Lewis and William Mann (American Philosophical Association,

1982). Lewis presented a paper, 'Eternity Again,' in which he critiques Stump/Kretzmann and points out that if Stump at t_1 compiled a list of what there was at t_1, she would include God – from which we could infer that, since God existed at t_1, he is not Boethian-eternal. William Mann's response, 'Eternity Redux,' points out that a list of what there is at t_1 is ambiguous between what there is *at t_1* and what there is *simpliciter*. I believe it would be still more accurate to say that the list is ambiguous between (1) what there is temporally at t_1, (2) what there is atemporally at t_1, and (3) what there is *simpliciter* ((3) being the genus of (1) and (2)). From these distinctions I believe we can see that statements about God which involve temporal indicators, e.g., "God exists now," "God existed at t_1," "God existed from t_1 to t_9," "God will always exist," do not in and of themselves entail anything about the mode of God's existence. More broadly, because of the ambiguity of such statements as "x existed at t_1," or "x existed from t_1 to t_9," I do not believe that it can be inferred from them that the mode of existence of x is temporal, i.e., is of the order of contingent duration. We will return to this point soon.

In brief, God's existence does not involve successiveness. He simply is. But his existence does involve duration. Hence, as Stump/Kretzmann point out so nicely, God's life involves atemporal duration – and, though that fact precludes appropriately making certain types of temporal statements about God, it does not preclude others. One does not have to enjoy temporal duration in order to exist when something begins to happen or ceases to happen, or while a temporal state of affairs obtains; one merely need enjoy duration, whether temporal or atemporal, when or while such things occur in order for it to be said correctly that one existed at the time or during the time when those things occurred.

DOES GOD POSSESS THE WHOLE OF HIS LIFE AT ONCE?

I want to argue, "Yes, God possesses the whole of *his* life all at once." God is, as Plotinus put it, "in repose, unchanging, self-identical, always endlessly complete," "at rest in unity" (III.7.11). His existence, nature, knowledge of absolute possibility, and will are forever unchangeable. As Aquinas put it, there is no before or after in God. "He does not have being after non-being, nor non-being after being, nor can any succession be found in His being. For none of these characteristics can be understood without time. God, therefore, is without beginning and end, having His whole being at once" (1975: 98).

A corollary of the preceding point is that two creatures that do not exist simultaneously with one another nonetheless exist simultaneously with the very same life of God because there is no change in the life of God by virtue of which it could be said correctly that the later creature did not exist simultaneously with the life of God in all the same respects in which the earlier creature did. I agree with Aquinas, then, that "Something can be present to what is eternal only by being present to the whole of it, since the eternal does not have the duration of succession" (1975: 219). There is nothing about God's existence, nature, will, or knowledge of absolute possibility that is past or future with regard to any event or entity in time. Hence, those events in time that do not exist simultaneously with one another nonetheless exist simultaneously with the whole of God as he is in himself. Events may exist later than one another, but they cannot exist earlier or later in relation to God because God does not exist earlier or later in relation to anything. He simply is. Because nothing has changed, is changing, or will change in the life of God as he is in himself, every creature that ever exists exists, when it exists, simultaneously with the very same life of God to which earlier and later creatures were and will be simultaneous when they existed or exist.

It does not follow, however, that because God possesses his life all at once that everything is all at once present in God. I would like to elaborate this point in the form of a reaction to the following statement by Aquinas: "God's understanding has no succession, as neither does His being. He is therefore an ever-abiding simultaneous whole -- which belongs to the nature of eternity. On the other hand, the duration of time [as distinguished from the duration of eternity] is stretched out through the succession of the before and after" (1975: 218). Here I suggest that Aquinas' Boethian conception of eternity is in need of modification. I agree that God possesses *his* whole being at once; there is no change, no before and after, no succession, no flow of duration in his life. He embraces the whole of his life all at once.

By contrast, as Boethius points out, "there is nothing placed in time that can embrace the whole of its life equally" (Stump 1981: 430). This, we have seen, is true even of an ever existing, unchanging creature. Hence, God enjoys *his* life all at once whereas a creature enjoys *its* life sequentially, even if it does not change, enduring forever identically. Stump/Kretzmann put this point nicely: "Because an eternal entity is atemporal, there is no past or future, no earlier or later, *within its* life; that is, the events constituting its life cannot be ordered sequentially from the standpoint of eternity" (Stump 1981: 434). The emphasis on "within" is by Stump/ Kretzmann; it seems intended to accentuate the point that God undergoes no change. The emphasis on "its" is mine and is meant to press the point that we should distinguish between God's knowledge of his own life and his knowledge of the lives of his creatures. Yes, God is eternal in the sense that he possesses the whole of his own life equally, i.e., unchangingly and everlastingly. All that he does not possess in this manner are the lives of his creatures. This lack does not indicate a deficiency in God or in our concept of God; such possession is, for reasons stated in the last chapter, impossible in principle. Now let me try to make a more convincing case for my claim that, though God possesses his life all at once, and therefore can be appropriately called eternal, he does not possess the lives of others all at once.

DOES GOD POSSESS THE BEING OF OTHERS ALL AT ONCE?

I have agreed with classical eternalists that God possesses his life all at once, but I do not agree that it follows from this that therefore God possesses the lives of all other beings at once. God cannot possess the lives of temporal beings at once because their lives do not exist at once; they exist sequentially. Hence, as I argued in Chapter 5, God does not and cannot know as actual what is future to us, nor does he know which of its possibilities a free creature will actualize. Obviously, then, when I say that God possesses his life all at once, I am playing off an ambiguity. "His life" can refer to (1) everything that is ever true of God, or (2) everything that pertains to God as a self-determining agent. I make this distinction because it seems that with regard to my own life, there is much that has happened to me that would be irrelevant to a biography of my life. I have undergone an enormous number of sensations, for example, that have had little or no significance in the development of my life. As Whitehead would say, I have been highly selective in what I have responded to, and I have been creative in how I have responded. Hence, the more revealing story of my life is of type (2), in which irrelevant detail is omitted and relevant details are correctly shaded for intensity. To be sure, if what someone wants is a type (1) story of my life, detail irrelevant to my life as a purposive agent would have to be included, but there is an important sense in which such detail was not and is not part of my life.

Similarly with God, if one asks, "Does God possess his life all at once?," the response should be, "In sense (1) or sense (2)?" In sense (1) he does not and cannot possess his life all at once because "his life" is taken to include all of the knowledge that he ever possesses, and, if my earlier arguments are correct, God's knowledge of creatures cannot exist all at once because they do not exist all at once. Hence, in any world in which changing creatures exist, God cannot in sense (1) possess his life all at once.

In sense (2), however, God does possess his life all at once. The ground of his existence is in his very nature and his nature is invariable; further, his knowledge of potentiality is everlastingly exhaustive, and his will is completely determined, without beginning or end. Hence, God has everlastingly known all he needs to know to determine his will, and he has everlastingly determined his will. In sense (2), then, it seems correct to say that God everlastingly possesses *his* life, instantaneously, without change, development, or sequence. All change and development are in the world, in which his will is being actualized in response to the choices of free agents. His knowledge of the choices of free agents and of the actualization of his will comes to him sequentially because that is the way they occur. But, as we have seen, this increase in God's knowledge is irrelevant to his existence and life as agent. Hence, the life of God as agent is an instantaneous whole because necessarily it has no beginning and no end and undergoes no internal change. There is nothing in God's life that involves sequential ordering except his awareness of the passage of potentiality to actuality.

We can now make a distinction between two senses of "eternity." In the Boethian sense, E_1, an eternal being has complete and simultaneous possession of all that ever exists. In a less inclusive sense, E_2, an eternal being has complete and simultaneous possession of his own life but not of the lives of free creatures that do exist or of any creatures that will exist. I have argued that E_1 is self-contradictory because it implies the possibility of something simultaneously being the case and not being the case. Hence, E_1 cannot be predicated meaningfully of God or anything else. E_2, I believe, gives us all that we need and can have in describing how God is in himself and how he is in general related to the world.

GOD AND EXTERNAL RELATIONS

Granted the preceding analysis, it seems to me that Aquinas was correct in saying that all relations between God and the world are external in the sense that such relations are real but any change in them is a result of a change in the world, not in God.[2] They are like Geach's Cambridge changes that do not make a difference in one term of the relation; e.g., the fact that the number of people who know of pi is continually changing does not make a whit of difference in pi (1972: 322). Similarly, the fact that the world is continually changing does not cause one bit of change *in* God's nature, will, or knowledge of potentiality, but it does, I have argued, make a difference in what God knows to be actual. Hence, the latter change is a real and internal change in God, not merely an external or Cambridge change. Consider, for example, the following statements: "God knows that today is the 60th anniversary of my birth," and "God knows the entirety of what happened during the third millennium after the birth of Jesus of Nazareth." Both of these statements are false, I believe — the first because the 60th anniversary of my birth has not yet arrived, and the second because the third millennium after the birth of Jesus of Nazareth has not yet elapsed. However, presumably each of these statements will become true, and each will become true because of changes in the world, not because of changes in God; the only changes that will result in God because of these changes in the world will be changes in his knowledge of what has come to pass. Changes in the world do not affect his existence, nature, knowledge of potentiality, or will. Hence it seems correct to say that all relations of the world to God are external because whenever these relations change, they change because of changes in the world, not because of changes in God, and because they do not result in any change in God other than a change in his knowledge of actuality.

Further indication of the externality of the relation of the world to God is the following. Recall my statements, "God existed at the time of my birth" and "God has now existed 44 years longer than he had when I was born." The temporal content of such statements, whether they be simultaneity statements or duration statements, is not and cannot be based on an event or unit of measure that comes from God because in God there is no change and therefore no moment of change or unit of duration on which to base temporal statements. Hence, all of the events, periods, and units of measure that are legitimately employed in temporal statements about God come from the world, not from God. The moment that anchors the reference of the statement, "God existed at the time of my birth," is the moment that I was born – not some moment in the life of God; the unit of measure that gives meaning to the statement, "God has now existed 44 years longer than he had when I was born," is based on my birth and our solar system – not on anything that has happened in God; and so it is with all legitimate temporal statements about God. They do not imply that God is temporal in himself.

CAN AN ETERNAL BEING BE OMNISCIENT?

An omniscient being related to a world that includes changing beings would have to know them as changing. An E_1 eternal being could not know anything as changing because, in order to know a thing as changing, one would have to know it first as x and next as not x. But one cannot know something first as x and then as not x without oneself changing. It follows that because an E_1 eternal being cannot change, therefore an E_1 eternal being cannot know a changing thing as changing, i.e., as undergoing change. Perhaps an E_1 eternal being could know *that* a thing changes, and that it changes from x to not x, but, because one cannot without changing know as it is that which changes, an E_1 eternal being could not know a changing thing as it changes. To see simultaneously a set of snapshots of a rolling ball or to see a time-exposure photograph of a rolling ball is not to see a ball rolling. Hence, an E_1 eternal being could not know perfectly that which changes. Therefore an E_1 eternal being could not be omniscient. But God is omniscient; therefore God must not be an E_1 eternal being.

What if, however, one were to insist that God can be both omniscient and E_1 eternal because, even though God does not change, he does know objects as they really are because they do not really change either; i.e., the appearance of change on the part of the objects is an illusion? This suggestion will not work because, as we saw earlier, even if the appearance of change on the part of every object is an illusion, so that God knows the object as it really is, i.e., as unchanging, still there is change in our experience, so he could not know the changing of our illusory experiences of these objects, and therefore he could not know our experiences as they really are. From this it seems that there is no escape because it is self-evidently true that an experience of change involves change. As surely as we exist whenever we think we exist, change is occurring whenever we experience change to be occurring — even though the change be only in our experience and not in something independent of it. Hence, if God is E_1 eternal, then, whenever our experience is changing, he cannot know our experience as changing and therefore he cannot know it as it is. But that is unacceptable. God is omniscient; therefore God knows things as they are; therefore God knows our changing experience as changing; therefore God is not E_1 eternal. He could, however, be E_2 eternal and know changing things as they are.

I agree, then, with Hartshorne and Kenny that the knowing relation must result in change in the knower insofar as what the knower is knowing is itself changing. Recall, however, that changes that come about in God's knowledge of actuality will not affect God's existence, nature, will, or knowledge of absolute possibility. We might say that changes in God's knowledge of actuality make a difference *in* him but not *to* him in these respects. That is, changes in the world cause God to begin knowing something as actual that was not actual earlier, or cause him to know the decision of a free agent (a decision that could not have been known earlier), but such changes and God's resulting new knowledge do not cause God to bring about in the world anything that he otherwise would not have brought about. The relation of God to the world, as I argued in Chapter 2, is not indeterminate in the sense that he is waiting to see what happens before he decides what to do; nor is it indeterminate in the sense that he has decided what to do, but only tentatively because he might change his mind as a result of seeing what we finally decide. His will has been eternally adequately resolved.

Richard Swinburne holds that if God knows all that he will ever do – as he would if his will is eternally resolved – then God cannot be free. Hence, Swinburne argues, as God must limit his knowledge of future creaturely actions in order that creatures might be free, he must limit his knowledge of his own future actions in order that he might be free (1977: 172–8). I criticized the claim regarding creaturely actions in the last chapter. The second claim is defused by divine EKP, which Swinburne either does not accept or has not seen the significance of. I agree that, if God did not have EKP but knew his future will, that would suggest that his will is determined – since if it were not determined it would seem more plausible that, given his ignorance of what could happen in the future, he would refrain from formulating his will until he was confident that he had adequate information or could wait no longer. But granted EKP, for which I argued in Chapters 2 and 3, it is more plausible to think that God's will is eternally resolved. This means that there is no future to God's will; it just is. Hence, God does not have to – indeed, cannot – limit his knowledge of his future willing. He is always willing all that he ever wills, and his eternal knowledge of what he wills no more implies that what he wills is not free than does the fact that he knows what I now will means that I am not free. Swinburne has written, "That someone P knows what someone else S is now doing in no way makes what S is now doing necessary" (1977: 173). I agree and add: That someone P knows what he P is now doing in no way makes what P is now doing necessary.

It is plausible then, to hold that God's will is free and yet has been eternally resolved and known by him. It follows that what our relation to God shall be is entirely up to us – within the context of the possibilities afforded to us by his grace. Hence, it seems to me that Aquinas was correct, at least in spirit, when he claimed that all relations of the world to God are external.

7

Divine impassibility in feeling

I HAVE ARGUED that God must be impassible in nature, will, and knowledge of absolute possibility, but that he must be passible in his knowledge of actuality and therefore of immediate possibilities. Each of these aspects of the issue of impassibility (other than the aspect of God's nature) has played a part in the long-running impassibility controversy – a controversy that is at the heart of or just beneath a number of early Christian disputes regarding patripassianism, theopaschitism, and docetism. However, none of the aforementioned aspects of the impassibilist controversy has aroused such intensity of emotion as has the aspect of impassibility in God's feelings. At least seven basic reasons have been given by passibilists in defense of their belief that the felt quality of God's inner life must be subject to change by what his creatures do and undergo. I will present these reasons thematically first, then relate them to their authors when I evaluate them later.

First it has been argued that *personality* requires emotional passibility. A being that is constitutionally unable to participate in the emotional life of persons, to be touched by their joys and sorrows, is not itself a person. It might be a sub-human creature, e.g., a turtle, or a sub-personal human in a catatonic or anhedonic state, but it is not a person. To be a person is to be able to participate in the emotional life of other persons, and that means to be subject to influence by what they are feeling, i.e., to be emotionally passible. Therefore, because personality is the highest category of individuality of which we know and because we must think of God in terms of the highest category of individuality, we must think of God as a person, and, because a person cannot be emotionally impassible, we must think of God as emotionally passible.

Second, God is not only a person; God is a loving person, and *love* requires emotional passibility. To love someone is to care about him, and to care about him is to care about what happens to him, and to care about what happens to him is to be affected by what happens to him; it is to be happy when things go well for him and to be distressed when things go badly for him. If a purported lover was emotionally unaffected by the good and bad fortune of his beloved, by her joys and griefs, it would show that he was no true lover, and if God, the greatest conceivable lover, is emotionally unaffected by our ecstasies and our agonies then it only shows that he is no lover at all. But God is love. Therefore God must be thought of as emotionally passible.

Third, *divinity* requires emotional passibility. Why? Because God is worthy of worship; indeed, he is the only being worthy of worship, i.e., of wholehearted praise, gratitude, and service. It is to this worthiness of worship that we refer by means of the term "divine." But, if God were emotionally *im*passible, then he would not be divine, i.e., he would not be worthy of wholehearted praise because he would be deficient in personality and love, as we have seen already. Further, if he were emotionally impassible, it would be a waste of time to express gratitude to him because he would not be affected by it in any way. Finally, devotion and service to God would be as meaningless as devotion and service to a stone because, being impassible, God's feelings would be unaffected by whatever we do, whether we do good or evil, and he could not be benefited by anything that we do, so how could we meaningfully devote our lives to him? But surely God must be thought of in such a way that devotion to him is meaningful and appropriate. Therefore we must think of God as emotionally passible. If he were not, he would not be capable of inspiring the unqualified praise, thanksgiving, and devotion that constitute a worshipful attitude, but he must be so capable or he would not be God. Therefore he must not be thought of as emotionally impassible.

Fourth, *justice* requires divine passibility in feeling. Because God is good, he hates evil and therefore is just, i.e., hates, opposes, and punishes sin, which is the commission of evil or the omission of obligatory good. However, if God is emotionally impassible, then he is moved by nothing that his creatures do. But, if he is moved by nothing that his creatures do, then he will not be disturbed by sin, and, if he is not disturbed by sin, he will not respond to punish it. Therefore he would neither care about it nor do anything about it and could not be described as just. But surely God must be thought of as just. Therefore he must be thought of as being angered by the occurrence of evil, and that means he must be thought of as emotionally passible.

Fifth, *omniscience* requires that God be passible in feeling. Obviously God in his omniscience must when we suffer know that we suffer. But in his omniscience he must know more than *that* we suffer; he must *know our suffering itself*, and it is impossible to know someone's suffering without suffering sympathetically with them. To know fully the feeling of another person is to have that feeling oneself. Hence, inasmuch as God must know our suffering when we suffer, he must himself have the feeling of suffering when we suffer. Consequently, he cannot be both omniscient and emotionally impassible. But he must be omniscient, so he must not be emotionally impassible.

Sixth, *morality* requires emotional passibility. God is ultimately responsible for the suffering of his creatures. He could have not created them at all, thereby precluding any suffering, or he could have created them and placed them in a world in which they could not suffer, or he could have created them just as he did but snatched them from existence before they ever suffered. Instead he has placed us in a situation in which all of us suffer and some of us suffer terribly. Consequently, it is only right that God should share our suffering, just as parents who impose a harsh penalty on a child feel suffering love for the child in its misery even though infliction of the penalty was brought on by the child's behavior after appropriate warnings from the parents. Consider also that when the child goes through adolescence, tormented by doubts about its physical appearance, tormented by romantic feelings unreciprocated, responsible parents do not ignore the child's emotional turmoil. They communicate with the child and are deeply touched by and concerned about what the child is undergoing. Moreover, even if the parents were inclined to avoid involvement with the child because of their own problems, they would realize that they had a moral obligation to share in the life of the child, and it is impossible to share in someone's life without being emotionally affected by what is happening to him. Hence, inasmuch as morality is binding on all persons, morality requires that God be emotionally involved with us, his suffering creatures.

Seventh, human *redemption* requires divine passibility in feeling. It is precisely by means of God's suffering love that sinful creatures are redeemed from their sinful ways and their lives are transformed. To be sure, *fear* of God might cause a creature to abstain or desist from sin, but fear does nothing to transform the heart and renew the soul. Hence, the image of God in wrath can be a very misleading image. Yes, God hates sin, but he is also grieved by it. In his love God suffers more intensely because of our sins than does anyone else because he knows our sins more completely than anyone else – our sins of desire and intention as well as action – and he cares about their impact on us and others more than we or others possibly could. Hence our sins cause him sorrow. When we realize the pain that our sinfulness brings to one who is not in the least deserving of it, one who suffers only because he cares about us, it is then that repentance is wrung from our hearts and that, as the biblical prophet Jeremiah puts it, our heart of stone is exchanged for a heart of flesh. Wrath triggers only fear and hatred; it is suffering love that brings about conversion of our minds, hearts, and affections. Hence, God can turn us and transform us only if he is emotionally passible relative to our behavior.

But surely he can turn and transform us. Therefore just as surely he is touched by our sins and sufferings.

The reaction of the sinner to his realization of the suffering that he is causing God is similar to the reaction of a child who finally realizes the grief that its behavior is causing its parents – a grief they do not deserve and that they suffer only because of their love for him. Obviously such a realization is capable of transforming the heart of a person, causing him henceforth to live morally out of gratitude when not tempted, and, when tempted, to live morally out of a refusal to grieve those who love him. It is not, then, the wrath of God that redeems us, nor even the love of God; it is the suffering love of God. A divine love that did not suffer with us and for us would be an odd sort of thing by which no heart would be touched or transformed. Indeed, it is God's vulnerability to suffering that makes morality meaningful and gives us pause in the face of temptation.

CRITICISMS OF THE DOCTRINE OF DIVINE IMPASSIBILITY IN FEELING

In the preceding section I have attempted to present as forcefully as possible the seven reasons I have found passibilists to give for rejecting divine emotional impassibility. In the remainder of this chapter we will examine the first five reasons and conclude with a survey of logical problems implicit in emotional passibilism. In the next chapter we will take up the last two reasons, morality and redemption, which are related closely to the problem of evil.

Personality

Does personality require passibility in feeling? That is, must a person's feelings be subject to alteration by what occurs to him or to others? In a comment on von Hügel, Hartshorne insists that the answer is "yes." "God," he writes, "must have a system of emotions, including suffering, if he is a person." Hartshorne adds that personality, "consists in part in a capacity to share the sorrows as well as the joys of others. Sympathetic suffering is no mere stepping stone; it is an element in the highest achievement or form of personality," and obviously God must embody the highest form of personality (1953: 160). It is not so obvious to me, however, that the highest form of personality must be emotionally passible. To be sure, in order for a thing to be correctly called "a person" it must exist, it must have awareness, it must have capacity for abstract thought and the use of symbols, and it must have the power of will. I would also agree that a person must have some feeling for things, an emotional life, as it were. But I do not understand why this dimension to personal life must be subject to alteration by changing circumstances.

We can imagine an individual who has the gifts of awareness, abstract understanding, will, and feeling, who works diligently and intelligently against poverty, injustice, and loneliness in his society, yet who is equally happy no matter whether he meets success or defeat. Unusual as such an individual would be, I see no reason why we should not think of him as a person. Indeed, we might envy him. Consider also the Stoics. They were not trying to cease to be persons by nursing the virtue of *apatheia*. They were trying to become persons with a proper attitude to the vicissitudes of life. Further, we find this attitude eloquently expressed by a contemporary woman, Rose Fitzgerald Kennedy, mother of John F. and Robert Kennedy. When an interviewer expressed his admiration for her fortitude she replied, "I have always believed that, no matter what, God wants us to be happy. He doesn't want us to be sad. Birds sing after a storm. Why shouldn't we?" (Amory 1983: 6). Clearly she is setting forth the ideal of emotional impassibility, and just as clearly she does not believe that it is incompatible with being a mature, sensitive person. Further, the ideals to which we aspire by right thinking and right effort we usually assume to be God's by nature. Hence, we may coherently think of a person as emotionally impassible, and we should think of God as such.

Love

But what *kind* of a person is God? Clearly God is a loving person, and, whereas a non-loving person might be emotionally impassible, it would violate the meaning of "love" to say that a person is both loving and untouched by the joys and tribulations of his beloved. Or would it?

To love someone, it seems to me, consists of (1) caring about the welfare of that person, (2) acting for the welfare of that person, and (3) taking pleasure in the welfare of that person. (1) is a disposition to act for the welfare of the beloved, and it is accompanied by the emotion that we call "caring." I see no problem with assuming that an emotionally impassible being could feel about and be disposed toward the welfare of someone else in this way. (2) consists of acting upon opportunities to benefit the beloved. I see no reason to think that an emotionally impassible being could not so act. The difficulty is with (3). Could an emotionally impassible being be rejoiced by the good fortunes of its beloved and distressed by its misfortunes? The answer is "no," of course, but I do not believe that implies that such a being could not take pleasure in the welfare of its beloved. Several points must be made to defend this claim.

First, it is simplistic and wrong to say, as Hartshorne does, that "Love *is* joy in the joy (actual or expected) of another, and sorrow in the sorrow of another" (1941: 116). If this were true in the simple, unqualified sense in which Hartshorne states it, it would follow that, because God loves everyone, he must rejoice with the sadist while the sadist tortures his victim, and grieve with the sadist when his victim dies and can no longer be tormented. But surely God is no more obligated than we are to share in the joys and sorrows of a demented mind. Further, sometimes people who are sound in mind but immature in character make mistakes in their judgments as to what merits their joy and their sorrow. Consequently they rejoice over things that should not be rejoiced over, or they sorrow over things that are not worthy objects of sorrow. When we recognize someone caught up in such a mistake, then, even though we love them, we do not sympathetically rejoice or sorrow with them. Indeed, our response may be the opposite of theirs; we may be dejected because of that by which they are elated, or we may rejoice because they do not get what they want. If God were to joy in the joy and sorrow in the sorrow of people in such instances, he would be joining in their mistaken judgment; but surely he cannot be mistaken. Hence, it is simplistic and wrong to say that to love someone is to joy in their joys and to sorrow in their sorrows.

What, however, if a beloved is not of a perverse mentality and has not misvalued something because of immaturity? What about the husband's grief over the loss of his young wife, or the pianist's anguish over the loss of his hand? Isn't it necessary that those who love these people will be disturbed by their sufferings? Richard Swinburne has argued that they certainly will because there is a *logical* connection between love, loss, and suffering. "Mental suffering and anguish," he writes,

> are a man's proper tribute to losses and failures, and a world in which men were immunized from such reactions to things going wrong would be a worse world than ours. By showing proper feelings a man shows his respect for himself and others. Thus a man who feels no grief at the death of his child or the seduction of his wife is rightly branded by us as insensitive, for he has failed to pay the proper tribute of feelings to others, to show in his feeling how much he values them, and thereby failed to value them properly – for valuing them properly involves having proper reactions of feeling to their loss. Again, only a world in which men feel sympathy for losses experienced by their friends, is a world in which love has full meaning.   (1977: 99)

Though Swinburne sees the connections between love, loss, and suffering as logical, he adds that they are not causally constraining. We can choose to cultivate or repress grief, for example, upon the event of a serious loss. We ought, however, to cultivate it (1979: 192). Because Swinburne sees the basic connections here as logical, it seems fair to assume that he believes that God, as a perfect person, experiences mental anguish and suffering because of his own losses and because of his sympathy for his creatures.

It is certainly the case that serious losses usually cause original or sympathetic suffering. Our concern is with whether such suffering is always appropriate. Is it possible that, if P_1 loves P_2, P_1's happiness could nonetheless not be marred by P_2's suffering? Certainly sometimes it is the case. Recently I saw a small child burst into tears upon some insubstantial fright. His mother, a few yards away, dashed to him with a broad smile on her face – a smile intended to reassure him and reflective of her knowledge that there was nothing for her child to be frightened about. The parent appeared to be participating emotionally in no way in the child's distress. Did that mean that she was a cold or perverse or insensitive person? Or did it mean that because she knew that there was no real danger to her son and that she could assure him of that, therefore there was no need for her to participate in his unhappy feelings? I believe the latter was the case, and I have seen this type of adult reaction numerous times.

Let us take up a more difficult example. Consider a parent who sees her child in pain as a result of disease for which there is not a known cure. Ordinarily such a parent would suffer with the child in its misery. But consider the same child later, suffering comparable pain but now from the implementation of a newly discovered cure. Though a loving parent would stay by the child, comforting it and assuring it at every opportunity that "everything's going to be all right," still I believe that joy over the cure being implemented could so fill the parent as to nullify emotional distress on the parent's part over the pain being inflicted by the cure. To be sure, in such a situation many of us would have mixed feelings; we would feel joy at the prospect of a cure but unhappiness over the pain involved. Yet, if the parent was so joyful over the cure that she was not emotionally distressed by the suffering of her child, I do not believe that we would fault her for being remiss or not really loving the child.

Regarding grief over the loss of a loved one, I am even more confident that there is no logical or moral connection such as Swinburne has outlined. A great deal depends on circumstances and metaphysical beliefs. Socrates was not anguished by his fate, and he wished that his friends had not been. Yet he was not at all an emotionally cold person, and he would not have judged his friends to be unloving had they because of appropriate philosophical and religious beliefs been undistressed by his approaching end. Ordinarily we are distressed by such events because they take from us things on which our happiness depends at the time, and because we usually do not think ourselves to know that the loss is not final. If we knew the loss to be final, then Swinburne would be correct about the proper emotional response. But what if such things were not necessary conditions of one's happiness? and what if one knew that such losses were not final? Surely such states of affairs would make a decisive difference in one's valuation of one's own losses and of those of others about whom one cared.

The most intriguing counterpoint to Swinburne's position that I have found is that of Helen Keller. Religion was extraordinarily important to her, and she had remarkable things to say about it, as can be seen in her book *My Religion*. Deprived since early childhood of sight, hearing, and speech, yet finally breaking through to the riches of language, she became a wonderfully sensitive, imaginative, and articulate writer. With regard to the loss of loved ones and the approach of one's own death she asked rhetorically, "What is so sweet as to awake from a troubled dream and behold a beloved face smiling upon you"? She went on to say, "I love to believe that such shall be our awakening from earth to heaven. My faith never wavers that each dear friend that I have 'lost' is a new link between this world and the happier land beyond the morn" (137).

Keller acknowledged that she could not but feel grief at the loss of a friend, but, contrary to Swinburne's recommendation, she fought against that sadness. With appropriate epistemological humility she acknowledged that death might be the end of personal existence. But she added: "Suppose there are a million chances against that one that my loved ones who have gone are alive. What of it? I will take that one chance and risk mistake, rather than let my doubts sadden their souls, and find out afterward. Since there is that one chance of immortality, I will endeavour not to cast a shadow upon the joy of the departed" (138). For the sake of our loved ones, then, we should resist the grief and sadness that their deaths tend to trigger, but which arise from the conviction that death is the end of life. After all, we would not grieve over losing the presence of a friend who was traveling to a wonderful country in which we would meet them ere long.

To Keller, then, "... death is not the end of life, but only one of its most important experiences" (203), and what lies on the other side of death is far more wonderful than anything we can now imagine. If we believe or have faith that this is so, then, "We can now meet death as Nature does, in a blaze of glory, marching to the grave with a gay step, wearing our brightest thoughts and most brilliant anticipations, as Nature arrays herself in garments of gold, emerald, and scarlet, as if defying death to rob her of immortality" (1927: 204). One could hardly make a case that Keller was an insensitive or uncompassionate person, yet it seems clear that she would disagree profoundly with Swinburne's conviction that we ought in the form of grief and anguish to pay proper emotional tribute on the occasion of our losses. Rather, I believe, she would say that we ought to cultivate joyful confidence that our deceased friends have gone on to a more wonderful world than this one and that we shall meet them there some day. Similarly, our other losses and our failures in this life should be appraised in the context of that wonderful larger setting.

It seems, then, that circumstances and beliefs can make it unnecessary, even inappropriate, for a lover to suffer with his beloved or because of loss of his beloved. But could there be circumstances that make it always unnecessary or inappropriate for God to suffer with his suffering creatures? God should sorrow for us, it seems to me, only when he knows us to have lost an irreplaceable good or to have suffered an irredeemable evil. He never will, however, because his omniscience and omnipotence enable him to replace every good and to redeem every evil. Indeed, a sound analysis of the concept of God requires that we hold that God would not have allowed evil were it not an unavoidable risk or stepping-stone contingent upon which is an end so good that those who choose and enjoy it will freely and readily agree that it is worth far more than whatever distress they went through to get it. In Leibniz's words, suffering in this life will be "later redressed with such profit that even the innocents would not wish not to have suffered" (1965: 120).

We cannot, then, rule out the possibility that God knows something about our destiny that renders it unnecessary and inappropriate for him to be disturbed by our suffering in this life. Moreover, it seems to me that he does have such knowledge if he knows that in order to enable us to choose freely for or against his kingdom he had to submit us to such risks of involuntary, even unfair suffering as we do in fact run, and that, whichever way we choose, our choice will be honored in such a way that neither our freedom nor his justice nor his goodness nor his bliss nor the bliss of those who dwell in his kingdom will be violated – and that those who do choose his kingdom will freely conclude that the joy of the end more than makes up for the suffering of the means.

Divinity

It has also been argued that divinity requires that God suffer with us. The sentiment behind this point seems to be that "the highest love is suffering love."[1] That is, God, as the supreme being, must embody all the highest categories of reality. Therefore he must be not only a loving person, but also one who suffers for his beloved. Such a person is more admirable than one who is incapable of suffering or who shies from suffering for the sake of his beloved. Therefore we must think of God as loving in a sacrificial way. Anything less would be something than which we could conceive of something greater; therefore anything less would not be something we could worship. But God must be worthy of worship; therefore we must not think of God as emotionally impassible.

This sentiment can be found in several sources. As mentioned earlier, in a 1912 publication, *Voluntas Dei*, Lily Dougall wrote from a Christian perspective:

If God suffers not, our Lord is no revelation of Him, nor is it possible to conceive the Creator as having the relation of Father to His creation, nor would it be possible for many of us to remain theists, for if the Creator must be faithful to His creatures it must be true that in all their afflictions He is afflicted; if He be not faithful He is not the Christian God.   (259)

There is a great deal going on in this statement, but part of it is that, if God did not suffer, many theists could not remain theists because they would no longer find God worthy of worship, i.e., of wholehearted praise and devotion. But the issue is broader than God's capacity for suffering; divinity must be passible to joy as well as sorrow. Hartshorne writes:

... if God has no good to acquire and hence cannot permit us the privilege of contributing value to himself, the sole worthy cosmic recipient of values, the only one able to receive *all* we can give, all the good we are (some of which escapes all human friends), then he is incapable of responding to our noblest need, which is that there should be a cause to which nothing of ourselves is merely indifferent, and nothing good is without positive value.   (1941: 118–19)

If God is not rejoiced by the good that we enjoy and do, Hartshorne asks, "if we contribute no value to the transcendent, why should we concern ourselves with it: All talk of serving a God thus described is absurd" (1970: 230). Schubert Ogden explains the problem this way:

... supernaturalists have traditionally maintained that the end of man is to serve or glorify God through obedience to his will and commandments. And yet the God whom we are thus summoned to serve is, in the last analysis, so conceived that he can be as little affected by our best actions as by our worst. As *actus purus*, and thus a statically complete perfection incapable in any respect of further self-realization, God can be neither increased nor diminished by what we do, and our action, like our suffering, must be in the strictest sense wholly indifferent to him.   (1963: 17–18)

The common sentiment of these authors is that the conception of a being who is not rejoiced by the good that we do or enjoy, and who is not grieved by the evil that we do or suffer, is not a conception of God, i.e., of a being worthy of unqualified praise and devotion. A being who is emotionally unmoved by us is not one who can give meaning and direction to our lives, who can call forth our finest efforts and highest sentiments. Hence, as Hartshorne says, our noblest need is for a passible God.

This position calls for several responses. First, it presupposes that suffering adds some good to the existence of a thing. That could be true only if suffering is either good in itself or good as a means. But in itself suffering is an evil. Hence, suffering would add no intrinsic good to God. Nor does there seem to be a way in which suffering could benefit God himself instrumentally. It could not benefit him as corrective punishment or as a warning of danger or as an incentive to be more sympathetic to the suffering of others. Nor could it increase his wisdom or confront him with moral dilemmas by which his character might be decided (though suffering does at times benefit us in all these ways) (Randles 1900: 115). But, if suffering adds neither intrinsic nor instrumental good to God, it is difficult to see why he would not be more praiseworthy without it, since in itself suffering is intrinsically bad, and suffering that is not redeemed by its consequences is absolutely bad.

My second objection is to the belief that suffering makes love admirable. That puts things backwards. It is love that makes suffering admirable. Suffering in and of itself is odious. But a person who for the sake of a beloved freely undergoes suffering is admirable. Suffering may, then, reveal the depth of one's love, but it does not create it or necessarily increase it. It is the love that lends merit to the suffering, not vice versa. The highest love, then, is not suffering love; it is love that is willing to suffer if possible and necessary. From this it follows that the greatest lover may be one who never suffers for his beloved because it is not possible or necessary for him to do so.

Third, if it were suffering that made love admirable, then the more suffering the better! And since God is infinite love, he must suffer infinitely or, if that be impossible because there is no maximal degree of suffering, he must be trapped in an endless vortex of ever increasing pain. But clearly the appropriate sentiment toward such a being should be pity not worship. Yet surely pity cannot be an appropriate feeling toward God unless our notions of God's majesty and self-sufficiency are shown to be illogical – as I do not think they have been.[2]

Fourth, if suffering love were the highest love, God would be indebted to sinners for his status as "suffering lover," since, if they had not sinned, he would not have suffered so much and his love would therefore not have been as admirable. Hence, God should be grateful to sinners in general for enabling him to be suffering love; he should be grateful to the most egregious sinners in particular for enabling him to achieve such heights of suffering love as he has so far achieved; and he should desire that future sinners sin yet more boldly that he might achieve yet higher heights of suffering love. But surely a position from which such implications as these follow must be faulty in its basic conception of God. It is absurd to think that God depends on sinners for his virtue.

Fifth, if God suffers with us, for us, and because of us, then religion properly understood becomes "pity for God" (Randles 1900: 145). After all, if God shares emotionally all the suffering of the world and also suffers his own misery over our waywardness, then he of all beings is most to be pitied. Further, if God is the highest object of pity, then he should pity himself above all others. Bertrand R. Brasnett was neither oblivious nor adverse to these implications of the doctrine of divine passibility. Consider the following statements from his *The Suffering of the Impassible God*. "We may believe," he says, "that God cares intensely when his will is disregarded, that he grieves, that he is angry, that he is troubled, for he is a living God in living personal relationship with his creation, and when it sins there is pain in the divine heart" (8). Furthermore, not only does it cause pain and grief to God when achievement of his will is delayed, but "he grieves for good unrealized as well as for evil done. Ugliness hurts and pains him, and beauty left unrealized is agony to him" (61). As a consequence, Brasnett adds, God's happiness fluctuates with the sinfulness and virtuousness of our behavior.

> When a good man turns to evil, and a bad man turns to good, these facts are not without significance for the life of God. To suppose that they are is to write God down indifferent to good or evil, as careless of the moral progress of his creation. But if God rejoices over the conversion of the evil-doer and sorrows over the good man who goes astray, his happiness and sorrow must vary in some degree as good or evil predominate upon the earth. (74)

Do not think, however, that evil-repented-of or unrealized-good-finally-realized relieve God of his suffering:

> So far as we can see, sin must cause to God an everlasting pain; for God has knowledge of its coming, he sees it present, and the memory of its foulness cannot pass away. We should therefore be ready to admit that in this sense God does not know, and has never known, the fullest happiness of which his life is capable. (71)

Brasnett should have added as a further implication that God never will know the happiness that he could have known had humankind been less sinful. As he does say, people who turn away from God condemn themselves and him "to unending pain and enduring agony..." (78)

Lest it be thought that Brasnett's 1928 sentiment was peculiar to his era, consider this 1976 statement by process philosopher John Robert Baker:

> God prefers creaturely fulfillment over creaturely frustration, and it is such a possibility of fulfillment that God presents the local agent. When such a possibility is spurned, it is a misfortune both to the local agent and to God. Even if the individual never feels any sense of loss or frustration because of the choice, there is a resultant suffering and tragedy in the life of God. In this regard we have moved beyond the first aspect of divine suffering, that of sympathetic participation. God does not merely suffer *with* us but *for* us. By analogy, one suffers when he sees a friend miss some intellectual or social achievement because of alcoholism, even though the friend (for whatever reason) never experiences any sense of loss. In the case of God, moreover, he has an accurate, realistic view of the creature's possibilities, so God's awareness of the loss is even clearer and more poignant than any local agent's could be.
>
> A further point needs to be made. This misfortune of the local agent occurs within the

encompassing life of God; and since essentially it is creaturely fulfillment that enriches the divine life, creaturely frustrations are misfortunes for the very life of God. God's own life is thereby limited. Of course, God makes the best use he can of such misfortunes.   (100–1)

A brief statement from Hartshorne shows that he is in sympathy with these sentiments of Brasnett and Baker. He writes that "God is not the being whose life is sheer joy and beauty, but the cosmic sufferer, who endures infinitely more evil than we can imagine" (Hartshorne 1941: 331).

The picture of God conveyed in these quotations strikes me as a portrait in sentimentalism. The religion of pity inspired by it should eventually dissolve into maudlin stupor because there is so little that any one person could do to relieve God's massive suffering. Moreover, it is obvious from centuries of human history that God's suffering is only going to get worse and worse. Poor God – and poor us, if we have no better concept of God than this! But, as I have been arguing, I believe we do, and I would like to attempt to discredit further the passibilist picture of God with the following points.

First, I agree that God cares intensely that his will be fulfilled, but his will is not that we love him; it is that we choose for him or not, and that, as a consequence, we become a part of his kingdom or not. In this sense God's will is always fulfilled. We always choose for him or not. Therefore he suffers no frustration of his will. But does God want everyone to be in his kingdom, so that he grieves if even one person rejects it? No. He wants everyone in his kingdom who freely chooses it – and that he will get. It would be foolish of him to grieve, grow angry, be troubled, or suffer pain over those who freely reject his kingdom, just as it is foolish for a jilted lover to pine away for someone who has freely chosen to pursue romantic involvement with someone else. According to theism, then, the exercise of our freedom with regard to God's kingdom is what this life is all about – a sentiment that is captured in Joshua's famous statement, "as for me and my house, we will serve the lord" (Joshua 24.15), and in an even more famous statement by Jesus, "Father, if it be possible, let this cup pass from me; nevertheless, not my will, but thine be done" (Matthew 26.39).

Second, the Brasnett-Hartshorne-Baker position holds that God is emotionally dependent upon humankind. Friedrich Nietzsche would have loved this idea. After all, in *The Gay Science* he merely killed God. But if God were as Brasnett-Hartshorne-Baker describe him (indestructible and emotionally dependent on humankind), then Nietzsche would have really had something to work with. Recall Brasnett's words: "Here God has given himself into our hands, we can wound and pain him, and make him suffer" (1928: 13). I can see Nietzsche saying with a grin, "Ahhh, so the old boy is real after all. This is even better! I may not be able to kill him, but

I can make him damn well sorry he ever created me. He will be like a vampire who cannot die though over and over I pound a stake into his heart! Sometimes I will curse him; other times I will ignore him; then I will flaunt my contempt of him; and when he thinks his heart must absolutely break because of my bad manners, I will create yet more effective ways of distressing his stupid sentiments.

"What if he casts me into hell for my mockery? If he does, then he will know that he has lost and I have won; remember, he loves me and must eternally grieve for me in my eternal damnation. And I in hell will continue with words and gestures of contempt and obscenity to remind him that he has lost and therefore is contemptible – that he could neither win my heart nor subdue my disdain. Of course, if he is too weak to face the prospect of such everlasting insolence, he might instead consign me to oblivion, snuff me out – but even then I shall have won. As Brasnett has pointed out, 'sin must cause to God an everlasting pain; for God has knowledge of its coming, he sees it present, and the memory of its foulness cannot pass away' – and above all the stench of my sins will not pass from the everlasting nostrils. So either way, hell or oblivion, I win, he loses. The only way he can win is to grant me heaven because of my courage and cleverness."

These Nietzschean reflections do seem correct inferences from Brasnett's statements that God "asks for the love of men and sorrows till he finds it," and that humans who turn away from God condemn him "to unending pain and enduring agony" (78). If God is in such a fix, it seems to me that we should pray *for* him, not *to* him – but to whom would we pray that God might be delivered from the likes of Nietzsche? Do we pray to Nietzsche? He, of course, would love it – and show his contempt for us, too! Or do we abandon the conception of emotional passibility in God because it is incompatible with the divinity of God, i.e., is incompatible with his worthiness of worship rather than pity? Logic seems to require that we do the latter.

Justice

An argument advanced by Lactantius (AD 260–330) is that God is just and therefore punishes sin, but he will punish sin only if he is aroused to that task by anger. Therefore God must be angered by sin; but, if he is angered by sin, he is emotionally possible to it. This argument can be found in Lactantius' classic statement, 'A Treatise on the Anger of God.' There he explains that God's authority and righteousness require anger: "Take away anger from a king, and he will not only cease to be obeyed, but he will even be cast down headlong from his height" (Lactantius 1979: 279a).

More generally, "Let any one consult his own feelings; he will at once understand that no one can be subdued to the command of another without anger and chastisement. Therefore, where there shall be no anger, there will be no authority. But God has authority; therefore also He must have anger, in which authority consists" (279a). Furthermore, because God is good, it is clear that he will love the pious and righteous, and hate the impious and unrighteous, rewarding the former and punishing the latter. However, rewarding virtue and punishing evil presuppose emotional reactions to them.

> ... as we ought to restrain those who are subject to our power, so also ought God to restrain the offenses of all. And in order that He may do this, He must be angry; because it is natural for one who is good to be moved and incited at the fault of another. Therefore they ought to have given this definition: Anger is an emotion of the mind arousing itself for the restraining of faults.   (274b)

Clearly, then, according to Lactantius, in response to sin God will experience "an emotion of the mind arousing itself for the restraining of faults."

Lactantius' language is unfortunately ambiguous. Does he mean by "anger" (1) the actualization of a predisposition to oppose and punish sinful behavior? Or does he mean (2) the state of mind we associate with displeasure, scowling, threats, and criticisms? The text seems to support (2) more strongly, but (2) leaves little dignity or autonomy to God. On this reading God is like an exasperated parent who fulminates from day to day at the stupid, irresponsible, and mean things that his child does. But such a parent is the emotional victim of the behavior of his child. He shows little imagination and has no emotional autonomy, integrity, or stability in relation to the child.

Still, a passibilist might ask, how can a parent, or God for that matter, remain emotionally untouched by the foibles of his children? Two responses seem appropriate. First, it seems to be a fact of human life that it is possible to punish behavior without being motivated to the punishment by an unhappy state of mind. Anger is not a necessary condition of stopping or punishing misbehavior. Second, not to be upset by behavior that deserves punishment does not imply that one does not care about the misbehaver and those affected by him. To be sure, it is common, perhaps natural, to feel and express anger in response to misbehavior, but all that is natural is not good. Hence, we should consider whether it is better to respond to misbehavior with inner turbulence, scowls, denunciations, and perhaps corporal punishment, or whether it is better to respond in a calm and concerned but firm and reasonable way. One problem with the "natural" model is that it does not help our children learn to cope with and overcome the unhappiness and irrationality of anger. Disapproval of behavior can be expressed and sanctions against it can be implemented without the person who does it being motivated by anger. Consider Mahatma Gandhi's principle of *satyagraha*, i.e., love-force, or Martin Luther King Jr's principle of non-violent resistance, which are based on vigorous, forthright opposition to injustice yet with love for the perpetrator. Such an ideal has been barely achievable by humans, and then only occasionally, I suspect, but it does seem to set the direction in which we should move. Moral anger is better than non-moral or immoral anger or rage, but moral anger still leaves us dependent on emotion, rather than principle, for motivation; it still meshes our lives with a highly flammable substance, and it transmits to our children the difficulties of coping with natural anger without having had the benefit of a model of responding to it with loving impassibility. In brief, emotional anger and the behavior that tends to go with it accomplish nothing constructive that could not be accomplished equally well with less unhappiness and lower risk of tragic side-effects through loving and moral emotional impassibility.

To conclude, Lactantius is mistaken in holding that anger is a necessary condition of authority, i.e., of the ability to subdue others; power seems to be a sufficient condition of authority in this sense. Further, justice or righteousness, in the sense of being opposed to evil, does not require anger; it requires only that one is aligned with the right ideal and committed to its promotion. Of course if all that Lactantius means by "the anger of God" is (1), i.e., his opposition to evil, without the emotional turbulence commonly connoted by "anger," then there is no problem. This is all he needed or ought to have meant. God's goodness ensures that he is opposed to evil and acts in opposition to it; his omnipotence ensures that he acts effectively against it; and his wisdom ensures that he can respond to evil without his response being either motivated or accompanied by turbulent emotion. Hence, God can be just and emotionally impassible.

Omniscience

Some thinkers hold that by virtue of his omniscience God must suffer because we suffer. Hartshorne writes:

To fully sympathize with and to fully know the feelings of others are the same relationship, separable in our human case only because there the "fully" never applies, and we never know the feelings of others but only have knowledge about them, abstract diagrams of how in rough, more or less general ways they feel. If we saw the individuality and vividness of the feeling we would have the feeling. As Hume said, without perhaps knowing what a contribution to theology he was here making, the vivid idea of a feeling is in principle coincident with its "impression," that is, with such a feeling as one's own.   (1941: 163)

John Baker expands this position sympathetically in his "The Christological Symbol of Christ's Suffering":

Let's say that God knows Jones is suffering. This might mean merely that God is cognizant of Jones' suffering. God, as the infallible spectator, is aware of the *fact* that Jones suffers. Hartshorne would reject this account of God's knowledge as inadequate. He believes that any intelligible doctrine of omniscience requires a complementary notion of divine participation – God experiences the experiences of creatures through "sheer, intuitive participation." Concretely aware of another's suffering, God feels that feeling of the other.   (97–8)

Baker adds that God does not mistake such feelings for his own but rather knows them as the feelings of his creatures.

I agree with Hartshorne and Baker that God as omniscient must not only know that we suffer but must also know our suffering. But I do not believe it follows that one who knows someone else's feeling must therefore share that feeling with them. If it were so, the implications for theology would be disastrous. God would have to be thought of as suffering, feeling stupid, feeling horny, taking pleasure in vicious acts, and so forth, because we humans do. Rather than accept such implications it would seem preferable to argue that God does not know any of our feelings directly because it is in principle impossible for any being to know directly the subjectivity of another. I suspect that this latter position – the contrary of process doctrine, but perhaps not of process implication – is more formidable than it generally has been recognized to be, but I shall not pursue it here inasmuch as I believe that God's omniscience can be explained as follows without entailing that in knowing our feelings he must share our feelings.

It seems axiomatic that to know, intuit, or feel someone else's feeling is to have that feeling oneself in some sense. If one does not have the feeling in any sense, it is a mystery how one could know it. But, if one does in knowing the feeling have the feeling, does not that imply that one will oneself feel happy, horny, depressed, in pain, or however the other person feels? I do not think so, and the reason lies in a kind of epistemic distance. Knowledgeable having of someone else's feeling would involve realization that the feeling was not direct but indirect, not original but derivative, not primary but secondary. Hence, we should make a distinction between feeling someone's feeling and having that feeling as one's own. It is, of course, one's own in the sense that one is having it, but it is not one's own in the sense that one feels that way oneself.

We can imagine, for example, an unusual human with the ability to feel directly the feelings of other humans. Perhaps he tunes into someone else's feeling about something and reports to that person, "I feel the same way." Perhaps he tunes into the same person with regard to something else and reports, "I feel quite differently." In the first case he feels the other person's feeling and also has it as his own. In the second case he feels the other person's feeling but does not also have it as his own, i.e., he does not feel that way himself; he only feels the other person feeling that way. Hence, to feel the feeling of another is to have that feeling as the feeling of the other, not as one's own feeling. To go a bit further, to know the feeling of another is to know that, if you were that individual, that is how you would feel – but it is not necessarily to feel that way yourself. Hence, it is conceivable that God can know our pain and pleasure, our joy and grief, our distress, relief, etc., without thereby having these experiences as his own.

What, however, if a passibilist says, "You are mistaken. In knowing the feeling of P_1, P_2 does have that feeling as his own. What more he knows by virtue of the epistemic distance that you mentioned is not that it is not his own feeling but that he has the feeling by virtue of knowing the feeling in P_1, rather than by virtue of whatever is causing P_1 to have the feeling. Hence, if P_1 suffers and P_2 knows P_1's suffering, then P_2 will suffer by virtue of knowing P_1's suffering."

The preceding analysis is not implausible, but I believe it claims too much. For example, P_2 by virtue of knowing that the depression he is experiencing is not originatively his own but rather P_1's will realize that he is not depressed though he is feeling depression. Perhaps a rough analogy here would be experiencing anger (muscle tension, increased heartbeat, heavy breathing, impatience, an impulse to lash out) while realizing that one is not angry but is experiencing the consequences of a shot of adrenalin. In such a situation one could meaningfully and correctly say, "I am feeling anger but I am not angry." Perhaps another analogy could be developed from a shot of insulin as a result of which one could say, "I am feeling depression but I am not depressed." As to the latter, people who are hypoglycemic sometimes learn to distinguish between being existentially depressed and being chemically depressed, i.e., being unable to enjoy ordinary sources of enjoyment because of some failure or frustration in life as distinguished from being unable to enjoy ordinary sources of enjoyment because of a chemical imbalance in the body, e.g., too much insulin produced by an overactive pancreas.

The point of these analogies is that, if one can distinguish in his own case when, e.g., a depression is really his (because primarily existential) and when it is not (because primarily chemical), then, if it is possible to know the feelings of another directly, it seems plausible that one could both feel that feeling, and therefore have it in the sense of experiencing its texture, and yet know that that feeling was not one's own, and therefore not necessarily suffer from it (or, if it is a positive feeling, not necessarily be rejoiced by it). With this analysis in mind, consider the following statement by Hartshorne:

> God cannot face his own death, whether nobly or ignobly; but he can face any and every real death threat with full participation in the sufferings of those whose death is in question. I agree heartily with Berdyaev and Whitehead in their repudiation of a mere spectator God who surveys creaturely sufferings and fears with "mere happiness" (Whitehead), i.e., without participation. But this would be only an abstract and inadequate knowledge of the creatures. The denial of divine suffering is "a profanation," as Whitehead implies. God knows fully and feels fully (for only feeling can know feeling) what our unhappy fears are like for us, and this without being afraid *for himself.* (1970: 263).

Hartshorne adds, "If this is a paradox so is any idea of adequate knowledge." I quite agree – but for reasons mentioned earlier I do not believe that such knowledge requires of God that he participate in (in the sense of having as his own) the sufferings of his creatures. As Hartshorne himself points out, it is impossible for God to participate existentially in our fear of death because he knows that he cannot die. Elsewhere Hartshorne points out that God can know the pleasure of the sadist without having that wicked feeling for his own, and that he can feel our fear without being afraid (1970: 214). In such examples Hartshorne implicitly acknowledges that God can know the feelings of others without having them as his own. It follows by implication that there is nothing in the nature of omniscience which requires that God be caused suffering or joy in his own life by virtue of knowing the sufferings and joys of others. Such a causal relationship would have to be grounded on some other divine attribute.

Notice also that, if it were the case that God could not know the feelings of others without having those feelings for his own, then divine omniscience would be incompatible with divine goodness, justice, and unity, so that the concept of God would be incoherent. For example, if omniscience entailed that God would have as his own the feelings of others, then in knowing the pleasure of a sadist at work God would have to have that pleasure as his own; but then he would not be perfectly good. Hartshorne seems to agree. "How," he asks, "can God feel the sadistic joy of a malicious man without being sadistic?" He answers:

> Jesus was not wicked simply because he could perceive the wickedness of others. God feels wicked feelings not as his own feelings but as his creatures'. This is the subject–object duality implied by the Whiteheadian category, "feeling of feeling" ... The first feeling is the "subjective form" of the experience, the second the "objective form." Both are feelings, but the second is the original (and temporally prior), the first is a participation in the second after the fact. Wickedness is in wrong decisions. God inherits our decisions, as ours, not as his. In feeling them he does not enact or decide them; for they are already decided. (1970: 241)

Having made a good start, Hartshorne moves too quickly from the topic of feeling to the topic of action. His first conclusion should be that God can feel the desires of the wicked without desiring what the wicked desire. The possibility of this discrepancy is crucial to the compatibility of omniscience and goodness.

   Also, if God were to have the desire of the sadist as his own, then, on the assumption that we are dealing with a sadist who feels no moral ambivalence about what he desires, God would have that desire as his own and feel no ambivalence about it. Therefore he could not stand in judgment on it or on any other feeling of desire or pleasure that creatures have without scruple. Consequently God could not be just, i.e., could not stand in judgment on evil. Further, God could not be unified with regard to his moral life because he, by virtue of knowing the feelings of both the sadist and a moral victim of the sadist, would feel both moral indifference and moral revulsion to the torment being inflicted. But surely we must think of God as having a harmonious inner life. We should, then, think of omniscience as not entailing that an omniscient knower must have as his own the feelings that he knows others to have. Hence, knowing the pain, depression, grief, etc., of another, God does not necessarily know himself as in pain, depression, grief, etc. Rather, I believe, he knows himself as eternally blissful and as knowing the pain, depression, grief, etc., of the other.

Suffering, time, and eternity

The conception of God as emotionally passible also generates problems in relation to time and eternity. For example, if God is E_1 eternal and suffers, then, because he is immutable in all respects, he is eternally transfixed by suffering. As a consequence God could never be perfectly happy, nor could his creatures if their happiness comes from a veridical vision of him, as, e.g., according to Thomists and Calvinists. Hence, those who hold an E_1 conception of God are forced to choose between divine impassibility in feeling and eternal divine suffering. It seems obvious that they should choose the former, as the classical tradition has.

   Some thinkers, however, have been so convinced of the necessity of God both (1) suffering with us/for us and (2) being perfectly blissful that they have tried to compatibilize these alternatives. Lily Dougall, H. P. Owen, and Gerald Vann, for example, take different approaches to the problem of the relation of divine suffering to divine bliss, but all seem intent on establishing that the two are compatible. Dougall's approach might be characterized as quantitative in nature. She declares in the closing statement of *Voluntas Dei*:

... as the shadow of a lark is to the flood of light in which it rises singing toward the sun, so is the sum of pain in creation, and God's suffering for creation, in comparison with the joy of a free, regenerate creation united to the joy of God.   (276)

God's suffering is real, as is the shadow of the swallow, but it is so dim as to be swallowed up in the glory that surrounds it. Dougall, like James Hinton in *The Mystery of Pain*, speaks also of God finding joy in sacrificial suffering for humankind, so that such suffering understood properly does not remain mere suffering; it becomes a source of joy.

Whereas Dougall compatibilizes divine suffering and divine bliss by emphasizing the miniscule quantity of the former in relation to the latter, Owen gives a sophisticated metaphysical analysis of the impact of God's inner joy on the suffering he sustains from the world. Having argued that God suffers with us, he goes on to say in *The Christian Knowledge of God*:

At the same time we must affirm that if God suffers, his sufferings are transfigured by the Joy that he, not merely has, but is within his uncreated Godhead. His suffering, like his wrath, does not and cannot form part of his own inner life; it is solely relative to man.

Admittedly, the idea that God's anger and pain are transfigured by his joy is a difficult one. Yet we need not find it self-contradictory if we grasp the fact that God is the self-existent Creator. This fact compels us to make three affirmations. Firstly, because God is self-existent his peace and joy cannot suffer increase or decrease; they are absolute and indestructible. Secondly, because he loves the world he is bound to be angered and pained by sin. Thirdly, since he is not a part of the world (or conversely, since the world is not a part of him) this anger and pain cannot be final; they must be wholly transformed by his beatitude.   (252)

This is a complex, sensitive statement. Among its valuable points is that we bring suffering upon ourselves in various ways whereas God, by contrast, is a source of only joy to himself. Hence, any suffering that he experiences must come from outside himself. But Owen claims, going beyond Dougall, that any suffering which comes to God from without is not merely overwhelmed by the divine joy but is also transformed by it.

Gerald Vann's appeal is not to the overwhelming quantity of divine joy or to its power to transmute suffering. His appeal is to the impact that knowledge can have on our feelings about things. He writes in *The Pain of Christ and the Sorrow of God*:

When Dante on earth sinned or was unhappy, did it leave Beatrice in heaven unconcerned? On the contrary, the involvement is greater to the extent to which the vision of the blessed is greater and deeper than was their awareness on earth. When Dante sinned, then, did Beatrice suffer? We cannot say yes without qualification, for that would deny her beatitude. But neither can we say not without qualification, for that would be to deny her love. We can only say that she had compassion, i.e., that she suffered with Dante, in the way proper to the blessed, the way proper to those who have telescoped means and end, who see the issue in the struggle, who see the good, which is love, emerging from evil and the evil only in terms of that triumphant good. For that involvement we have no words, for our human experience cannot know it; but at least we can see it as transcending of joy and sorrow, a transcending of both which destroys the love-reality of neither.   (73)

Vann's passage is about two fictional characters, but it is clear from the rest of his essay that this is mere background against which to defend his point that, though God suffers, his suffering should not disturb us because his eternal knowledge of our future enables him to enjoy an eternal bliss that contains but transcends the earthly dialectic of sorrow and joy. In the mode of a counterfactual, Owen's point seems to be as follows: *If* God were not aware of the good purpose and end of all things, he would merely suffer because of his love of us. He is eternally aware of such a purpose and end, however, so he does not merely suffer; but neither therefore does he know the joy that is known only after release from suffering. Rather, he knows a bliss that transcends the duality of mere suffering and joy, a bliss that transcends the categories of present human experience.

Interesting as they are, it seems to me that none of these attempts to compatibilize divine suffering and divine bliss is successful. Each seems to be an implicit denial that God really suffers. As a result these positions, in spite of disclaimers by their authors, seem like double-talk whereby it is said that, though God suffers, he does not suffer – that the suffering is there but is drowned out, overwhelmed, transformed, transmuted, transcended, dissolved, or whatever, by the essence or knowledge of God. However, suffering that is not felt does not exist. Suffering exists only as experienced. If God's suffering is eternally overwhelmed, transformed, or transcended by his joyful essence or knowledge, then he never suffers. If the compatibilist position were true, the most we could say would be that God would suffer were the possibility not dispelled by his essence or his knowledge – but it is, so he doesn't.

Nor could the passibilist help his case by insisting that one can suffer without being aware of one's suffering, so that God can suffer even though awareness of his suffering is blocked by the bliss resulting from his essence or knowledge. To hold that God is suffering but that awareness of his suffering is blocked by the bliss resulting from his essence or knowledge would imply that there is something about his own immediate experience of which God is ignorant. This appears on the face of it incredible and implies that God is neither omniscient nor one.[3]

There is a further problem with Owen's position. He claims that God's essence brings him only joy and that God suffers only because of his relation to free creatures. This claim breaks down under analysis. Because God is responsible for the existence of everything other than himself, and, because he therefore is responsible for the existence of those who cause his suffering, he is responsible for his suffering. To be sure, he may not be directly responsible, inasmuch as free creatures could have chosen to act according to his will, but he is at least indirectly responsible because he could have chosen not to bring free creatures into existence or he could have circumscribed their freedom so that they could not have chosen alternatives that would cause him suffering. But he did not; and surely his actions follow from his essence, whether necessarily or freely, and therefore his essence, if God suffers, is not a source of only joy to God.

Since God knew he would suffer if he created this world, then, given that suffering in itself is an evil, why did he create it? Presumably Owen would answer, "For the sake of a greater good than could be had without it." But for whom would that greater good be? Presumably not himself because, according to Owen, in himself God is perfectly happy and therefore needs no eudemic supplement. Further, as we shall see, prior to the creation of creatures he could have no obligation to them, so he would have no obligation to create them. Owen, then, gives us no reason why God would create a world which he knew would cause him suffering, but that very knowledge provides a reason for thinking that God would not create such a world.

We will return in Chapter 9 to the question as to why God created the world. For now let us look at a plethora of additional questions that need to be answered by passibilists who believe that God is temporal. If God is temporal but knows the future, does he exist in dread at the suffering he knows he will undergo? Is he tense in expectation, clenching his teeth, so to say, at the pain that is to come? Is he regretful but resigned toward the suffering that he and his creatures undergo?

Things get even more problematic if God does not know future free actions but knows everything that can happen. Does God in this case hope (pray?) that humankind will deliver him from great suffering? "If possible, deliver this cup from me?" Knowing that humans could refuse to reciprocate his love of them, did he before they existed suffer painful anxiety as to whether they would reject him?

Things get trickiest when, *à la* Hartshorne, God knows neither future free actions nor all possibilities. Did God not know when he contributed to our creation that we could cause him to suffer? If he did not, the discovery must have come as quite a shock. Additionally, have humans committed sins so bizarre, so extensive, so grievous that once upon a time God could not have foreseen these things as real possibilities? Is this the kind of background against which we are to interpret Genesis 6.5–6: "The Lord saw that the wickedness of man was great in the earth, and that every imagination of the thoughts of his heart was only evil continually. And the Lord was sorry that he had made man on the earth, and it grieved him to his heart"? In brief, it seems to me that passibilists must answer some of these questions in the affirmative and therefore are not speaking of a being worthy of worship.

Now let us focus on a problem raised by the temporalist view of God held by Hartshorne. Hartshorne claims that God's inner life is a mixture of joys and pains the relative proportions of which fluctuate with the choices of free agents. There are, however, two sources of God's joy: his own abstract essence and the behavior of other free agents. The former, as Owen also claims, is an unvarying source of joy whereas the latter is a varying source of joy and the only source of God's suffering.[4] Regarding the joy that God derives from himself, Hartshorne writes:

> God primordially and forever enjoys the vision of his own necessary essence, the fixed and absolute element in his experience. This element is absolutely perfect, the contemplation of it yields a satisfaction that is untarnished, in the sense that it is all that the enjoyment of anything abstract could possibly be.   (1953: 162)

A little later Hartshorne adds that, though God is "the being who, infinitely more literally than any man, feels the sorrows and pains of other persons than himself, vicariously suffers them," we should also understand God as "preserving in himself always an enjoyment of an absolute, though not concrete perfection – his own contemplated essence" (1953:163). However, Hartshorne, as Brasnett, understands this ever-present, unchanging ingredient of God's total experience to be mixed with the ever-changing pains and pleasures that come to him from the world.

Hartshorne's position is sensible as far as it goes, but there is an important omission. There seems to be no ascertainment of the weight that God's enjoyment of his essence contributes to the total package of the quality of his experience at any moment. Does God's essential happiness constitute 50% of his happiness at any given time, so that free creatures can affect only the other 50%? Or is the ratio somewhat different? 1% happiness from his essence and 99% happiness/unhappiness from others? Or vice versa? In brief, just how passible is God with respect to his happiness? Without a rather specific determination I do not understand how Hartshorne can defend the following position:

> ... since at all times God enjoys an infinite past, the wealth of happiness which he possesses is never less than infinite. Though not completely beyond tragedy or the possibility of increase in happiness (nor the risk of falling short of the maximal possible increase), yet is he superior to us in happiness, with a unique, incomparable superiority, as the gap between the finite and the infinite is unique.   (1941: 240)

It is equally true, though Hartshorne fails to say so, that, because God "enjoys" an infinite past, the "wealth" of suffering that he possesses must also never be less than infinite – since according to Hartshorne there have always been free creatures and therefore presumably always creaturely choices that through ignorance, malice, or tragic alternatives led to suffering. Again, then, we are driven against the question, "How do we weigh the infinite happiness that God derives from the world, plus the constant happiness that he derives from his essence, against the infinite suffering that is inflicted on him by the world?"

It seems to me a hopeless task to try to answer this question by empirical or philosophic methods, and so it seems inappropriate for Hartshorne to paint such a rosy picture of his God as he did in *Man's Vision of God*, 240. Unless he can defend some extensive percentage of extent or degree of happiness that God always enjoys from his essence and the world, he cannot even defend the position that God is always more happy than unhappy, much less that he is always infinitely happy.

Further, Hartshorne's "God's-happiness-depends-on-us-but-he-is-always-infinitely-happy" position seems by implication to devalue God's feelings for us. If finite creatures are genuinely free, as Hartshorne claims they are, then a large majority of them could make choices that cause God more pain than pleasure. Yet Hartshorne says that God is always infinitely happy. How can this be? Is it because the extent to which God's happiness is passible to our actions is miniscule compared to the extent to which God's happiness is derived from his essence? (If "yes," go back to the problem in the preceding paragraph.) Or is it rather the case that, though it is logically possible in Hartshorne's system that free creatures could make God more unhappy than happy, God has stacked the deck by means of causal laws so that we cannot in fact do that? Yet how could he stack the deck since according to process metaphysics God cannot unilaterally institute laws of nature? There are no such *things* as causal laws; there are only free individuals. Causal laws are mere abstractions from the behavior of free individuals.

Further, if God has control over creaturely awareness of possibilities, so that, though he cannot determine which alternative a creature will choose, he can control which alternatives it will choose among (as process philosophers generally hold), then, because God is the sole beneficiary of history (Hartshorne denies that any individual other than God can have everlasting life), we must ask why God has presented to creatures the alternatives that have enabled the horrors of history. Why has he not instead presented to creatures only alternatives that fall far short of the possibilities of sadism, tyranny, and racism?

Hartshorne might reply that great good can come only from a situation that involves the risk of great evil as well. Whether that is true or not it should be noted again that the great good is, in Hartshorne's system, ultimately for God, not for those who exist but briefly then vanish forever except from God's memory. To be sure, insofar as things go well, creatures do enjoy good achieved. Indeed, they are the primary beneficiaries, God's enjoyment being dependent on theirs. God, however, is the sole everlasting beneficiary. To be sure, God suffers with the world as well as rejoices with it, according to Hartshorne, but it should be noted that the evil that creatures suffer lies eternally unredeemed in their oblivion whereas the evil that God suffers is, according to Hartshorne, being forever diluted by new experiences of good (though this contention, too, we have seen reason to question).

The compassion and morality of a God who cannot grant life after death yet who cooperates with the occurrence of the Holocaust is questionable, to say the least. To be sure, the process God has an infinite, everlasting appetite for happiness and depends inescapably on the world for some portion of his happiness, but even so one would think that, given his inability to redeem broken lives after death, he would offer creatures a narrower range of alternatives. His happiness might thereby be less, but so would the suffering of the world. Indeed, granted the immutable compassion and moral integrity of the process God, plus his inability to grant life after death but his ability, according to Hartshorne, to have restricted the choices of creatures so as to have precluded the horrors of history, I believe the horrors of history count decisively against the existence of the process God. Were there such a God, he would not have allowed these horrors to come to pass knowing that he could not redeem their innocent, involuntary victims. In the next chapter I will say why I believe those same evils are compatible with a classical conception of God.

Two final points of criticism. First, with regard to the classical notion of divine judgment followed by heaven or hell, such as Brasnett seemed to hold, it should be noticed that, if humans are genuinely free, then it is possible that no one will choose God's kingdom. If none does, Brasnett should hold that God will be everlastingly emotionally devastated. Or what if a slight majority of all free creatures elects against God's kingdom? Will that condemn God to be everlastingly slightly more sad than happy? It would seem to be so if traditional passibilists are correct – and because it seems so I believe their position should be rejected as an inadequate conception of God.

Second, neoclassical passibilists such as Hartshorne seem to be inconsistent in their position about God's feelings toward those who reject his will. To be sure, I believe that Hartshorne's passibilism is more coherent than Dougall's, Owen's, and Vann's because he insists that "the happiness of God is tinged with tragedy in such a way that the regrettable remains regrettable, even as entering into deity" (1953: 153). But, when he also says that God is always infinitely happy, and when he seems to indicate that God's suffering is always and necessarily heavily outweighed by his joy, he seems to speak at odds with himself: God loves each of us more tenderly and dearly than anyone else does, suffering with us and for us more poignantly than anyone else, but, if we reject him, act in contempt of his will, and torment our fellows, he will not be so bothered that his happiness will not always continue to be infinite and growing. In brief, I do not believe this position is consistent. Either God's happiness can be seriously and constantly damaged by the world, or God is not so emotionally passible as Hartshorne claims. In brief, passibilists should either draw the harsh conclusions that Brasnett drew or abandon their position.

8

Evil, morality, redemption

I HAVE CLAIMED that the enormity of evil in human history seems a
conclusive disproof of the existence of the process God but not of the
classical God. The difference turns upon the kingdom of good that the
classical God can establish, according to classical theists, but the process
God cannot, according to process theists.[1] Whether this kingdom is in
every case worth the price of admission is, I believe, a judgment that can be
made adequately only from the vantage point of membership in the
kingdom. There are, however, those who believe that this judgment can be
made independently of such membership. Consider Edward Madden and
Peter Hare, who insist with Dostoyevsky's Ivan that a good God, even of
the classical description, would not have created a world with so much
suffering as this one. Such a statement suggests that God could have
created a world with *some* suffering – but not *this* much! Therefore,
Madden and Hare conclude, there is not a God. But this line of argument
cannot succeed in any conclusive way against the classical conception of
God because it has to be based on a specific limit to permissible suffering,
and any such limit would have to be, so far as I can see, established
arbitrarily.

The position of Arthur Schopenhauer, by contrast to that of Madden
and Hare, is more tractable. Schopenhauer declares that if there is the least
iota of creature suffering, then there cannot be a God.[2] It is not a quantity
of suffering that is incompatible with the existence of God; it is the
existence of any suffering at all. Two responses to Schopenhauer seem
appropriate. First, I do not believe that logical analysis of the concept of
God reveals that no amount of suffering is compatible with the existence of
God. It seems, for example, too easy to construct counter-examples
involving higher values, whether athletic, artistic, intellectual, or spiritual,
that can be achieved only through some degree of suffering, pain, or
discomfort – values that we freely choose to pursue in spite of our
knowledge of the cost in pain. Second, on a personal level, as distinguished
from a logical level, I do not share Schopenhauer's sentiment about
suffering. Though I were to suffer greatly, if I could be shown that the
suffering was necessary to the enjoyment of a good so exquisite that for the
sake of it I would, if necessary, go through my suffering all over again, I
would have no complaint against God. I would be grateful for the

opportunity that he had graciously extended to me. Hence, I believe that those who claim that any creature suffering or "this much" creature suffering is incompatible with the existence of God show a lack of logic, a lack of imagination, arrogate to themselves a decision that should be left to each of us, and presume to answer a question that can be answered knowledgeably only from the appropriate vantage point, the kingdom of God – in which we obviously are not now. Further, those who do not enter the kingdom will never be able to make the judgment on adequate grounds – though they have answered in advance on inadequate grounds that God's kingdom is not worth the price.

There is another issue here, however, because even if it would not be appropriate for God to be disturbed by the sufferings of those who will enter his kingdom later – since he knows that a good awaits them that in their own judgment will more than make up for the suffering they have endured – nonetheless, shouldn't he be disturbed by (1) the rejection and (2) the suffering of those who choose against his kingdom? Let us consider these points separately. The first point is that a loving God would be grieved when we reject him and his kingdom, when we return his love with spite or indifference, when we reject the good and pursue evil. As Dr A. Fairbairn has said of God, our sins are "the sorrow in the heart of His happiness" (Randles 1900: 147), and, as Bertrand Brasnett has said, God "asks for the love of men and sorrows till he finds it" (Brasnett 1928: 78). How, then, could God be said to love us if he is unaffected when we reject him and his kingdom? To be rejected by one's beloved is necessarily a painful experience for any genuine lover.

Or is it? It seems to me that it depends on what the lover desires for the beloved. The thrust of classical theism, as I understand it, is that there is a God who has created us in order that we might choose for or against his kingdom. In order to make that choice genuinely ours, God had to create us as free creatures, which means that he had to make it possible for us to choose for or against him without any direct or indirect manipulation by him of our choice. Obviously such freedom involves the possibility of us choosing against God. If we do so, will God be grieved? No. To say that God loves us is to say, as we have seen, that he cares about our welfare and provides for it. The highest possible provision for our welfare is in his kingdom, in which we have been invited to dwell, but which we can dwell in only as free citizens. Hence, God shows his love for us by creating us and by providing us with the dignity of making our own choice for or against his kingdom. If we choose against his kingdom, he will not be distraught. His fundamental will for us is not that we choose his kingdom but that we choose between his kingdom and its alternative.

God is like the father of the prodigal son. He makes every provision for our welfare, allows us to reject it, but welcomes us back warmly if we return. He does not, however, chase after us – nor did the father of the prodigal son (at least so far as the story reveals). Were God to pine away over those who reject his kingdom, he would be as immature as a jilted lover who pines over what could have been if only the beloved had chosen differently, and who runs after the beloved making demeaning efforts to win her back. Such feelings and behavior are not realistic or mature, nor do they respect the freedom and dignity of the beloved. They do not recognize that the beloved has freely chosen to be someone who does not pursue a romantic relationship with the lover, and they do not recognize the right of the beloved to make such a choice and have it accepted and respected by the lover. Indeed, it is clear that the possessive lover's feelings and behavior are really an insult to the beloved because it is obvious that the lover does not love the beloved as she is; rather, the lover loves what he would like the beloved to be. He loves an amalgam of certain features of that person and certain features added by imagination. If he really loved *that* person, he would want her to make her own decisions, and, if her decisions did not include him in her life, he would respect that and not be grieved by it because he could not maturely grieve over not being part of the life of a person who did not want him in her life.

Similarly, I do not believe it would be appropriate for God to grieve over those who freely reject him and his kingdom. Hence, I am opposed to the implications of Richard Swinburne's statement that "God is *anxious* to have friendship with man" (1981: 158, emphasis mine; also 1979: 273). It does not seem defensible to say or suggest that the meaning of human life is to provide companionship for God. John Hick takes a position similar to Swinburne's when he says that "man has been created by God for God" (1976: 254). As a consequence of this belief Hick holds that the world is "a place of soul-making, an environment in which creatures made as rational and personal in the image of God can grow towards the finite likeness of their maker," apparently in order that they will be worthy friends of God (1973: 54; also 1978: 83–90).

By contrast, I believe it is more compatible with the theistic tradition to say that man has been created by God for freedom. To be sure, by means of our spiritually significant decisions, our souls are shaped in one way or another, but our spiritually significant decisions are basically for or against the kingdom of God, and we are as free to reject it as to accept it. Were we not, then God would not be playing fairly with us; he would have given us the feeling of freedom without the substance of it. But surely he is playing fairly, and so our freedom is as radical as it seems. "It is good," as Richard Swinburne writes, "that God should not let a man damn himself without much urging and giving him many opportunities to change his mind, but it is bad that a man should not in the all-important matter of the destiny of his soul be allowed finally to destroy it" (1981: 154–5).

John Hick repudiates the preceding position and argues that all free creatures will be saved eventually. His reason is that if they were not, that would represent "a definite failure on the creator's part," who has created us for himself (1973: 70); but God cannot fail; therefore we cannot reject his kingdom forever. To be sure, "It remains logically possible that any (or all) will eternally persist in rejecting God; but it is also morally and practically certain that in unlimited time, in a universe ruled by a love that is actively seeking their deepest good, each will come into harmony with the divine ground of his own being" (1973: 72).[3]

I disagree with Hick because I believe it is more plausible that God has created us for freedom than for himself. Hick's position does not fully acknowledge the dignity or decisiveness of freedom. His God everlastingly besets the free creature until it makes the preferred choice. A choice other than the preferred choice is not allowed to be final. That means that there is only one final choice that we are free to make – and that makes a mockery of our freedom. Hence, I agree with this sentiment of Swinburne's: "Free will is a good thing; and for God to override it for whatever cause is to all appearances a bad thing" (1981: 154). To override it would be a violation of the dignity that God has given us in our freedom. If in our freedom we choose against the kingdom of God, that is no failure of God's. He did not create us to choose him; he created us to choose for or against him – and that we shall do, willy nilly.

"But," you might be thinking, "mustn't God at least be disturbed by the fact that those who reject his kingdom will go to hell and suffer eternal torment? After all, even a parent who agrees that his son deserves the severe criminal punishment being inflicted on him is anguished by the suffering that his son is undergoing. And, whereas one might respond that even in this case the parent might not be anguished because he believes the suffering will benefit his son, hell can benefit no one because from it there is no reprieve." There is merit to that point, but I believe the appropriate response is that we should not rush to conclusions as to what will become of those who reject God's kingdom.

As far as conceptual analysis is concerned, one alternative to hell is that God will simply consign to oblivion those who reject his kingdom. By having chosen not to live under God's rule, those people have chosen not to live at all since there is no possibility of life apart from God (on the assumption that there is a God). Hence, after their decision against citizenship in God's kingdom, they will simply be dropped from existence. With their passing into oblivion and with the establishment of the kingdom of God, all involuntary suffering will become a thing of the past.

In such a case I do not see any reason to believe that God would be grieved by the passage of some into everlasting oblivion. They would have merely got what they insisted on: independence from God.

The preceding is, of couse, only one alternative to the traditional conception of hell as eternal torment. Consider another: perhaps God will give everlasting life to every person, including those who reject his kingdom. These latter will be established everlastingly in a kingdom of their own, forever sealed off from a sense of the presence of God or of things divine. To be sure, even that would be unfair to a Walter Kaufmann or a Bernard Williams, who repudiate the desireableness of everlasting life, but there is no reason why God could not make voluntary oblivion a permanent option in his alternate kingdom (Kaufmann 1963; Williams 1973).

Either of the preceding alternatives to hell strikes me as more compatible with the attributes of God, especially love and justice, than does the traditional notion of hell. I do not, however, believe that we can infer from the concept of God specifically how he would handle those who choose and those who reject him as Lord (or, for that matter, how he would decide who had decided which way). What we can infer with certainty from the concept of God is that, however God handles those who reject his kingdom, it will be in a way that is compatible with his goodness and eternal bliss, and with the everlasting happiness of those who do choose and inhabit his kingdom. To think that God cannot work things out so that he can respond respectfully to our free choices without disturbing his own bliss or that of those in his kingdom is to think of God in an unworthy way. From this it follows that God can be emotionally impassible and loving.[4]

But what about those who choose God's kingdom? Won't God rejoice over them? And would not such rejoicing imply that he is emotionally passible to our good fortunes if not our bad? For the following reasons, again I answer "no." First, our choice for or against God's kingdom will not make a difference in his love for us, and therefore he will not as a result of his love for us increasing or decreasing have a corresponding change in the pleasure that he takes in us. Second, though he will enjoy forever the citizens in his kingdom, as they will enjoy him, we should make a distinction which allows that those who choose and enter God's kingdom will not in the ordinary sense increase his happiness. To be sure, given my E_2 conception of God, I believe that God does not know eternally but, rather, discovers who chooses his kingdom, but I believe that upon this discovery he takes pleasure extensively, not intensively, in each individual who chooses to be a citizen of his kingdom.[5]

To say that something makes an extensive but not an intensive contribution to God's happiness is to say that it makes a contribution, but not one that increases or decreases the intensity or purity of God's happiness. Aquinas uses this distinction in a discussion of the body's contribution to our happiness after death. But can resurrection, i.e., reacquisition of a body, possibly contribute anything to our happiness in God's kingdom? John Morreall has argued that reunion of the soul with a body after death could not alter the degree of our happiness because our happiness after death, according to Aquinas, will come from a vision of the essence of God, and obviously happiness enjoyed from such a vision could not be in need of supplementation – so why should there even be a resurrection? What could it possibly contribute to our happiness after death (Morreall 1980)? Aquinas answers that "when the body is reassumed happiness will grow, not in depth but in extent" (Aquinas 1964a: 4.5.1). Or, as a different translation has it, "with reunion of the body [to the soul], happiness will increase, not intensively, but extensively" (1964b: 4.5.1). I believe the point Aquinas is making can be illustrated by thinking of a delicious kind of food that can be made with spices. It is equally delicious whether it is made with vanilla or lemon rind, with basil or oregano, with a single spice or a combination, with this combination or that, or with no spices at all. The dish is merely different, not better, by virtue of being spiced or unspiced, or by being spiced in one way rather than another. Hence, it seems correct to say that the spices make an extensive difference to the taste of the dish but not an intensive one.

Similarly, I submit, God's happiness is affected extensively, not intensively, by who and how many choose life in his kingdom – and, indeed, by whether anyone at all does. God will be happy in more persons or fewer persons, in these persons or those persons, depending on who and how many choose to dwell in his kingdom. But however *we* choose, he will be perfectly happy because the perfection of his happiness is entirely from himself; it is our good fortune, according to theism, that he has chosen to share his felicity with us – if we so choose. Hence, when we choose for or against God's kingdom, we are choosing for or against our own happiness, not God's.

Does this mean that we cannot enrich the life of God? Yes and no. Yes, we can enrich it extensively; no, we cannot enrich it intensively. What we affect is the "texture" of God's happiness, not the intensity or purity of it. Some people see this position as preposterous. They will not have a God whom they cannot enhance or wound – whose happiness they cannot manipulate. Lily Dougall has written from a Christian perspective:

If God suffers not, our Lord [Jesus] is no revelation of Him, nor is it possible to conceive the Creator as having the relation of Father to His creation, *nor would it be possible for many of us to remain theists*, for if the Creator be faithful to His creatures it must be true

that in all their afflictions He is afflicted; if He be not faithful He is not the Christian
God.   (1912: 259; emphasis mine)

What are we to make of such an attitude? It seems to me that any person
who is bothered by the idea that God would be just as happy if that person
chooses for or against his kingdom is someone who does not want God to
be able to be happy without him – who wants to have some degree of
control over the happiness of God, and presumably of other people as well.
This strikes me as an unhealthy attitude. If we love someone, we should
want them to be able to be happy without us – even though we would
prefer that they be happy with us. To desire otherwise seems more
indicative of megalomania and insecurity than of love.[6]

To conclude this discussion of love and divine impassibility in feeling, I
believe that, because of God's personal perfection, his will for us, his
control of the parameters of our destiny, he can be perfectly happy no
matter what happens to us in this life and no matter whether we choose for
or against his kingdom.

MORALITY

Some would go on to say that, even if it were not true that God must suffer
with us because he loves us, nonetheless he would suffer with us because he
has a moral obligation to do so and is perfectly moral. Along this line Lily
Dougall has written, "The pregnant praise of the writer of 1 Peter, 'a
faithful creator,' cannot be read without reminding us that creation must
mean an obligation to another. In other words, we cannot think of God as
creator and without obligation" (1912: 55). One of God's obligations is
that he should make the struggles of his creatures his own and be united
"in entire sympathy with his whole creation" (1912: 55, 56). Another
author, Bertrand Brasnett, begins by arguing by means of an analysis of the
attribute of divinity that God *can* share our pain (an argument that we
have taken up already), and goes on to argue that, because God can share
our pain, if he will not do so then he is not moral. In Brasnett's own
words, "... we cannot regard a God as moral who stands aside and refuses
to share in the pain of the world that he created" (1928: 131). But,
according to Brasnett, obviously God is divine, i.e., worthy of worship,
and therefore able to suffer with us, and just as obviously he is moral and
therefore does suffer with us.

Does one who makes it possible or inescapable that another will suffer
have a moral obligation to share the suffering of the other for which the
one is directly or indirectly responsible? I think not. I see no reason to think
that a responsible parent whose baby while out on a family picnic is stung
by a wasp has an obligation to share in the pain and alarm of the child. I

believe there would be an obligation to comfort and help the child, but not to share its unhappiness – though the parent was significantly responsible for the misery of the child by having brought it into existence in the first place and having taken it on a picnic in the second place. Moreover, a responsible parent who *inflicts* unhappiness on his child in order to discourage behavior that is judged to be harmful to the child's health or character would have no obligation to share the child's misery as it sits in a corner complaining bitterly. Indeed, the parent would appropriately take *satisfaction* in the child's misery if he believed that infliction of such unhappiness was the only effective way to discourage the child from a repetition of its misbehavior. Now let us relate these points to God.

God is obviously responsible directly or indirectly for all of the sufferings that we undergo. Our suffering is either caused by him directly or is caused by things that he has willed into existence. But, because God is good, he would neither allow nor cause us to suffer unless such suffering was instrumentally ingredient to the achievement of a good such that we each would agree that the suffering was an understandably unavoidable risk and was more than made up for by the good to which it was a means. God would understand this eternally, and from such a perspective it does not seem that he, anymore than the responsible parent, has an obligation to suffer because of the suffering that he has intentionally allowed or caused.

But, critics will want to know, what do we make of the suffering of idiots, incapable of making a decision for or against God's kingdom, and of children whose lives are cut short by painful death before they can make a decision? Such instances are tragic and not to be taken lightly, but I do not think the interests of such people are better served by concluding that their suffering proves there is no God. If there is no God, their suffering is senseless and apparently final; if there is a God, then given God's infinite resources their suffering is redeemable, and, God being good, I believe it follows that he will redeem their suffering. Indeed, in such instances it seems to me that, though God has no obligation to suffer with such people, he would (if he were not perfectly good by nature) have an obligation to redeem their suffering by giving them an opportunity to choose for or against his kingdom – which entails that he should continue and develop their lives so that they will have such a choice.[7] Because he is perfectly good by nature, however, I believe he would do this by virtue of his natural beneficence and not because of an obligation.

Now let us put the Brasnetts on the defensive by appealing to Baron von Hügel's point that to love someone is to will that they never suffer unless suffering would be beneficial to them (Hügel 1926: 212). What are we to think of someone who wants his beloved to suffer when the suffering would be non-beneficial? Such a desire strikes me as perverse or arising from some mistaken assumption. Would a morally sound adult who is experiencing career failure believe that his parents ought to suffer with him because, after all, it was they who made his suffering possible by bringing him into the world? Would an adult whose parents caused him anxiety and embarrassment by refusing to loan him money to keep from having his new jacuzzi repossessed be right in thinking that his parents ought to share in his embarrassment and anxiety for not having loaned him money that they could have spared? Surely not, in either case.

But let us make it harder on ourselves. What about a person born with a painful, incurable affliction that is not terminal. Would he be right in thinking that his parents ought to suffer with him? If he were morally mature would he *want* his parents to suffer with him? To both questions I believe the answer is "no." A mature person who loved his parents would because of his love be grateful to them for their beneficence, and hope that they would not suffer because of his suffering. Indeed, out of concern that knowing his problems might cause them unhappiness, he might not tell his problems to them, or he might tell them but assure them that they should not be worried, that they should merely stand by him as he works through them.

A critic might insist that these examples provide no basis for a defense of God because, whereas the parents of the child, let us assume, had no way of knowing that he would be born with a painful affliction, God always knows the real risks of such events and has the resources to avert them. But he doesn't. So in such cases doesn't the individual have a right to insist that God, too, should suffer? Again I believe the answer is "no" – as difficult as such an answer is to accept when one reads, for example, about a 7-year-old boy who saved his 4-year-old sister and a 3-year-old neighbor from an escaped cross-breed wolf-dog but could not escape himself. The wolf, weighing more than 100 pounds, dragged the boy some 70 feet before his father was alerted and chased off the wolf – which soon was shot. The boy lived but was bitten terribly. One of his ears was found in the wolf's stomach; surgeons reattached it as best they could; part of the other ear and an eyelid were lost, and there were ugly slashes across his chest and back. He required more than 1,000 stitches and developed serious behavior problems that he did not have before.

What are we to make of such a horrible case? Doesn't it prove that there cannot be a God? Or that God is powerless to prevent such things? Only if it is impossible that there could be an adequate reason for permitting such a thing. I do not see, however, how anyone could establish that it is impossible, especially given what I believe is the fact that it is the child alone who has the right to say whether he would go through it all again for the sake of the kingdom of God – and he could make that judgment knowledgeably only from the vantage point of citizenship in the kingdom of God. I do not see that we have enough knowledge to conclude that the child would have been better off had it never been born. As Socrates said, the best may be yet to come, and, as St Paul said, what is to come may be worth far, far more than the pain and even terror that some of us experience in this life.[8]

Further, it seems to me that we have a moral obligation to hope that theism is true regardless of how the evidence is running. Let me back up and work my way into this point by entering a piece of dialectic that Edward Madden and Peter Hare initiate. In their book, *Evil and the Concept of God*, they note that among the reasons that theists give for being theists are existential reasons, i.e., experiences of mystery, forgiveness, inner transformation, etc. Madden and Hare acknowledge the relevance of such experiences but quickly point out that "there are existential grounds which pull the other way for those initially sensitive to the suffering of others or those who become sensitive through discussions of the problem of evil" (72). This is a troublesome statement for two reasons. First, it seems to imply that theists in general are insensitive to or uncaring about the suffering of others – only atheists being realistic about such matters – whereas in fact such a claim would be absurd and could be disproved easily by a survey of the kind and amount of relief work that is done by theists as well as atheists. Second, it is to overlook the point that sensitivity to innocent suffering justifies, at worst, ambivalence toward the question of the existence of God – that ambivalence taking the form of belief that there is probably no God yet hope that there is. Why hope that there is a God? Because of compassion for those who have suffered innocently; because of desire that their suffering not have been senseless and terminal, i.e., unredeemable past death.[9]

As long as it is logically possible that evil be defeated, that innocent suffering is not meaningless and final, it seems to me that we have a moral obligation to hope that that possibility is actual. Therefore we have a moral obligation to hope that there is a God because, if there is a God, then innocent suffering is not meaningless or final. Consequently, whereas we have one moral obligation not to think of or present theism (or any other hypothesis) as any more likely to be true than the evidence indicates, we have another moral obligation to hope that theism is true no matter how strong the evidence against it, unless it is conclusively demonstrated to be logically impossible.

But couldn't we just hope for the redemption of innocent sufferers without hoping for the existence of God? No, because without God evil could not be *defeated*; it could only be *counterbalanced* or *outweighed*.[10]

Why? Because, if there is no God, i.e., no intelligent being responsible for the existence, structure, and parameters of our world, then at least some innocent suffering is absolutely meaningless, purposeless, senseless, and consequently unredeemable – just a tragic fact about reality. The seeming meaninglessness, absurdity, and waste of innocent suffering and tragic loss are overcome only in the existence of God. To be sure, the Holocaust was enormously tragic – but without God it is even more tragic. Indeed, a far greater evil than the evils of history would be that the evils of history will not be defeated because there is no God. This seems to me a terribly important point that Dostoyevsky's Ivan failed to consider.[11]

To be sure, it would be better if innocent suffering is outweighed by good for those individuals, or at least counterbalanced, rather than not, but it would be better yet if it were redeemed, i.e., if it were understood to have been a necessary risk for a good that could not have been enjoyed without it, a good in the retrospective light of which the sufferer would agree that, though it was regrettable that the possibility of innocent suffering eventuated in innocent suffering, it was not regrettable that the possibility of innocent suffering was established inasmuch as it was a necessary condition of a good worth far, far more than the risks involved and the suffering endured (again: this is a judgment that only those who understand the reason and enjoy the good can appropriately make). As a matter of the heart, then, theism is a refusal to despair of hope for innocent sufferers, a refusal to believe short of indefeasible proof that evil is meaningless and terminal.

The position I have been developing *re* the problem of evil is a version of what Madden and Hare call the "all's well that ends well" view. Of their five criticisms of this view, the following one seems important to comment upon:

> The price that is paid for long run good is too high; the incredible amount of misery endured by sentient beings, and its unjust distribution, ruins the value of any possible goals. The end does not justify the means. The notion that all's well that ends well ignores the wounds along the way. Some will never heal. A selection to read here is 'Pro and Contra' from the *Brothers Karamasov*. No doubt, on the day of resurrection, Ivan says, I too will join the chorus, "Hallelujah, God, thy ways are just!" I too shall sing, as the mother embraces her son's murderer, "Praise God, I see why it had to be!" But, he concludes, I loath myself now for the very thought of doing that then. I renounce the ultimate harmony altogether, while I still can, while there is still time. For the love of man I now renounce it altogether.   (1968: 63–4)

In the first statement of this passage Madden and Hare claim that the amount of misery that has come to pass is logically incompatible with there being a God. This claim contradicts others in which they allow that success for the theodicists is always a logical possibility (1968: 14, 110). If the latter is true, then they cannot claim with logical consistency that, because of "the incredible amount of misery endured by sentient beings," there could not be a God. I am less troubled by this contradiction, however, than by their conviction that they know there is no way that even an infinite being could justify and redeem the suffering that has come to pass. It seems to me much more probable that an infinite being could have justified reasons for allowing or doing things that we could not now clearly understand than it seems probable that Madden and Hare, *et al*, have exhausted the possible reasons that an infinite being could have for allowing/doing what has come to pass and have seen correctly that none of them is acceptable.

Further, Ivan's love of man is a strange kind of love. He seems to hope that there is no God because, if there is, there will be an obscene spectacle during which God is praised and glorified in spite of all he has put us through. Ivan does not seem to care that, if there is no God, the suffering of the innocent will have been senseless and final. If he really cared about the innocent, wouldn't he hope that somehow sense could be made of their suffering and that their wounds could be healed? He seems more concerned that his cynicism be vindicated than that the innocent be redeemed. He does not allow that his praise of God "on the day of resurrection" might be because then he will understand the why of it all. His sentiment seems predicated on the assumption, as in Madden and Hare, that he knows that there is no way that the misery of history could be justified and redeemed, so that any post-resurrection hallelujah choruses to God by those who have suffered innocently could occur only after the minds of those people had been cynically manipulated by God. But in such a case there would, of course, be no God; at best evil would be counterbalanced or outweighed; at worst, good rather than evil would be defeated.

I have more admiration for Bernard Garrity in Taylor Caldwell's *Answer as a Man* than for Ivan. Bernard is a tough old Irishman who is bitterly critical of God and religion. When his daughter-in-law Katie, a truly innocent sufferer, dies of consumption, Bernard launches a vicious philosophical assault upon the local priest. After the priest leaves, Bernard's grandson Jason (Katie's son), says to Bernard: "You were right. God is our enemy. That is, if there is a God. I don't believe it. The world would be a different place if he existed." But Bernard replies, "Jase, if there is no God... there isn't anything for Katie, either. She deserves a God." I agree and hope for all the Katies of the world that there is a God who can make sense of their suffering and defeat it (Caldwell 1980: 121).

Yet isn't it the case, as Madden and Hare argue, that though it may be possible for there to be a successful theodicy the evidence is against it, so that even though we ought to hope that there is one we ought to concede that there probably is not? I do not think so. Madden and Hare allow that the existence of God and the existence of some evil are not incompatible with one another (Madden and Hare 1968: 38–9). They further allow that "success always remains a logical possibility for the religious cosmologist" (14). It follows that it is always possible in the larger scheme of things that evil is defeated; but if it is always possible that evil is defeated, i.e., that the world is more good than it would have been had the evil that it has known not been possible, then the evil of the world can never be counted legitimately against the existence of God.

From the facts that Madden and Hare are speaking of a God who is infinite in wisdom, goodness, and power, and that "success always remains a logical possibility for the religious cosmologist," it seems to follow that evil in itself cannot count against the existence of God. Because evil, as Madden and Hare allow, can be contributory to a greater good than could have existed without it, it follows that *vis à vis* the existence of God, evil can gain evidential status only contextually, i.e., from the entire story of history. Obviously that story is not presently available to us. Hence, we cannot ascertain now whether evil is to be counted against the existence of God. Consequently, the question of the existence of God must be adjudicated independently of the fact of the existence of evil. To count evil against the existence of God would be to assume that it is undefeated, which would be to assume that there is no God, which would be to beg the question of the existence of God.

If on other grounds it can be established that there *is* a God, then theists have a right to be confident that evil is neither senseless nor terminal, for, if there is a God, then there is a successful theodicy. Hence, Madden and Hare are mistaken when they say that if the theist "does not have a genuine answer to the problem of evil he has no right to say that he *knows* that God exists" (57, 73). To know that there is a God is to know that there is a successful theodicy – whether or not one knows precisely what it is. Questions of the nature and status of evil are secondary to questions regarding the nature and existence of God. Hence, it is illogical ever to abandon or reject belief in God because of evil.

In conclusion, there seems to be no good reason why a responsible parent or God would have a moral obligation to suffer with its suffering child, but there are good reasons to think (1) that there is something wrong in the sentiment of those who want their friends to suffer with them, (2) that for the sake of innocent sufferers, we have an obligation to hope that there is a God, and (3) that evil as far as we know it now cannot be counted against the existence of God.

REDEMPTION

Some believe that God suffers with us and for us in order to redeem us, that is, to save us from doing and suffering evil. The point seems to be that it is by means of the suffering of God that we are saved and transformed. First some passages to this effect by Lily Dougall:

> Wherever invisible Deity is not conceived of as suffering, wherever man ceases to identify God with human weal, wherever man conceives that he cannot hurt or help God, there I think there will be found that whatever the concomitant intellectual brilliancy, human progress is in a *cul de sac*.
> ... the Creator must suffer, as well as rejoice, in the endurance of an autonomous creation. [Hence] some generous response on man's part to the ideal of Omnipotence suffering from human cruelty is a condition of man's more permanent development...
> (1912: 164–5)

Dougall goes on to say that the development of sympathy for divine suffering is a condition of human fitness to enter the kingdom of God.

Later Dougall states that, though God suffers in all the wrongs of his creatures, his suffering is "efficacious for the righting of all wrong." Indeed, it is by divine suffering that the world is saved:

> The world is saved by joyful realisation that God has taken all our wrong and pain upon Himself, and is Himself its certain remedy. How joyful is the certainty that in so far as any of God's creatures, in sympathy or by suffering violence, freely take upon themselves the wrong and pain of others, their suffering, as one with His, has saving efficacy!
> (275)

We, then, can share in God's act of salvation by sharing in his suffering. Bertrand Brasnett brings out even more pointedly the redemptive impact that awareness of God's suffering can have:

> The thought of God as a great sufferer may well be a depressing thought to those who have caused that suffering, yet when they know that by turning away from sin they can turn the divine sorrow into joy, surely then the thought of God as "the most miserable object of our pity" becomes a powerful stimulus to holiness and righteousness of life.
> (1928: 142)

It remains to evaluate these sentiments.

It does not strike me as obviously true that divine suffering is a necessary condition of human redemption. Nor does it seem to me that proponents of passibilism have their values straight when they claim that it is by knowing the suffering that we can and do cause God that our hearts are convicted of the meanness of sin and rendered more sympathetic. To take up the last point first, I submit that we should be convinced of the wrongness of our behavior whenever it intentionally causes non-beneficial suffering to our fellow creatures. We do not need to think about the possible effect on God before realizing that teasing a child about its harelip would be wrong. It would be the innocent pain in the heart of the child that would make it an immoral act – not some sympathetic suffering that God would undergo.[12] Further, if we are insensitive to the feelings of the child, I do not see why our hearts would be changed by realizing that we cause God as well as the child to suffer. If we are not sensitive to the suffering of the child, why would we be sensitive to the suffering of God – except perhaps out of odious self-regard?

If process philosophers were to respond, "But God, as the supremely sensitive being, suffers even more than the child, and so we should be more sensitive to his suffering than to the child's," I would be incredulous. That child's whole world would be taken up by its self-consciousness of its harelip and being teased. At the very least, as Hartshorne points out, God always has the perfection of his own nature plus the lovely things of the past and present to enjoy as a counterbalance to his suffering from the ugliness and tragedy of our past and present behavior. Hence, it is primarily the prospect of innocent creature suffering that should sway us from sin – not the prospect of secondary divine suffering.[13]

What about the argument that God's suffering love causes us to adopt a godly life because, once we discover that God "asks for the love of man and sorrows till he finds it" and that when we turn from him we cause him "unending pain and enduring agony," we find our ungodly inclinations paralyzed by our sympathy for God? I quite agree that sometimes such concern for others, our parents for example, causes us to refrain from an action that we know would cause them suffering. But I do not believe that this consideration applies to God. In the first place, as pointed out earlier, it would give us a power over God that seems incompatible with his divinity. In the second place, it presents what strikes me as an undignified picture of God. Freedom is given to be exercised however one chooses to exercise it. It would be unthinkable for God to be shocked, surprised, or disappointed at how we use our freedom – as though he did not know that we could or would do *that*! And it would be inappropriate for him, when we choose against him, to try to get us to change our minds by pursuing us relentlessly with pleading, whining, and tears. Such behavior would only show his gift of freedom to have been insincere – and surely it was not. If we, like the prodigal son, ask for our "share of the inheritance" that we might leave and be on our own, God grants it. Like the father of the prodigal, he accepts our decision regarding his kingdom, and awaits our return with infinite patience, greeting us warmly should we return. But he does not chase after us in distress with sighs.

It does not seem, then, that God must suffer in order for us to realize what is morally right and wrong or to find a motive for resisting immoral temptations. Moreover, when what we need to be saved from is not doing evil but suffering it, it is help that we want, not fellow-suffering. E. L. Mascall makes the point nicely: "when we are in trouble what really helps us is not sympathy, in the sense of imaginative or even an actual participation in our suffering, but concrete practical help" (Mascall 1949: 142). Mascall was building on a point by Aquinas: "To feel sad about another's misery is no attribute of God, but to drive it out is supremely his" (Aquinas 1964a: 1a.21.3).

It is certainly my impression that in an emergency people do not ordinarily sympathetically feel the suffering of the person in need; they just act immediately so as to help in some way. If someone were to help me in such a situation I would not hold it against her for not having suffered with me either before, during, or after the event. In fact, I would be glad to discover that my helper had not been aesthetically repulsed or emotionally traumatized by my plight. Further, I would fault the character of anyone who thought the less of my benefactor merely because she had not been negatively affected by my experience. Finally, I would admire someone all the more for not only being a good samaritan, but for also being able to avoid emotional disturbance in an emergency situation.[14]

What I have been doing in the last two paragraphs is asking why passibilists want a fellow-sufferer when the help they need can be extended without suffering. Before developing that point further, a caveat is in order. Some people note that the experienced physician who has become inured to the traumas of the hospital emergency room is able to be more helpful than the new intern who is traumatized by the sights, sounds, smells, and stress of the emergency room; similarly, the experienced crisis counselor who knows the importance of getting at the real feelings of a client, reflecting them back, and helping the client work through them therapeutically, yet not getting caught up in them personally, is able to be more helpful than the less experienced colleague who still gets emotionally involved in his clients' problems. People who note these facts sometimes conclude that, because we are able to be more helpful when our thinking and actions are not disturbed by emotional trauma, i.e., when we are emotionally impassive to physical injury and emotional distress as are the experienced physician and counselor (at least relatively so), it would be better for God, too, to be emotionally impassive.

The problem with this position is that though we know that emotional trauma can interfere with *our* ability to act promptly and correctly – so that ordinarily it would be better for us to be emotionally impassive in emergency situations – the same consideration does not apply to God. As Hartshorne and Baker have pointed out, because of God's omnipotence and omniscience it cannot be the case that anything, including his inner life, could interfere with his judgment or action (Baker 1976: 98;

Hartshorne 1957). Hence, it should not be concluded, because empathy sometimes interferes with our ability to help, that God, since he can always help, never empathizes. The issue of divine empathy must be settled on other grounds because it follows from divine omnipotence that God can always help whether he empathizes or not.

To return to the question of redemption and impassibility, I am assuming that traditional passibilists would agree that, unless God's suffering were redeemed by some greater good, we could not allow that God suffers. We have seen, however, that suffering in itself is an evil, and that it could in no way benefit God himself. Consequently, it must be the case according to passibilists that God's suffering benefits us, his beloved creatures, in ways in which we otherwise could not be benefited. Hence, we are redeemed by God's suffering, and God's suffering is redeemed by our salvation. Bertrand Brasnett expresses this sentiment in the following statement: "In our day the traditional view, that God is impassible, is challenged on many sides. Men feel, and perhaps will feel increasingly, that a God who is not passible, who is exempt from pain or suffering, is a God of little value to a suffering humanity" (1928: ix). The passibilist position, then, is something like the following: "It is important to me to know that God suffers with me and for me. It proves that he really cares. It enables me to relate to him. It softens my suffering. If I felt that he did not share my suffering, I would feel that he did not really care about me, and so I could not really care about him."

Perhaps this sentiment and my own simply represent an emotional impasse – two people with different intuitions or emotional needs. Still, I believe that this is an issue that can be resolved by conceptual analysis, especially once it is noted that all the benefits associated with divine grace can be enjoyed even if God does not suffer. Whether or not God suffers with us and for us, we can still feel gratitude to him for the blessings we have received and for the hope that we have. Whether or not God suffers with us and for us, we can be confident that he is aware of us, that he cares for us through his providence in this life and the next, and that he is present to us – at the very least in order to ensure that his way is among the alternatives with regard to which we can exercise our freedom. To be sure, God cannot be present to us as fellow-sufferer; but, rather than being disturbed by that, we should be glad, even as we are glad when our friends do not undergo suffering that is non-beneficial to them. God can, however, be present as an exquisite sense of tenderness or strength or forgiveness or purity whereby we are touched and whence we draw new life and direction. Finally I would urge that the look of blissful loving equanimity on God's face in the midst of our suffering is not a sign of aloof indifference; it is a sign that in the long run all is well because all occurs within the parameters of God's power, wisdom, and goodness.[15]

SUMMARY AND CONCLUSION

Conceptual analysis of the concept of God reveals that none of the divine attributes requires suffering of God. Consequently, because divine suffering would be evil in itself, would have no instrumental value for God himself, and would provide no benefit to his creatures that could not be had without it, we should reject divine emotional passibilism. A more defensible position is that God's purpose in creating us is to give us the opportunity to choose freely whether we want to be part of his kingdom. If we reject his kingdom, he will respect that choice and respond in a manner compatible with his perfect goodness.

Regarding those who do not get to make a choice because of circumstances such as an early death, it seems to me that we can reasonably expect a further opportunity of choice to be provided to them. As to those who suffer innocently or beyond what is just, analysis of the concept of God warrants confidence that God has the will and the resources to ensure that those who see the goal of all things and understand the means to that goal will agree that the means were warranted even if some of the consequences were regrettable – but regrettable not because they meant everlasting or even temporary sadness for God, but because they meant involuntary, non-beneficial suffering for creatures. Still, it is better that it have been possible for such suffering to occur than not, and we can be confident that God would not have allowed it to occur unless he could redeem it, i.e., defeat the evil inherent in it. Hence, the theist agrees with Paul of Tarsus that "neither death, nor life, nor angels, nor principalities, nor things present, nor things to come, nor powers, nor height, nor depth, nor anything else in all creation, will be able to separate us from the love of God . . ." (Romans 8) Paul concluded the preceding statement: "in Christ Jesus our Lord." With that final assertion only Christians would agree, but up to that point it seems to me that Paul has said something to which all classical theists – whether Jewish, Christian, Muslim, or otherwise – should agree profoundly.

In closing these reflections on emotional impassibility in God, I would like to say something about the possible significance of this divine attribute for human life. The more I have reflected on the virtue of impassible love, the more I have wished I were possessed of it. If I were, it would mean that when people I love are sad I would care about them and do what I could to comfort them, but I would not be saddened by their sadness. It would mean that when people do things that I believe are wrong (cruel, irresponsible, unjust) I would not become angry, i.e., emotionally perturbed, yet I would act to persuade or prevent them from their behavior. It would mean that when I believe loved ones correctly rejoice in something I would be happy for them and with them, but, because the existence and intensity of my happiness would come from my confidence in the goodness, wisdom, and power of God, my happiness would not be dependent in these respects upon others.

At the same time, I would like people to relate to me in the manner of impassible love. Should I fall into sorrow, I would like them to comfort and encourage me, but I do not want them to sorrow with me or for me. I do not want their happiness to depend on mine – what a terrible responsibility for me and misfortune for them were it so! Yet when I am happy I would like them to share in my happiness – extensively, not intensively. Finally, when I do something wrong, I want to be corrected, responded to appropriately, and if necessary stopped from continuing or repeating my infraction, but I would like this to be done by people whose attitudes evince a calm and steady concern for me and others, rather than evincing the anger that can be so easily misconstrued as hatred or condemnation and that so frequently has unintended destructive consequences.

The virtue of emotional impassibility is so foreign to our ordinary emotional life that at first it seems alien and impossible of achievement. Perhaps it is impossible for a human to achieve. Perhaps such a change would require a biological mutation or a transformation of nature by grace. In either case I believe we would be better off. We would move in the direction of Buddha's tranquil compassion as seen in his tender response to the grief-stricken woman who carried her dead child to him. We would move in the direction of Socrates calmly and solicitously warning those who condemned him to death that they were harming themselves, not him. We would move in the direction of Jesus on the cross praying for his executioners, "Father, forgive them, for they know not what they do" – feeling neither anger nor despair, only love and concern.[16]

9

Why does God create?

CLASSICAL THEISM holds that, because God is free, he did not have to create a world. That he created this world rather than another possible world or none at all was the result of a free choice. There has, however, been vigorous opposition – ancient as well as modern – to this position. I have isolated four reasons for thinking that God must create a world: (1) morality, (2) divine goodness, (3) divine happiness, and (4) the logic of the concept of existence. Each of these reasons has some initial plausibility, but in my judgment none of them finally succeeds. I will defend this judgment by examining pertinent quotations.

Morality

In 'The Unchangeableness of God,' Philo takes up the question, "Why did God create?" In his response he also answers the question, "Did God have to create?" That response is as follows:

God has bestowed no gift of grace on Himself, for He does not need it, but He has given the world to the world, and its parts to themselves and to each other, aye and to the All. But He has given His good things in abundance to the All and its parts, not because He judged anything worthy of grace, but looking to His eternal goodness, and thinking that to be beneficent was incumbent on His blessed and happy nature. So that if anyone should ask me what was the motive for the creation of the world, I will answer what Moses has taught, that it was the goodness of the Existent, that goodness which is the oldest of His bounties and itself the source of the others.   (1930: 63–5)

Why, then, did God create? Not because creatures deserve his beneficence, but because his blessed and happy nature places an obligation upon him. Did he, then, have to create? Yes. Being by nature perfectly good he could not fail to fulfill an obligation.

Hartshorne, too, has put forth an argument from morality to divine creation. He writes, "since any world is better than none at all (there is no value in nonentity), it would be wrong or foolish of God not to create. But God cannot do wrong or be foolish" (1970: 264). Clearly, inasmuch as it would be wrong for God not to create a world, he has a moral obligation to create one. And, inasmuch as he cannot do anything wrong, he must and will create one.

I do not find these arguments from morality to the necessity of creation to be convincing. Though God had an obligation to create a world, it would not follow that that was his reason for creating the world. One can have an obligation to do something yet do it for some other reason, such as love or prudence. But for now let us examine whether, as Philo and Hartshorne seem to hold, morality would obligate God to create a world if he had no other reason to do so.

If God had an obligation to create a world, to whom would he have that obligation? Either it would be to himself or to someone else. I do not understand how God, an essentially perfect being in no need of improvement and incapable of evil, could have an obligation to himself or what it would mean for him to have such an obligation. Nor is it clear that Philo or Hartshorne means that God has an obligation to himself to create a world. Hence, I will assume that they mean that God's obligation is to someone other than himself. On the assumption of the argument, however, there is no one other than God. The *desideratum* is: If there were no individuals other than God, would God have an obligation to create at least one?

The only other possibility seems to be that God has an obligation to possible individuals to create them. But Hartshorne is explicit that possible individuals are not authentic individuals, nor can good or evil be done to them. I agree.[1] It seems, then, that possible individuals are not things to which we can have obligations. It follows that there is and can be no individual, actual or possible, to whom God could have an obligation to create a world.

One might object, "God's obligation to create a world is an obligation to creativity, to reality, to goodness." None of these, however, is a proper source of moral obligation precisely because none is an individual. Obligations to abstractions or principles are not basic; such obligations derive their authority from their relation to the fulfillment of obligations to individuals.

Now let us look at some additional objections to these suggested objects of obligation. On the assumption that creativity could be a proper object of obligation, to say that God ought to create a world because of an obligation to creativity would be question-begging. The question is whether the claim that God has such an obligation can be justified.

If one says instead, "God's obligation to create a world is an obligation to reality," we need to recall that on the assumption of the argument, nothing has yet been created, so the reality to which God has this obligation consists of himself and the plenum, which together constitute reality prior to the creation of a world. I have already expressed my belief that it does not make sense to speak of God having an obligation to himself, and it does not seem that he could have an obligation to the plenum. In addition to not being an individual, the plenum does not care about which of its possibilities are actualized, or whether any are, and there is no way in which God can benefit or harm the plenum. It is not better off for having its possibilities actualized rather than not actualized. Hence, I see no basis for thinking that God has an obligation to the plenum to actualize its possibilities, or to reality to create a world.

Finally, does God have an obligation to goodness to create a world? First we must ask for the locus of goodness. If goodness is identical with God, then God's obligation to goodness would be an obligation to himself – a notion that seems to be without merit. If goodness is not identical with God, then it is something distinct from God that stands over him as an ideal and standard. I do not understand, however, what metaphysical basis or moral authority such a thing could have in its independence from God. Given my metaphysics, goodness which is not identical with God in any respect would have to be identical with the plenum as a whole or a part of it. If it were identical with the plenum as a whole, then the plenum would stand over against God as an ideal and standard, but the plenum does not have that kind of definiteness; it is not the ideal possibility, either concretely or formally. It is the passive basis of all possibilities, and it is indifferent to whether good, bad, or evil possibilities are actualized, so it could hardly function as a moral or aesthetic ideal. If we were to identify goodness with some possibility of the plenum, rather than with the plenum as a whole, we would be saying that God has an obligation to a possibility. To be sure, we can have an obligation to actualize a possibility, but our obligation is not to the possibility; it is to an actual individual to whom we have an obligation to actualize that possibility. Hence, the idea that God has a primary obligation to goodness as a possibility seems to be indefensible.

Parenthetically, I believe that a *reductio* can be worked upon the idea that God has an obligation to goodness to create a world. If such an obligation to goodness entails that God has an obligation not only to create a world but to create all the goods that he possibly can, as it would seem to, then the resulting scenario is of God trying to accomplish the impossible, ever producing goods at a geometrically increasing pace, yet always knowing that he is never getting the least bit closer to producing all the good that he could (because of the jointly infinite resources of his power and the plenum). Hence, because of the inexhaustibility of the total set of possibilities, accomplishment of such an obligation is impossible in principle and therefore is not a legitimate obligation. If a proponent of this position were to respond, "Then God's obligation is not to create all the good that is possible but, rather, all the good that he possibly can," I would object that this, too, seems a meaningless notion because of God's infinite resourcefulness. No matter how much good is being created by him at any given moment, more could have been being created by him at that very moment. In brief, the principle of plenitude makes God a slave to creativity. But God properly conceived is a slave to no thing. Hence, he should be thought of as free to create or not create.

Divine goodness

Joseph F. Donceel, S.J., takes a similar but subtly different route to the conclusion that God must create a world. He bypasses the question as to whether God has an obligation to create, focusing on whether it is inevitable that God will create a world because of his nature. Donceel's conclusion is a form of theological compatibilism: because of God's goodness, and in particular his loving nature, he cannot help but create; however, inasmuch as he creates because he wants to, and not because of external or internal compulsion (such as moral constraint), he creates freely. In Donceel's own words, "It seems, therefore, that we may conclude: It makes sense to say that God, out of the superabundance of his love, will necessarily create some universe, but not necessarily this or that universe" (Donceel 1979: 146).[2] However, "Something that is motivated by love is, insofar as it is thus motivated, free" (146). Notice that Donceel, unlike Philo, is not saying that God's goodness obligates or constrains him to create a world. However, he is saying implicitly that God could not have chosen not to create a world. Indeed, he says explicitly, "That which is motivated by infinite love will necessarily happen, yet it will happen in total freedom" (146). Hence, the existence of a world is the necessary result "of God's overflowing love, which wishes to share" (147).

It seems clear that God's creation of the world was both free and not free, according to Donceel. It was free inasmuch as God created it because he wanted to; it was not free inasmuch as he could not have chosen not to. The last clause amounts to saying that that is just the way God is, a creator because of his infinite love – not that he is by his love constrained to create. Rather, that is just the way infinite love is – creative of others. This is in my judgment a more attractive argument than the moral argument but still not convincing. Its major premise (basically the Dionysian principle noted in Aquinas by Kretzmann) is that a loving being is necessarily a being that creates another. Apparently this premise is held by Donceel to be intuitively obvious, since little effort is made to justify it, yet it does not seem impossible or even difficult to conceive of God not having created a world even though he is a loving being in the sense that he loves himself and would love anything that he created.

We have seen that it would be mistaken sentiment for God to create out of pity or compassion for possible individuals. If he did create because in his love he could not stand to think of those poor possible individuals just sitting there insentiently, so to say, it would appear that he creates in order to relieve *his* unhappiness over their plight – since it is not a plight of which they are aware. He could never overcome his unhappiness in this respect, however, because, no matter how many possible individuals he actualized, there would always be even more who remained merely possible. Fortunately Donceel denies that God creates in order to satisfy any need of his own, and so is not subject to the preceding criticism.

Is it the case, then, that God creates for the sheer joy of creating, for the pleasure of bringing other enjoyers-of-existence into actuality? If so, then either he does so freely (in the sense that he could have done otherwise) *or* (ruling out external compulsion and moral obligation) he does so because without a world he would not be as happy owing to impoverishment or sadness. I gather that Donceel would not affirm the latter disjunct, yet he has ruled out the former. Therefore he would reject this "for the joy of it" interpretation of why it is that infinite love must create a world. If so, he is left with a bare assertion: infinite love because it wants to share necessarily creates a world. If this assertion is true, it is analytically true, but to many it does not seem analytically true, and so we must wait on its proponents to illuminate the necessity of the relation between its predicate and subject. At present it seems reasonable to say at most that the divine goodness determines what kind of a world God does not create, but not whether God creates a world.

Divine happiness

Now let us turn to the idea that God does create for the sake of his happiness. Earlier we saw Hartshorne's statement that God would be a fool not to create (1970: 264). Why? Because, according to Hartshorne, it is by means of the world that God's life is enriched. Hence, were he not to create a world he would be foolishly responsible for his own aesthetic poverty. But God is no fool; therefore necessarily he creates. Further, because the notion of unsurpassable happiness is incoherent (1941: 36), God will always be creating and thereby continually enriching his life. Hartshorne elaborates these points in the following statement:

Self-preservation is not a problem for the necessary being. God "needs" only one thing from the creatures: the intrinsic beauty of their lives, that is, their own true happiness, which is also his happiness through his perfect appreciation of theirs. This appreciation *is* love, not something extra as a motive to love. God "needs" happiness in which to share, not because the alternative is for him to cease to be, for this is not a possible alternative, but because the exact beauty of his own life varies with the amount of beauty in lives generally. *Some* other lives he must have, but his perfect power consists in this, that no matter what the creatures do with their free will they cannot bring about the destruction of the cosmos as such, they cannot reduce God to solitariness. All they can do is to determine *how much each new event adds* to the sum of event-values already stored in the memory of God. God has need for the maximum possible addition, not in the sense that he must have it "or else," but in the sense that it is to his interest to have it.

(1941: 163–4)

Hence, if God had the power to create a world, he would do so, and he would do it in such a way as to maximize his happiness.

I have two reactions, one conceptual and one moral, to this position. The conceptual one has to do with whether unsurpassable happiness is conceivable. Hartshorne believes it is not; I believe it is. I believe I can consistently and meaningfully conceive of a being that is by nature perfectly happy in the intensive sense explained earlier. The intensity of the happiness of such a being could neither wax nor wane, and therefore would be unsurpassable. What could cause a being to be so fortunate? Being perfectly satisfied with its nature and its circumstances.

Perhaps we can best approach this notion in two phases. Let us say generally that happiness is a product of satisfaction with one's self and one's circumstances and that unhappiness is a result of dissatisfaction with one's self or one's circumstances. The permutations of these elements are as follows:

	SELF	CIRCUMSTANCES
HAPPY	S	S
UNHAPPY	S	D
UNHAPPY	D	S
UNHAPPY	D	D

Aldous Huxley may have had some such scheme in mind when he wrote of alpha people and beta people in *Brave New World*. Each was perfectly content being the type of creature it was; indeed, each was repelled by the idea of being any of the other types, and each was perfectly happy with its circumstances. In brief, those creatures could not have been happier. One might say, "But that's fiction. Real people aren't that way." People do, however, say such things as "I could not have been happier" or "I could not be happier" – an obviously empirical claim that, it seems to me, puts the burden of proof on those who disagree.

The critic might concede, "Okay, any member of a given species might be perfectly satisfied with its nature and perfectly adapted to its circumstances. But we can always conceive of another species whose happiness is on a yet higher level." For example, a perfectly happy angel is happier than a perfectly happy human in the sense that, could one individual experience both states of happiness, he would prefer the happiness of the angel even though he would know that if he chose the happiness of the fortunate human he would be perfectly satisfied. It is, then, conceivable that there are an infinite number of levels of happiness on which finite beings might be created. However, does this consideration apply to God, an infinite being?

Presumably one finite species could be created capable of a higher happiness than another species by being created with greater powers of sensitivity in terms of (1) degree of pleasure that could be enjoyed or (2) range of objects that could be enjoyed, the full satisfaction of such powers being provided by appropriate circumstances. But the power of enjoyment that God has and the primary objects that he has to enjoy, viz., himself and the plenum, are such that greater ones are inconceivable. Further, the circumstance that he enjoys, viz., the perfect amenability of the plenum to his will, could not conceivably be improved upon. He holds the key of the gate to contingent existence. Anything that occurs he must cause directly or approve the occurrence of in view of objectives that he has.

God, then, should be perfectly happy with himself and his situation, in which case it does not seem true that he must actualize a world in order to become happy or that by actualizing a world he would increase his happiness. As Philo suggests, and I believe should hold, God creates a world for the sake of the existence and happiness of creatures. God's own happiness is perfectly and eternally secured by means of his nature and his providential control over the plenum. Because God has a purpose for creatures that requires the possibility of great suffering, and, because he has the intention, wisdom, and power to insure that an end is being achieved that justifies all evil that transpires, he need not be saddened or rejoiced by what transpires in history.

Logic

The fourth argument for thinking that God must create a world begins with analysis of the concept of individual existence. Hartshorne, particularly fond of this argument, writes, "For an individual to exist is always for it to be actualized in concrete states, none of which (unless the first one) is absolutely necessary for the existence of that individual" (1970: 150). That is, to exist as an individual is not to exist as a mere essence but, rather, to have some aspect of accident or contingency.[3] I, for example, must be in some specific posture as I type these words. I happen to be sitting, though I could have been standing or kneeling – indeed, my wife believes that the latter would be the more appropriate posture for me to take before my typewriter.

Generalizing this point to God, Hartshorne writes:

Since God has no beginning, one can drop the qualifying "unless the first one" and say that, conceiving him by analogy with ordinary individuals, his existence must consist in his nature being actualized in states which do not follow necessarily from his individual essence. That, nevertheless, God "exists necessarily" means that his individual nature is inevitably and invincibly actualized *somehow*, but just how, in what actual states, is a further and contingent truth about him.   (1970: 150)

I agree with Hartshorne on this point and believe that Aquinas' talk about God being completely necessary is either mistaken or misleading. The latter seems more likely because of Aquinas' distinction between absolute and conditional necessity in God. As I noted earlier, in that distinction Aquinas acknowledges that there is freedom in God – that not everything about God is necessary, that some things about God (such as his not having created the world without a beginning) could have been otherwise had he so chosen.

Hartshorne deserves credit for having cleared up the mistake of thinking that everything about God must be necessary. There must be a contingent aspect to God if he exists. Why? Because as an existent he must exemplify one of the mutually exclusive sets of alternatives available to him. As Hartshorne puts it, "there must always be some appropriate concrete realization of the abstract divine nature" (1970: 234). Hence, God's abstract nature "must be concretized somehow, but there is no must about the particular how" (1970: 234). The particular how is entirely up to God.

Does this mean that God must create? In a sense, yes. As Hartshorne insists, God is creator of himself – not in the sense that he brings himself into existence, but in the sense that he makes himself, for example, to be creator of a world with a beginning rather than of a world without a beginning, or of a world with intelligent beings in it rather than of a world without intelligent beings in it. Hence, no matter what God does, he is involved in creation. Hartshorne defends his position by arguing: "For a creative being not to create at all is for it not to exist as creator. At most it would be potentially creative. But the reality of creativity is the very basis of possibility or potentiality itself" (1970: 264). Hence, God is necessarily a creator, at the very least of himself in his contingent aspect.

Does this mean that God must create a world? Certainly not, according to Hartshorne's position, for two reasons. First, according to Hartshorne, the world "is not an individual but simply 'all individuals other than God'" (1957: 82). From this it follows that, if God must create a world, he must create an individual other than himself. According to 1970: 264 God would be "wrong or foolish" not to create a world, so obviously he will create a world, i.e., create at least one individual other than himself. But, according to the process position, no individual can create an individual other than himself. Hence, God cannot create an individual other than himself; therefore he cannot create a world. At most he can attempt to persuade already extant individuals to create themselves according to his preferred alternatives for them.

Hartshorne might reply, "But that is all I meant when I said that God must create a world, viz., that he must persuade extant individuals in such a way as to bring a universe, i.e., a world, out of chaos." This move, however, is rendered impossible by positions that Hartshorne takes elsewhere in *Creative Synthesis and Philosophic Method*. For example: "Both God and world are, then, necessary beings; but since subject includes object, the two are really but the one necessary being, God-as-experiencing-a-world – some world or other, no matter what" (1970: 170). Later Hartshorne states,

... the Anselmian controversy should teach us that one thing could not merely happen, the divine existence or failure to exist, and likewise the existence of some world or other, or its failure to exist. What can happen (if divinity is conceivable) is only God in such and such a state knowing such and such a world, or God in some other state, or knowing some other world (1970: 259).

If the existence of a world is necessary, as Hartshorne says it is, then there will be a world no matter what God does or does not do. Hence, God does not have to create a world; indeed, God cannot create a world, for that which is necessary can be neither created nor destroyed.

There will, then, be a world whether God wants one or not. God's only possible influence is on what kind of a world he will have. Were Hartshorne to say, "But in creating one kind of world rather than another, God is creating a world," I would rejoin that his statement is at best misleading and at worst false. A sculptress can from a block of marble create a statue of this kind, or another kind. In creating any kind she is creating a statue. She also, however, has the option of not creating a statue of any kind. Hence, she has an option that God does not have. God cannot not create a world, but she can not create a statue.

If it were the case that no matter what she did she created a statue, then she would be like God, but she would not be able to create a statue from that which was not a statue, just as God, according to Hartshorne, cannot create a world from that which is not a world. She would have always already created a statue and therefore could only create a statue from a statue; i.e., she could only create a different statue out of the extant statue. She could not create a statue in the most fundamental sense of creating it from that which was not a statue. Equally, God, given Hartshorne's conception, cannot bring a world into existence from that which is not a world. Hence, God cannot create a world; he can only create a different world. It seems indefensible, though, to think that the real-life sculptress can create a statue in the most radical sense whereas God cannot create a world in a similarly radical way.

Still, I believe that Hartshorne is close to the truth in what he has said. I agree that, if God exists, then something other than God must exist. There must be two necessary things that constitute reality, but they are God and the plenum, not God and a world. I agree that God must know something other than himself, but I believe that the something that he knows necessarily is the plenum, not a world. I further agree with Hartshorne that God must will something freely and therefore have a contingent or accidental feature, but I believe he could will not to actualize any of the possibilities of the plenum, and thereby not create a world, being creator of himself but of no individual other than himself.[4] Hence, the one necessary being is God-as-experiencing-the-plenum, not God-as-experiencing-a-world. Exemplification of the class of contingent things is necessary, but exemplification of the class of contingent things other than God is not. Nor would it be appropriate to call the plenum a world in Hartshorne's sense. It is not an individual; it is the possibility of individuals.

Hartshorne might, nonetheless, argue as follows to the necessary existence of a world: "There is in fact a world; therefore there is a God; God could not have created the world out of nothing; therefore there has always been a world." This last conclusion, however, is too strong. Because God could not have created the world out of nothing, either there has always been a world *or* there has always been something out of which God could create a world. The second alternative seems more plausible and is what has been put forward under the notion of the plenum. Hence, the existence of the world may imply the existence of God, and the existence of God would imply the existence of the plenum, but the existence of God and the plenum would not imply the existence of a world. God's creation of a world follows from his freedom, not his essence.

Hartshorne might respond to my position by insisting that the notion of a bare plenum is nonsense and that, therefore, some of the possibilities of the plenum must be actual at all times, thereby making it the case that there is a world at all times. Such a reply would not be without merit, but for two reasons I am not persuaded. First, I agree that the notion of a bare particular is nonsensical. The plenum, however, is not a particular; it is the substantive possibility of particulars other than God. Hence, I do not believe it falls victim to criticisms of the notion of a bare particular.

Second, if a premise from which Hartshorne proceeds to his conclusion that there must be a world is the proposition that at least one determinate of every determinable must be actual, then he is proceeding on a false assumption. If that premise were true, it would be necessary that God create at every moment an exemplification of every possible species. Even if we ignore the impossibility (according to Hartshorne) of instantiating an infinite number of species simultaneously, it would follow that, for example, the species of octagonal blue things would always have to be instantiated. But surely it is not incumbent upon God to make sure that there are always blue, octagonal individuals. Might it be the case, however, that, though the necessity of exemplification does not hold at the level of species, it does hold at the level of genus? Here, too, there are problems. For example, color and smell are genuses, but there is no difficulty in conceiving a world in which there is neither. Hence, not every genus must be instantiated.

The correct conclusion seems to be that only those genuses are eternally instantiated that are necessarily instantiated. But those genuses are just the ones that are instantiated in the existence of God and the plenum, assuming that these are genuine possibilities. It seems, then, there is no necessity that there be at least one individual other than God. The only determinables for which there must be actualized determinates are those that would be satisfied by the existence of God and the plenum. In order to be what he is essentially, i.e., a creator of himself and a potential creator of individuals other than himself, God must have the plenum but he need not have a world; in order for the plenum to be what it is essentially, i.e., the possibility of individuals other than God, the plenum needs God but there is no logical necessity that its potentiality for individuality be actualized.

Penultimately, I do not understand why Hartshorne makes an exception of God to an ability that humans seem to have. It is true that I, for example, cannot not respond to that which is given to me, but I can choose not to create from it, that is, not to act upon it so as to bring about the emergence of novelty. I can choose to ignore it or to refrain from acting upon it. Why does God not have the same choice in relation to that which is given to him, viz., the plenum? Or, on the Hartshornian assumption that a world is always given to God, why could not God refuse to act upon it, allowing it to regress to a lower level of complexity and therefore a lower level of capacity for suffering?

Finally, I take note of a concern expressed by St Augustine in his *City of God*, XII, 15: "when I consider what God could be the Lord of, if there was not always some creature, I shrink from making any assertion ..." He adds, "I dare not say that there was ever a time when the Lord was not Lord" (395). Augustine's is a proper concern for one who believes in *creatio ex nihilo*, but when that doctrine is replaced by *creatio ex plenum* it becomes clear that, even if God had never created a world, still he would have always been Lord of the plenum.

DIVINE MAGNANIMITY

I have argued that it is not the case that God must create a world because of moral obligation, his goodness, the achievement of happiness, or the logic of existence. A critic might reply that thereby I have removed all reasons why God might create a world, but obviously there is a world, and so my theology must be faulty.

I agree that my description of God implies that God's creation of the world is inexplicable on a deductive or causal model of explanation, but that is irrelevant to the conception of God that I have been developing. God, I have argued, is subjectively free with regard to creation of a world; from that it follows that God's creation of a world cannot be derived deductively. But does this not mean that God's creation of the world was purely arbitrary? Yes and no.

On the assumption that God is free with respect to creation of a world, it follows that his creation of the world was arbitrary in the sense that he did not have to do it, i.e., he could have refrained from doing it. Further, it was arbitrary, within limits, which possible world God actualized.[5] In both cases we are dealing with the inexplicability of a free action, whether divine, human, or other.[6] An action that is free cannot be deduced from facts about the agent or his circumstances. Consequently, the most that an explanation of a free action can accomplish is to provide the reason why the agent did what he did in spite of the fact that he did not have to do it. To be sure, some think that the libertarian doctrine on which I am proceeding here is incoherent. But if it is not, and I think it is not, then all that must be done to discredit the idea that, if God did not have to or need to create the world, he would not have is to provide a plausible reason why he might have done so in spite of having been able to do otherwise. The following strikes me as a plausible reason.

Philo in addition to having said what he ought not to have said, viz., that God created the world because it was incumbent on him owing to his goodness, also said that in creating the world "God has bestowed no gift of grace on Himself, for He does not need it, but He has given the world to the world, and its parts to themselves and to each other ..." (1930: 63). The latter statement seems to me correct in spirit if not in all details. God as an enjoyer of existence knows that enjoyment of existence is good, and, though he is not free to choose between doing good and doing evil, he is free to choose between creating centers of enjoyment additional to himself or not creating them. We have seen that, for reasons examined earlier, by not creating centers of enjoyment additional to himself God would not be wronging himself or others. Nonetheless, in spite of the fact that his happiness is eternally perfect and secure, he might freely decide to actualize additional persons. To be sure, he would not do it for his sake (he does not need other persons for his existence or happiness), and he would not do it for the sake of others (by supposition there are no others), yet he would know that it would be good for there to be enjoyers of existence other than himself – but not "good" in a moral sense that would imply a good obligatory on God. Perhaps an analogy will help.

Imagine a young woman who by an atomic armageddon is rendered the last human in existence. She discovers a magic lamp, rubs it, and out pops a genie. At first the genie leaps about making gleeful sounds of freedom. Finally he whirls up in front of the bedazzled woman and says, "For that, my dear, I will grant you happiness! You know," he adds thoughtfully, "I used to *ask* people if they wanted to be happy, but they always said 'yes'. It got to be a bore. So now I automatically confer happiness and follow it up with a choice on which people do differ. Specifically, do you want to be happy with children or without children?"

Ginny, the young woman, begins pursing her lips to say something but the genie interrupts, afraid that she will make a quick decision, rendering his services no longer necessary, dispelling him back into the lamp in a flash. "Don't rush!" he urges. "I'm in no hurry. Take all the time you want! Especially consider that you really will be happy whether you choose to have children or not. The only difference will be what you find your happiness in and whether there will be others to enjoy existence." "Well," Ginny reflects out loud, "it would be nice if there were others to go on enjoying existence after I die." "Oh me," says the genie, "it's been so long that I'd quite forgotten to tell you. I'll make you immortal, too. You get three wishes, in a way. But everybody," the genie emphasizes with an outward sweep of his hands, "asks to be happy and live forever, so happiness and immortality are standard equipment now. Your only option is whether to have children." Ginny asks, "Would my children be happy?" The genie is a bit evasive but assures her that, though there might be some difficult times in their lives, at the last, yes, they would be happy, even eternally happy – or at least they would get what they wanted. Ginny now knows what she wants to do, but she can tell by the pleading look on the genie's face that he is hoping she will not announce her decision and thereby dispatch him to his lamp. So she considerately tells him she would like more time to think, and he, sensing that she has already made up her mind, mock-warns her (just in case his superiors are watching) that he will return in 24 hours for a decision.

Would Ginny be selfish, wrong, or foolish not to choose having children? She certainly would not be being foolish if the genie could indeed deliver on his promise of making her just as happy without children as with them. Further, it is difficult to understand why she would be morally wrong not to choose children given the fact that she would not be hurting them, since if she did not choose for them to exist they would not exist to be hurt, and she would not be bringing the existence of human life to an end, since she would exist forever. Further, it would seem to be a category mistake to say that she would be selfish not to choose children; she would not be choosing her own welfare over the welfare of anyone else, since no one else would exist. In brief, it seems that Ginny would have the moral as well as the subjective freedom to choose to have children or not. I can imagine her going either way. Indeed, she could decide the issue by a random method such as flipping a coin. But she could also do it by considering the different goods that would come from the different choices and deciding for the one set of goods or the other, for the things she could accomplish without children or the things she could accomplish with them. She has a good reason to choose either way. Whichever way she chooses, the goods of that way would be her reason for choosing that way, but they would not be a constraining or obliging reason.

God, unlike Ginny, does not need a genie to enable him to be eternally happy and have children. He is his own genie, so to say.[7] If he wills there to be a world, there will be, and if not, not. If he wills a world, the good of that world is his reason for willing it; if he does not will a world, the good of reality without a world is his reason for not willing a world. The divine decision to create a world is, I suggest, a perfect example of magnanimity.[8]

A psychological egoist might reply, "But a magnanimous human gets pleasure from her acts of magnanimity, and that is the cause of her doing them." I agree that a magnanimous person ordinarily takes pleasure in her magnanimous acts, but that is no proof that desire for such pleasure is the cause of her doing such acts. A person might enjoy brushing her teeth, but that does not mean that the enjoyment thereof is her motive for brushing them, or that she would cease brushing them if she ceased enjoying it. To be sure, she brushes her teeth for the sake of a good. Similarly, it seems true that a person would not perform freely a magnanimous act if it were a matter of indifference to her. As Swinburne emphasizes, she must see some good in it (1977: 141ff), but if she is free then the good that she sees in it cannot be a constraining good, and it need not be for her own good. It is fallacious to infer that because an intentional free act can be performed only in order to bring about something that is perceived as good that therefore the agent must perceive it as for her own good and be motivated to it primarily for that reason.

The preceding analysis applies especially to God prior to creation of a world. His decision then is not whether to enhance the happiness of extant creatures; it is whether to actualize creatures at all. As we saw earlier, it would be unwarranted to feel sorry for possible individuals because they were not enjoying themselves or to want to make them happier by actualizing them; prior to creation of a world there are no such individuals to enjoy or not enjoy themselves. Then there is only the possibility of selves other than God. Hence, pity or affection for possible selves could not be

God's motive for creation, and the motive of self-benefits is ruled out by God's very nature. To be sure, if God creates a world he will take pleasure in it, but not a greater or lesser pleasure than he would have enjoyed otherwise, only a different one. What God does in his freedom determines the texture but not the intensity of his happiness. There seems, then, to be no possible motive for God's creation of the world other than pure magnanimity.

In brief, it seems conceivable that a person could decide to create or benefit others though he would have been just as happy without doing so. If that is not possible, then the concept of magnanimity, i.e., the concept of a free being intentionally doing something good but without doing it for his own benefit, is a pseudo-concept. Certainly if I must and can act only for the sake of my own pleasure, then I am not subjectively free in the fullest sense; rather, I am an engine driven by the calculation and pursuit of egocentric utility. Hence, whether the concept of magnanimity is a pseudo-concept turns upon whether the libertarian conception of subjective freedom on which it is based is meaningful and free of self-contradiction. I believe it is, but it would take us too far afield to explore the issue further here.

Our critic might continue, "But the magnanimous person takes pleasure in anticipation of the happiness and gratitude of her beneficiary, and, if all goes well, she takes further pleasure in the actual happiness and gratitude of her beneficiary. Surely these are at least partial causes of her magnanimous behavior." Two responses seem appropriate. First, the fact that a benefactor receives pleasure from her beneficiary's pleasure does not imply that she acted in order to receive such pleasure, or that she would not have so acted if she had known that she would not receive such pleasure. Were she motivated by a desire for such pleasure, then, of course, her motive would not have been magnanimous, though it might have seemed so. Second, we can identify conditions under which her act would have been truly magnanimous and others under which it would not have been, and that helps establish that the concept of magnanimity on the part of a free being is coherent. To be sure, whether humans ever are truly magnanimous is a factual issue, but in relation to God it is a conceptual issue because, if God is eternally free and perfectly happy, then it seems to follow by conceptual analysis that, if he creates a world, he must do so magnanimously, i.e., without regard to his own benefit.

In conclusion, God's omniscience entails that his life will be enriched by the effects of his magnanimity, and the fact that he is loving entails that he will take pleasure in the world he creates, but, as we saw earlier, such enrichment will only diversify God's happiness: it will not improve it. God's happiness is from himself. The content of his happiness would have been different had he not created a world, but the perfection of his happiness would have remained. Hence, his own pleasure could not be his motive for creating the world. He would have been equally happy without it. He needs nothing for himself. Clearly, then, he did not create the world for his own sake; nor did he create it for the sake of others. Prior to creation of the world there were no others to do anything for the sake of. Rather, he created a world not that he might enjoy existence but that others might do so. It is this realization that causes believers to marvel at God's graciousness and to give thanks for his supererogatory act of creation. On the hypothesis that God freely created the world in order that there might be additional enjoyers of existence, God's act of creation is no more a mystery than is any other free act, none of which can be deduced logically or causally from the nature or circumstances of its performer. In creating the world, God did a good thing, but it was not a good that was necessary, compelled, required, deserved, or obligatory. It was a gratuitous good – full of grace and graciously done.

10

Creation and freedom

SCIENTIA DEI, CAUSA RERUM (VOLUNTATE ADJUNCTA)

WE HAVE GIVEN a good deal of attention to the nature of God's knowledge of the world, but we have not yet considered what is, at least initially, one of Aquinas' most baffling doctrines, viz., the doctrine that God's knowledge is the cause of the world, i.e., the doctrine that "scientia Dei est causa rerum." Aquinas was no doubt respectful of this doctrine because it can be found so clearly in the writings of St Augustine. Consider the following passage from Augustine's *The Trinity*, book VI, chapter 10:

> ... although the times come and go, nothing comes and goes in the knowledge of God. For these things which have been created are not known by God because they have been made; rather they have been made, even though changeable, because they are known unchangeably by Him. (213)

Later, after asserting that God knows "all future temporal things," Augustine adds this *caveat* in book XV, chapter 13:

> But He does not, therefore, know all His creatures, both spiritual and corporeal, because they are, but they, therefore, are because He knows them. For He was not ignorant of what He was going to create. He created, therefore, because He knew; He did not know because He created. He did not know them differently when they were created, than when they were to be created, for nothing has been added to His wisdom from them; it has remained the same as it was, while they came into existence as they should and when they should. (485)

Aquinas did not accept this doctrine merely because of Augustine's theological authority, however; he also saw it as clearly entailed by God's impassibility. According to Aquinas, God is pure act and therefore cannot be acted upon by the world. Obviously, then, God cannot learn from the world how the world is; but he knows how the world is, therefore rather than his knowledge being caused by the world it must be the case that his knowledge is the cause of the world (1975: 1.16.6).

Norman Kretzmann has illuminated marvellously some of the difficulties in this doctrine (1983: 644–9). In particular he seems to have shown that this doctrine on its most obvious interpretation implies determinism, and that this implication is not nullified by Aquinas' insistence that our actions are contingent because though the ultimate cause of them, i.e., God's knowledge, is necessary, the intermediate causes of them are contingent. Kretzmann examines and dismisses diverse ways of trying to get Aquinas off the deterministic hook. He approached the idea that I believe would get Aquinas off that hook, but then he pulled back, so I would like to develop it here.

Aquinas makes explicitly a distinction between God's knowledge and God's will. In the *Summa Theologiae* he writes, "God's knowledge with his will adjoined is the cause of things. Hence it need not be the case that *whatever* things God knows are or have been or will be, but *only* those he wills to be, or permits to be" (1964: 1a. 14.9.3.). In *The Disputed Questions on Truth* he wrote:

> ... knowledge *qua* knowledge does not indicate an active cause any more than does a form *qua* form ... And so a form is not the source of action except through the mediation of a power ... And so an effect never proceeds from knowledge except through the mediation of a will ... Thus between God's knowledge, which is a cause of a thing, and the caused thing itself two sorts of intermediaries are found: one on God's side – viz., the divine will – the other on the side of the things themselves considered as certain sorts of effects – viz., the secondary causes by means of which the things proceed from God's knowledge.   (11.14)[1]

Note that Aquinas distinguishes here three causes of the existence of a contingent thing: God's knowledge, God's will, and the contingent things by means of which the desired effect is achieved (when it is not created *ex nihilo*). If God passively knew the effect as occurring, he would not have to will it (since it would have already to exist in order to cause his knowledge), and so God's will would be otiose. Just as clearly, if God did not know the possibility of that effect, he could not will it. Consequently, it seems to me that in this context our most plausible assumption is that Aquinas is speaking of God's knowledge of all possibilities.

Aquinas obscured his view of this form of God's knowledge by the way that he drew his distinction between God's simple knowledge and his knowledge by vision. The latter covers all that ever has been, is, or will be actual, and only that. The former is restricted to all things that never were, nor are, nor will be (1975: 1.66.8; 1964: 1a. 14.9). Together these two classes yield EKP, but Aquinas does not seem to have thought of God as knowing that class independently of and logically prior to the other two. Still, I believe that it was lurking in the background of his thinking, as can be seen from the way in which it helps clear up his position, as demonstrated above and in the following statement: "Now just as in our case things are the cause of knowledge, so divine knowledge is the cause of the thing known" (1975: 1.67.5). The first clause of this statement is a version of Aquinas' famous position that there is nothing in our minds that was not first in our senses. Part of his point is that we do not know independently of actuality what is possible. Our knowledge of possibility is derived from our knowledge of actuality. Actual things cause our knowledge of actuality and thereby provide the basis for our knowledge of possibility. Conversely, as I argued in Chapter 3, God's knowledge of possibility is not contingent on his knowledge of actuality (see Aquinas 1964: 1a.14.8). Further, given the necessity of God to the actualization of contingent things, as argued in Chapter 4, if God did not have EKP, he could not create anything because he would have no knowledge of anything that could be created. God's knowledge of possibility, then, is an important cause of the existence of things other than God, even as the carpenter's knowledge is an important cause of the house that he builds.

As Aquinas notes in the quotation from *On Truth*, though, mere knowledge of what is possible is not a sufficient condition of the actualization of any specific one of the possibilities known. As he puts it in 1964: 1a.14.8, "a knowledge-form is indifferent to opposite courses, since one and the same knowledge covers contraries ..." Theoretical knowledge covers, for example, the possibility of a house being white or red or yellow, etc. We could intentionally make it one of those colors rather than the others only if we knew the range of possibilities. But merely knowing those possibilities would never get the house painted. To get it painted our knowledge must be supplemented by our will selecting one of the colors for application. God's knowledge, then, is not *the* cause of things; rather, it is a cause of things. When it is supplemented by the divine will, then, and only then, does the possibility that is known become actualized. As Aquinas puts it so precisely in 1964:1a.14.9, "God's knowledge taken in conjunction with his will is the cause of things" ("Dei scientia est causa rerum, voluntate adjuncta").

If all that God has is EKP on its usual interpretation, however, i.e., what *could* happen, then, though we have cleared up one difficulty in Aquinas' position by showing that he did not mean that mere knowledge is a sufficient cause of things, we have not escaped the consequence of determinism because, if all things will be fully determined as God decides on the basis of his knowledge of what is possible, then the only contingency relevant to the world is in God's will, not ours. God having willed, our willing is necessary.

Even here, though, there is a way out. I am, however, unable to verify the existence of this escape hatch by appealing to statements by Aquinas. I am limited to saying that it makes such sense of other things that he says that it is plausible to think that he was operating, wittingly or not, on the assumption of what is here called for, viz., the doctrine of *scientia media*. According to this doctrine, God knows not only how things could be; he knows also, when free creatures are involved, how they would be under any set of circumstances. For example, God knows not only what I could do if I were offered a certain amount of money in certain circumstances to pass a failing student; he knows what I would do. He knows also what I would do in other possible worlds in which the bribe is a different amount or takes a different form or my circumstances are different in some way. God knows, then, an exhaustive set of logically possible worlds, and he also knows which of those logically possible worlds containing free agents can be actualized because those worlds have the free agents doing only those things that they would in fact do, and he knows which of those logically possible worlds cannot be actualized because they have free agents doing things that they would not in fact do.

We can imagine, then, that God's decision procedure, temporal or not, is something like the following regarding creation of a world. First, he considers whether to create a world. He decides "yes, a world." Second, he separates logically possible worlds from logically impossible worlds so as not to waste time on the latter. Third, he considers whether to create a logically possible world with free agents in it. He decides "yes, free agents." Fourth, he separates actualizable logically possible worlds that contain free agents from non-actualizable logically possible worlds that contain free agents. Fifth, he decides which actualizable logically possible worlds containing free agents are satisfactorily good. Sixth, he actualizes W^* as the best possible actualizable logically possible world containing free agents, or as a satisfactorily good such world.

Clearly, then, on the classical model of God's creation of a world, God's *natural knowledge*, "by which he knows his own nature and all the things which are possible to him either by his own action or by the action of free possible creatures", and his *middle knowledge*, i.e., "his knowledge of what any possible creature would do in any possible world", play important causal roles in the Aristotelian sense of a formal cause.[2]

Now it can be noted that neither God's natural knowledge, nor his middle knowledge, nor his free knowledge, i.e., his knowledge of all that is ever actual (which knowledge he has by virtue of his knowledge of the possible world that he wills to be actual), compromises the freedom of the agents of the world that God wills unilaterally into existence. To be sure, the free agents of the actual world had no voice in the decision to actualize that world, but it is logically impossible for them to have had such a voice because, if they had existed to have a voice, then a world would have already existed. Hence, no creature can will a world from possibility to actuality. Its existence already constitutes a world. Creaturely freedom is limited to possibilities *in* a world. Hence, if God knows what free creatures would do with their freedom in any possible world were it to be made actual, it in no way takes away from the freedom of their actions if he wills into existence that possible world in which he knows them to do these things rather than those things.[3]

If God did not unilaterally will some world into existence, there would be no opportunities for real creatures actually to act. Moreover, on the Molinist assumption that I believe Aquinas shared, or would have accepted, God cannot help but know what free creatures will do in any world that he creates. Hence, when God creates a world with free creatures in it, he cannot help but know what they will do, but his willing that world in no way causes free creatures to decide what they decide. His willing merely occasions their actions, i.e., makes it possible for them actually to do what by virtue of his middle knowledge he knows they would do in their freedom. For example, by virtue of his middle knowledge God knows eternally a possible world in which I have a certain background, am put in certain circumstances, and decide freely to devote myself to research and writing on the topic of divine impassibility – even though there are numerous attractive alternatives. By virtue of knowing that possible world, God knows what I will do if he actualizes that world. Hence, by actualizing that possible world, of which this one is the actualization, God in no way nullified or compromised my exercise of my freedom even though he knew what I would do in my freedom. He has merely made it possible for me to do actually what he knew I would do, in spite of alternatives, given the opportunity actually to do it.

To summarize what I have proposed, Thomists, if not Thomas, should hold that God's knowledge is the cause of things in that, if God had no knowledge of possibilities apart from actuality, then he could not get things started inasmuch as, at least logically, he exists prior to contingent actuality. But, because mere knowledge of possibility does not entail a choice among mutually exclusive possibilities, God's knowledge of possibilities must be supplemented by God's willing one of those possibilities to the exclusion of the others. But on the assumption that regarding the actual world God must know what we will do (as well as what we are doing and have done), and that what we will do is free, it must be stipulated that God has middle knowledge, i.e., knowledge of what we would do were certain circumstances made actual. On this supposition God can without violation of our freedom know what we will do freely by knowing which possible world he wills to be actual.

The preceding development of Aquinas' position makes it as clear, consistent, and plausible regarding divine creation and human freedom as I am presently able to make it. I find this position, as developed, very attractive. It gets Aquinas past Kretzmann's imputation of determinism, and it shows how God could know our future free actions (by virtue of them being present to him in the mode of middle knowledge) without our freedom being violated. Still, for reasons expounded in Chapter 5, I do not believe that *scientia media* is possible, and therefore I do not believe that this development of Aquinas' position is viable.[4]

CAN FREE INDIVIDUALS BE CREATED?

Traditionally it has been assumed that, if free creatures can exist, then of course it is possible for God to create them. Process philosophers have shown, at the very least, that the answer to the sub-title of this section is not so obviously "yes" as has been thought – even on the assumption that it is possible for free individuals other than God to exist. Moreover, process philosophers would probably shorten my sub-title to, "Can individuals be created?", because they generally hold that individuals, divine or not, are necessarily free. Perhaps they are correct that individuals are necessarily free, though I am not yet convinced. Fortunately we do not need to resolve that issue prior to dealing with the possibility of the creation of free individuals. Hence, I will continue to speak of free individuals.

In one sense process philosophers would say, "Of course free individuals can be created – but only by themselves. Can God create a free individual? Yes – himself. Can he create any other free individual? Yes and no. He creates every free individual other than himself by contributing to its self-creation by presenting it with various real possibilities, shaded valuatively, by means of which it creates itself. But he does not and cannot by efficient causation bring free individuals into existence from non-existence. Hence, he cannot create a free individual; he can only contribute to its creation of itself." As Lewis Ford says in *The Lure of God*, "freedom is precisely that which cannot be derived from any external agency, including God..." (18). Consequently, God never creates other free individuals; rather, he is confronted with them and lures them into appropriate paths of self-creativity.

A classical theist might respond to Ford by saying, "But we must make a distinction between the power of freedom and the exercise of freedom, i.e., between the capacity to act freely and acting freely. God creates us with the capacity to act freely, but of course he does not and cannot exercise our freedom for us. If he were to determine the content of our free actions, and not merely our capacity to act freely, he would destroy our freedom in the process of determining it. Hence, he is responsible for the existence of our freedom but we are responsible for its exercise."

Ford is correct, however, that this distinction by itself is no help to the theist. Ford's major premise in support of this point is that freedom cannot exist without being exercised. More specifically, yes, we can make a distinction between the power of freedom and the exercise of freedom, but it must be a purely formal distinction because the power of freedom cannot exist without being exercised. A free individual cannot take or be given a holiday from the exercise of its freedom. Hence, a free individual must always be self-determined. It follows that God cannot create a free individual other than himself because any free individual must be engaged in the exercise of its freedom even in the first moment of its existence. But any individual created by efficient causation, i.e., created by an external force, even though it be God, could not in the first moment of its existence be engaged in the exercise of its freedom because everything about it in its first moment of existence would have been determined from outside it. Hence, God cannot create a free individual other than himself because he would have to determine everything about it and therefore it could not be free.

The critic might respond, "Of course that is true of the first moment of existence of the individual, but after that moment God can turn control of the individual's behavior over to the individual itself." Such a response would, however, ignore this point of significance: there must be a first moment to the existence of the freedom of a transient free individual. But God could not get such an individual out of the mode of being completely determined into the mode of being subjectively free because, no matter what he did to it from moment to moment, it would still be completely his product. On the classical model, then, if God does not create an individual by efficient causation, it will not exist, whereas, if he does create it by efficient causation, it will not be free.

God cannot, then, create us by efficient causation at one moment and make us free at the next. Either we are free from the first moment of our existence or we are not free at all. As Jean-Paul Sartre says and Ford, I believe, would agree, "man is freedom." If God cannot make us free in the first moment of our existence, it is implausible that he could do so in any subsequent moment given that, according to classical theism, at every moment after creating us God must sustain us in existence, and to sustain us in existence means to continue creating us, or to recreate us, from moment to moment. There is, then, no moment at which God can release his complete control of us (as Plato might put it) yet we continue in existence on our own. Because the classical God cannot get us into existence without initially determining everything about us, he cannot make us free at some subsequent moment. Hence, we must simply accept it as an axiom that there are free individuals other than God, or we must give up the belief that they are free.

Though I believe the preceding position is formidable, I do not believe it is conclusive. Inasmuch as process philosophers hold that transient free individuals do come into existence, it seems to me no less anomalous to say that God brings them into existence by efficient causation than to say that that's just the way reality is, viz., transient free individuals pop into existence inexplicably.[5] To be sure, process philosophers do not say that transient free individuals just happen to exist; they say that such individuals create themselves out of the past. But surely from the locution "create themselves" it can be inferred that they were already in existence in some form – otherwise they would not have been around to create themselves and therefore could not have done so. Once this is noted it becomes clear that it is not being said (or should not be said) that free individuals create themselves from scratch (pulling themselves into existence by their bootstraps, so to say), but that they create themselves in the sense of making themselves different from however they find themselves to be. Hence, to say that they create themselves is to leave unanswered the question as to how they are initially given to themselves.

To go at this problem from another angle, consider that free transient individuals must be created initially (1) by nothing, (2) by other transient creatures that are not free, (3) by other transient creatures that are free, (4) by an infinite being that is not free, (5) by an infinite being that is free, or (6) by themselves. (1) seems absurd. I will let others argue for (2), (3), and (4). Process philosophers can defend (6) only at considerable expense. Because it does not make sense to think of individuals creating themselves in their first moment of existence, and no more sense to speak of them just popping into existence *ex nihilo* (without even the benefit of divine fiat!), if one denies that something other than themselves is responsible for their first moment of existence, it can be inferred that they only appear to be transient, that they have never come into existence, that they have always existed and, indeed, necessarily exist.

This is, of course, just the kind of position that process philosophers have fought hardest to discredit, but it is the position to which they are wed if they insist on self-creation. Why? Because if they hold that individuals are self-created, then they have stepped onto a slippery slope to which there is no bottom; the self that creates itself must have been created by itself, which must have been created by itself, *ad infinitum*, so that there never was a beginning of the individual. Corollaries are that every individual has always existed and always will exist, so that the number of individuals in existence is always the same because each individual always creates itself but never another. Rather than accept these implications that are so close to Samkhya Hinduism and so contrary to process axioms, I would think that process philosophers would prefer to abandon the position that free individuals cannot be brought into existence by efficient causation.[6]

Our preferences will remain irrelevant, however, until we can make divine creation of free individuals plausible, so we turn now to that task. Two points seem particularly relevant. First, I am sympathetic to the following objection of process philosophy to classical theism: If God creates individuals *ex nihilo*, they are always in every respect entirely dependent upon God; hence, there is no respect in which they could be free.[7] As process philosophy has insisted, then, finite individuals cannot be free if they are created *ex nihilo* or if pantheism is true. It seems to follow that the existence of transient free individuals, such as classical theism assumes, presupposes the existence of something that was not created by God but which contains the possibility of the actualization of free individuals by God. Such a something is the plenum. To go at this another way, if there are free individuals other than God, either they must necessarily exist or they must be actualized from something that God does not create in every respect, something that provides a basis of contingent autonomy for them.

I have argued already that this basis of contingent autonomy, viz., the plenum, is not self-actualizing; God must actualize all of its primary possibilities. To distinguish between primary and secondary possibilities of the plenum is to hold that, whereas the plenum cannot actualize its own possibilities, an individual actualized from the plenum can freely actualize some of its possibilities. Hence, in actualizing some (process philosophers would say "all") individuals from the plenum, God is actualizing freedom other than his own.

This position is particularly plausible if one holds a substance theory of the individual according to which the individual can endure across moments so as first to exist and then act. But merely to hold a substance theory of the individual does not explain how it is that an individual that is not free at one moment can become free at the next. Plato addressed this problem in the *Statesman*, secs. 269–70:

There is an era in which God himself assists the universe on its way and guides it by imparting its rotation to it. There is also an era in which he releases his control. Thereafter it begins to revolve in the contrary sense under its own impulse – for it is a living creature and has been endowed with reason by him who framed it in the beginning. Now this capacity for rotation is of necessity native to it ...   (1034)

But is it not the case that if God "releases his control" of the universe it will of necessity immediately collapse into non-being? Plato's conviction was that it will not – that it will have enough momentum to proceed on its own for at least a while, but he provided little in the way of justification for this conviction.

Leibniz tried to do better. He was driven against the problem of the duration of transient individuals by occasionalists and pantheists (1965:

101–12). Pantheism holds that there is no problem because there is only one individual, viz., God. Everything else is a mere modification of the one individual. Hence, God cannot create an individual other than himself; he can create only modifications of himself. Occasionalists hold, by contrast, that God can create individuals other than himself, but those individuals have no "persevering existence"; they exist only at a moment and consequently are neither affected by other finite individuals nor affect them. But this means that God is entirely responsible for what occurs in each occasion of finite existence, so such occasions, Leibniz notes, do not involve true individuals because to be an individual is to act and be acted upon, to affect and be affected by other individuals.

Leibniz's argument against these positions is Anselmian: they "deprive the commandments of God of all lasting effect and all future efficacy" and require of God "ever renewed efforts." That is, they deny that God can endow an individual with "persevering existence" so that it can "endure for some time" without further action by God. But we can conceive of a being that can so endow an individual; therefore we can conceive of a being greater than God; but that is impossible, so we must conceive of God as able to endow individuals with persevering existence. To be sure, Leibniz is not saying that an individual could come into existence apart from the will of God or could continue in existence in spite of the will of God. He is saying that God can will an individual to exist from t_1 to t_n without having to concern himself from t_1 to t_n with maintaining that individual in existence. Such an individual has been invested with the power of existence and action until such time as that power is directly or indirectly interrupted by God.

I believe Leibniz's argument is sound, and that, therefore, there is time enough in the existence of an individual for one and the same individual first to come into existence and only subsequently acquire the capacity for free action. This is, of course, contrary to the process position that individuals exist only for a moment and, therefore, must be free then or never. Still, to establish that the "persevering existence" of an individual would provide time enough for such a change to take place does not disarm the earlier argument that, if God cannot make us free in the first moment of our existence, neither can he do so at a subsequent moment.

The first process objection to the claim that God could bring about this metamorphosis would be that there *is* no subsequent moment of the individual – and, if there is not, a criticism could hardly be more conclusive. I have agreed with Leibniz, however, that this conception of God's creative power is inadequate. God can endow an individual with persevering existence. Still, a process philosopher who was persuaded might reply that, even so, it is a mystery what God could do in some subsequent moment of the transient but enduring individual to transform it from being non-free to free. I am sympathetic to this objection to a magic moment subsequent to the first moment of an emergent individual at which God causes that very individual to change from not being subjectively free to being subjectively free. Hence, what I would like to do now is attempt to show that it is conceivable that God can actualize an individual who is free from the very first moment of its existence.

Consider that, when one has not yet decided to select among alternatives of which one is aware, one's freedom has not been violated or compromised *vis à vis* those alternatives. Let us say, for example, that you are in the process of deciding which of several records to listen to while reading Plotinus. (Gustav Mahler?) If God had created you at the moment, giving you the requisite knowledge to consider alternative records and then select among them, he would not have compromised your freedom with regard to your choice; you could go on from that first moment to choose any one of the available records or to decide that none of them was appropriate accompaniment to the reading of Plotinus.

In such a case what God would have decided for you was that you would erupt into existence deciding on a record, but that decision by God would not violate your freedom to decide on any one of the records – or none at all. Moreover, by casting you into existence with a specific configuration of circumstances and intentions, God would not be violating your freedom; he would be enabling you to choose freely. He would not be exercising your freedom for you; he would merely be engaging you in the exercise of it. Hence, by creating us as deciding but undecided, i.e., as creatures essentially involved in the exercise of freedom, God would not have precluded or compromised our freedom; he would have made it actual.

A critic might reply, "What you say is reasonable as far as it goes, but it fails because we do not come to self-consciousness in an undecided state. Rather, we discover ourselves to have numerous specific values and projects, i.e., to have already decided a great deal. Either we decided those things ourselves (in which case our freedom is not compromised), or God decided them for us (in which case we are not free), or they have been determined for us by such factors as genetic endowment and environmental history (in which case, again, we are not free). Obviously, therefore, if we are going to hold that we are free, we must also hold that we are responsible for our decisions even in the first moment of our lives, i.e., that we have created ourselves."

First, it seems wrong to characterize decisions that exist in the first moment of one's existence as decisions that one could have made freely. Inasmuch as we are speaking of the first moment of the existence of a transient individual, we are speaking of a moment the content of which could not have developed from a prior self-consciously deliberative period as the individual did not exist prior to that moment. Consequently, I do not believe that the things that were already decided in that first moment could have been decided at all, much less freely, by the individual whose first moment it was. The critic is correct that there must already be things decided in the first moment of an emergent individual's existence, but he is wrong that those decisions could have been made by that individual.

Second, even if God were directly or indirectly responsible for a set of decisions with which we begin our existence, decisions that we discover ourselves involved in rather than having made, I am not convinced that this would preclude our being free. For a finite being to be free means for it to be able to alter itself – no matter how it came to be the way it is. Decisions are themselves data for decision-making, and so the decisions made for the individual in the first moment of its existence are the initial data for its own decision-making. To be free means to be able to redecide decisions, i.e., to make decisions about decisions that have already been made. That the decisions about which one's initial decisions are made are not one's own does not prevent one from being free in relation to those decisions or exercising one's freedom with regard to them.

Moreover, it appears that a free individual cannot begin to exist unless it be given a self that has been decided for it. This initial self of the individual enables it to learn what it means to have a self and provides it with a self to which to react, to choose for or against. Indeed, our most profound freedom is with regard to whether to continue to be the kind of person we find ourselves to be or to change ourselves in certain respects. Most basically, then, the freedom of an individual is its power to preserve or change itself. But it would not be possible for an emergent individual to give itself a self to which to react in its first moment of existence. Hence, that the original self of a free individual is not decided by it but is brought about for it is not problematic; rather, it is a necessary condition of an individual existing and being free.

In brief, an emergent individual can create itself only if it has a self to begin with – a self about which it can make a decision; but its initial self must be given to it by something or someone other than itself. Hence, the process of creativity, i.e., of self-creation, can get under way for an emergent individual only by that individual first being constituted by something or someone other than itself.

Ford might object to the preceding argument that it supposes that the essence of a free individual is created for it by another, but "our very freedom precludes any individual essence beforehand" (1977: 186). Jean-Paul Sartre took a similar position in his famous lecture on existentialism as a form of humanism – his point being that, when God creates, "He knows exactly what He is creating" (1957: 14). He creates according to an essence that fills up any space that might have been left to man's freedom. But does it? It seems to me that the use of "essence" by both Ford and Sartre involves a mistaken understanding of classical theism and an idiosyncratic use of "essence".[8]

The essence of something is generally understood to be that without which it could not be the kind of thing that it is. Consequently it does not make sense to talk about anything, even God, choosing its original essence. In order to make any choice a thing would have to exist, and in order to exist it would have already to be a kind of thing, i.e., be an instantiation of an essence; therefore it would have already to have an essence which it could not have selected for itself. Hence, nothing can choose its own original essence. We have, then, no freedom of choice with regard to our initial and fundamental essence.[9]

An individual might, however, be free to choose among various concrete forms that its essence can take – a point that Hartshorne has elaborated nicely under the distinction between the abstract and the concrete. But, in order to make a choice among existential possibilities for one's essence, one must have an essence and that essence must already exist in some concrete state (otherwise one would not be actual). Hence, in our first moment of existence we must have specific particularity, but we cannot have created or chosen it for ourselves. Clearly, then, it must be created for us, along with the essence of which it is a concrete expression. The possibility of being free is not precluded by such gifts; it is actualized by them – specifically, by the gift of our essence, viz., freedom, and the gift of a self and circumstances in relation to which to exercise our essence subsequent to our first moment of existence.

In conclusion, what is required for the actuality of a transient free individual is an individual who is aware of at least one possibility of an actuality, who has the capacity to actualize or to refrain from actualizing that possibility, and who is aware that he has that capacity. Such freedom is compatible with the actuality in which the possibility is discerned not having been created by the individual even though that actuality be the self of the individual. Indeed, initial creation of the individual by another is a necessary condition of both its existence and its freedom. The self which it initially discovers itself to be, but not to have created, and the circumstances that it initially discovers itself to be in, but not to have created, constitute its initial data for decision.[10]

11

How to create the best possible world

IN CHAPTER 7 we asked whether the world as we know it could have been created by a supreme personal being. The question exists because there is evil in the world. To be sure, there is also good. But is the world sufficiently good to warrant believing that it could have been made by God? My answer was that, given an all-inclusive historical sense of "world," the world is sufficiently good, so far as we know, to have been made by God. Now we want to modulate that question into its final form: Is the world so good that it could be the best possible world? Some have argued that if it can be proved that this is not the best possible world, then it can be inferred that there is no God, inasmuch as God, a supremely perfect being, would create only the best possible world.

Robert Adams has argued that, if this is not the best possible world, we cannot infer validly that there is no God. God is under no necessity or obligation to create the best possible world. If he creates a world at all, it is sufficient for him to create a *good* world. Genesis 1.31 states that when God saw all that he had made he said that it was *very good* – not that he could not have done better. Bruce Reichenbach would add that of course God did not say that he could not have done better. The idea of a world than which none better could be made by God is incoherent. A world can always be improved upon, and God is omnipotent. Therefore God cannot create a world upon which he cannot improve (Adams 1972; Reichenbach 1979 and 1982).

These positions by Adams and Reichenbach have been widely accepted, but I shall argue against both of them.[1] Before doing so I would like to clarify what I will and will not mean when I say that God can or cannot create the best possible world. There is one sense in which it seems obvious that God cannot create the best possible world. If we proceed on the assumption that the best possible world includes morally free creatures (MFCs) but no moral evil, then it seems clear that God cannot unilaterally create such a world. Whether there is moral evil in a world containing MFCs is not entirely dependent upon God; therefore God cannot unilaterally create such a world; hence God cannot unilaterally create a best possible world. Nor is it the case that God knows of a possible world that he can actualize in which there are MFCs but no evil. What he does know that he can actualize is a possible world in which there are MFCs and the possibility of no moral evil. But he, as we, must wait to see what MFCs will do with their freedom.

Note that a possible world containing MFCs is a possibility that contains possibilities (real alternatives), but God does not know which of these possibilities will be actualized if he actualizes that possible world. In a world containing MFCs, the MFCs become co-creators with God of that world. God determines whether to create W_1 or W_2. God having, let us say, actualized W_1, the MFCs decide whether it will be W_{1a} or W_{1b}. Hence, God, as we, must in some respects wait to see which possible world the actual world will become. Note that by contrast a possible world without MFCs would be a possibility without possibilities. It would be William James' "block universe" in which there are no real alternatives to what occurs.

In this first sense of "best possible world," then, God can no more create unilaterally a best possible world than a human can sing a perfect duet by herself. She might sing a perfect accompaniment in a duet, but whether the duet is perfect depends to some degree upon her partner, over whom she does not have complete control. Still, one might object that even in this first sense God can create a best possible world because, though he has no control over the free actions of MFCs, he can bring good out of evil. Thereby, unlike the musical accompanist, he can, so to say, make up for the mistakes of his partner. More specifically, God can counter-balance or cancel out any evil that MFCs do by bringing out of it an equal amount of good. Indeed, we should think of God as not only counter-balancing evil with good, but *overwhelming* evil with good – making it an occasion for even greater good than would have been without it, thereby not merely overcoming evil but humiliating it.

There is something appealing in this position. I believe that we should hope and perhaps believe that God can bring some good out of all evil (in the sense of gaining from it some positive value for us – a valuable insight, perspective, or sensitivity that we might not have had otherwise). However, the belief that such a wonderful divine ability would cancel out the evilness of evil or enable God to augment the good in response to evil seems mistaken. First it blinks the fact that, even if God brings good out of evil, the evil will still have existed. But evil is regrettable; therefore it would be better had it not existed even though God is able to bring some good out of it. Second, if one says, "But because of the good that God brought out of it, the world is a richer place – is better off," then one is proceeding on a principle that is pernicious because it makes the heights of the good that God can do a function of the depths of evil to which MFCs descend. Were that principle true, we should be grateful to Hitler for enabling God to bring about a greater good than he could have brought about without the

Holocaust; further, we should hope that even greater horrors will come to pass so that God will be enabled to bring about even greater counter-balancing goods than those that Hitler made possible.

Surely the preceding is a morally untenable position. We should hold that, though God brings out of the Holocaust goods that otherwise could not have existed, the world would have been better off without the combination of those goods and the terrible evil that occasioned their emergence. More generally, surely we should not hold that the great and perhaps unsurpassable good of God's kingdom is contingent upon the actuality of evil. To be sure, if it is true that actualization of the greatest good is contingent upon the existence of MFCs who freely choose God's kingdom, then actualization of the greatest good is contingent upon the *possibility* of evil – the possibility of evil being a necessary condition of the existence of MFCs. However, this great good does not require that MFCs ever *do* evil, nor is any moral evil necessary for eventuation of the great good of God's kingdom. To use Bruce Reichenbach's language, moral evil is "gratuitous or pointless," i.e., it is neither logically nor causally necessary for the existence of the great good of God's kingdom (Reichenbach 1982: 39). Moreover those who rejoice in God's kingdom will count their joys much more worthwhile than whatever they suffered in this life, but they will not be glad for a single act of moral evil that they or others performed. They will be glad only for the possibility of evil that made it possible for them to exist and choose God's kingdom.

To summarize, if by "best possible world" we mean a world that contains MFCs and no moral evil, then obviously God could not create such a world by himself; at most he could create a world in which such a state of affairs was a possibility. Is there, however, another sense in terms of which we might seriously discuss whether God could create such a world? I think so. It is the sense in which the musician might provide perfect accompaniment to a partner who falls short of perfection. It is the sense in which we might speak of creating a perfect environment for a species of animal or a perfect series of experiences for a developing child. The earlier sense of "best possible world" focused on what MFCs do with the world once they have it. The second focuses on the fitness of the world for achieving the ends for which MFCs were created in the first place. In this sense it seems to me that God can create a world optimally suited to MFCs, a world for MFCs than which none better could be conceived, a world for MFCs that both respects their freedom and provides for their welfare in ways than which none better could be conceived.[2] In this sense a world might contain moral evil by virtue of the free choices of MFCs yet still be the best possible world for MFCs.

Such a world as a world would be *unsurpassable* in potential value for its MFCs by any other possible world. But would such a world be *unequallable*? That is, is the notion of "best possible world" in the second sense one that necessarily has a single referent, or is it the case that it could be satisfied by more than one possible world? This was an issue of grave concern to G. W. Leibniz. He was convinced that the concept of a best possible world must refer to one and only one possibility. To the contrary opinion that there might be an infinite series of possible universes better than one another, he replied, "If this opinion were true, it would follow that God had not produced any universe at all: for he is incapable of acting without reason, and that would be even acting against reason" (1966: 111). Leibniz seems committed here to a kind of rationalistic determinism. God can do only what is best, and what is best cannot be in any way indeterminate or else God could not do it.

Leibniz has at least a *prima facie* point: if there were better and worse worlds but no best possible world, God would of necessity when he created a world have to create a world inferior to one that he could have created – which is hardly fitting. Further, since such worlds are infinite in number, he would have no principle for selecting one to actualize rather than another. Robert Adams might reply that such a situation is quite okay because even if God could create a perfect world he would be under no obligation to do so and therefore could simply create a good world, as the Bible says he did. Such a reply would be of no comfort to Leibniz, however, because it does not remove the anomaly of thinking of God as creating an inferior world, and it does not explain how God, who does not act arbitrarily, i.e., without sufficient reason, could select such a world to actualize.

I believe Leibniz is correct against Adams that, whenever God acts, he acts in a best possible way because of the excellence of his nature. The necessity implied here, however, is the necessity of "will-do-because-of-essence" rather than the necessity of "must-do-because-of-coercion-or-obligation." It is this necessity of "will do" following from essence whereby Donceel means to explain the necessity of creation, and, though I believe he is wrong that a loving God will necessarily create a world, the distinction of modes of necessity that Donceel has employed in his remarks (1979: 146) helps us understand why God *will* always do the best possible thing though it would be misleading to say that he *must* do it.[3]

Reichenbach rejects this essentialist explanation as to why God is good because it implies that God is not morally praiseworthy. His argument may be developed as follows: either God is morally praiseworthy or he is not, and surely God is morally praiseworthy. But only significantly free persons can be appropriate objects of moral praise. Consider Reichenbach's definition of significant freedom, D_3: "A person is significantly free, on a given occasion, if he is then free either to perform or to refrain from performing an action that is morally significant for him" (1982: 45). It follows that, because God is morally praiseworthy, he is free to do or refrain from doing that which is moral. From this it follows that God is not good because of his essence but "because he always does, intends, and is disposed to do good acts" – even though he really could choose to do otherwise (1982: 148).

Though it is not entirely clear to me, Reichenbach's position seems to result in part from a belief that, if God were not morally praiseworthy, it would be because he was not significantly free, and, if he were not significantly free, then he would not be free at all – but surely God must be thought of as free. I agree that God should be thought of as free, but not as morally free. Reichenbach's position fails to identify moral freedom as a species of a broader freedom that I shall call "subjective freedom." For an individual to be subjectively free with regard to an action is for that individual to be able to do it or refrain from it, and whether the individual does it or not is entirely up to him, i.e., whether the individual does it or not, he could have chosen to do otherwise given the very same circumstances.

The preceding is a more general definition of libertarian freedom than is Reichenbach's D_3. D_3 defines a species of subjective freedom, viz., the subjective freedom to choose between good and evil, as though it were the genus. But in addition to moral freedom there is obviously another species of subjective freedom, viz., non-moral freedom, i.e., subjective freedom with regard to possible actions that are not morally significant. However, non-moral freedom is not "non-significant" freedom, as D_3 implies by calling moral freedom "significant" freedom. Here we have the freedom of one person to propose marriage to another or not; here we have the freedom of a couple to choose to have a child or not; here we have the freedom of an artist to choose one subject or another for her next creative endeavour; here we have the freedom of a scientist to pursue a hunch or drop it. Any of these situations could become a moral one, of course, but none need be so.

Granted these distinctions it is clear that God in his omnipotence could be subjectively free without being morally free and therefore without being morally praiseworthy. However, that God is not subjectively free to do evil does not imply that he is not objectively free to do evil. He is objectively free to do evil, i.e., he has the power and opportunity to do evil. Failure to make this distinction can lead one to conclude that since God has, for example, the power to inflict meaningless suffering on an infant therefore he has the freedom to do so. Yes, he has the objective freedom (given an appropriate situation) because he has the power and opportunity to do so, but because of his essence he cannot will to do so – he cannot even try to will to do so; therefore he is not subjectively free to do so though he is objectively free to do so. From this it follows that when God acts he can do only good; but if he can do only good then he is not morally praiseworthy. Reichenbach concludes that, if God is not morally praiseworthy, then he is defective in virtue. But are moral praiseworthiness and its necessary condition (moral freedom) perfections without which God would be defective? I would like to argue that they are not.

Moral freedom is at the very least a power. To the theist it is a power with a meaning. It is the power that enables us to choose for or against the morally good, and therefore for or against God's kingdom. Inasmuch as morally free beings are neither morally good nor evil by nature, they are assayed as morally good or evil by reference to their actions, intentions, and dispositions, but with the realization that because of their moral freedom, whether they are morally good or evil now, they could reverse themselves in the future. Is it conceivable that God could become morally evil in the future? If God is morally free, then it is conceivable that God really could become morally evil. But this seems impossible.

In classical philosophical theology, such as Reichenbach and I are engaged in, the character of God is not established by looking to see what he does; it is axiomatic that God is a perfectly good being. Hence, it is as impossible that God could choose (and therefore become) evil yet remain God as that a circle could become angular yet remain a circle. As a being than which none greater can be conceived, God must be thought of as essentially good, i.e., as conforming in his actions to the canons of goodness, however those canons might be grounded. God is, then, perfectly good and subjectively free but he is neither morally free, nor morally good, nor morally praiseworthy, nor is it regrettable that he cannot be any of these things.

It is because of his essential goodness that believers can be absolutely confident of God's perfect and everlasting goodness. Were God only morally good, we could never be confident of his goodness in the future because a morally free being is one who by nature always has the power to break his promises or otherwise do evil. But surely we can be certain of the goodness of God; therefore his goodness must not be contingent. Further, if the purpose of moral freedom is to enable individuals to choose for or against the kingdom of God, then – given the nature of God's knowledge and will as developed in Chapter 2 – it would be a category mistake to predicate moral freedom of God because it would not make sense for him to have freedom to choose for or against his own kingdom.

Consider as an aside that perhaps the moral freedom of subjectively free creatures is transient. That is, perhaps by choosing for God's kingdom

MFCs are making a choice that will lead to termination of the exercise or even existence of their moral freedom. Jesus, for example, taught his followers to pray "lead us not into temptation" and "deliver us from evil." These petitions could be answered in two ways in the kingdom of God. On the one hand there could be in God's kingdom no temptations to do evil even if we remain morally free; on the other hand in God's kingdom we could be transformed so as to be no longer susceptible to the kinds of things that in this life tempt us to do evil.[4] Thinkers like J. L. Mackie and H. J. McCloskey might ask "Well why didn't God make the world and people like that in the first place?" but that would be to ignore the theist's position that the purpose of this phase of history is precisely to give MFCs an opportunity to choose between good and evil – to choose to become insusceptible as well as impassible to lust, greed, rage, and such (Mackie 1955; McCloskey 1974).

In conclusion, because God is good by nature, he is not and cannot be morally praiseworthy. That does not mean, however, that he is praiseworthy in no respect. To be praiseworthy is to be worthy of appropriate expressions of being highly prized, of being strongly approved, of being judged as pre-eminent. Surely, then, God is praiseworthy. He is uniquely pre-eminent in wisdom, power, and goodness; in worship he is appropriately acknowledged as such. Moreover, he is worthy of being prized above all others for these qualities. These and his other attributes appropriately inspire awe and gratitude.

Have I begged the issue at hand by saying that God is supreme in goodness? I think not. To be good and to be moral are separable. A moral person, i.e., one who does what he does because he believes it is required or at least not forbidden by the canons of goodness, is not necessarily a good person. He might be tragically mistaken about what is good and what is evil. A good and moral person is one who not only chooses to do what he believes is right though he could do otherwise; he is also one who does what in fact is right, i.e., required or permitted by the canons of goodness. God by definition is such that he knows perfectly well what is right and what is wrong, never does what is wrong, and could not do otherwise. God is perfectly good, then, not in the moral sense, nor merely in the sense of possessing his ontological properties perfectly (though that of course is true), but also in the sense of being by nature such that he will never violate the canons of goodness, whatever they might be and however they might be grounded.

Having agreed with Leibniz that God is by nature good and will because of his excellence create the best possible world, if he creates a world at all, I now register two points of disagreement. First, it seems impossible that there could be one and only one best possible world. Second, I do not understand why God, any more than ourselves, should be paralyzed by equally attractive alternatives. Regarding the first point, the notion of an unsurpassably good world, i.e., a best possible world, does not seem to be incompatible with the further notion that it is possible that there is more than one unsurpassably good world. (I will soon defend the notion of the coherence of an unsurpassably good world.) Indeed, reflection seems to reveal that there must be more than one possible unsurpassably good world, if there is any at all, because any such world could be paralleled by another world involving variations of the first world that would be axiologically insignificant. For example, say that W_2 is a mirror image of W_1, i.e., they are identical in every respect except that what is on the right in W_1 is on the left in W_2 and what is on the left in W_1 is on the right in W_2. I fail to see how this could make one of these worlds better than the other (I am assuming that God is not a "righty" or prejudiced in favor of such). The same would be true of W_3, which is identical to W_1 (a world in which people like ourselves exist) except that in W_3 people's internal organs are reversed in location and the people are predominantly left-handed. A little imagination quickly reveals a limitless number of such structural variations, and a bit of aesthetic imagination produces even more. Hence, if my insight here is correct and if the notion of a best possible world is coherent, then there are an infinite number of best possible worlds, i.e., of worlds axiologically equal that could not be surpassed in value.[5]

Leibniz presumes in the following passage to undermine my line of argument:

I call "World" the whole succession and the whole agglomeration of all existent things, lest it be said that several worlds could have existed in different times and different places. For they must needs be reckoned all together as one world or, if you will, as one Universe. And even though one should fill all times and all places, it still remains true that one might have filled them in innumerable ways, and that there is an infinitude of possible worlds among which God must needs have chosen the best, since he does nothing without acting in accordance with supreme reason.   (1966: 35)

Leibniz was aware that possible worlds, even in his all-inclusive sense, could vary by ever so little. Still, he was convinced that it must be possible to rank them hierarchically such that one is absolutely best. Whether he believed that this is necessary in order to enable God to act or because any difference between two worlds must involve a value difference between them, is not clear. Neither position seems defensible.

I argued earlier that God should be thought of as free, and that freedom often, perhaps always, especially for God, involves some element of arbitrariness in selection among alternatives. Further, though I agree that all possible worlds can be ranked valuatively, I see no reason to think that each can be ranked hierarchically relative to every other, i.e., that no two possible worlds are equal in value. For reasons set forth two paragraphs ago, quite the opposite seems true, viz., for every possible world there is an infinite number of others equal to it in value. If this is correct, then the theist should conclude that, if God decides to create a world, he must select among an infinite number of possibilities because he can actualize only one of them, given that, as Leibniz says, a world spans "the whole succession and the whole agglomeration of all existent things."

God's freedom regarding creation is, then, twofold. First, he can create or not create a world. Second, he can create whichever best possible world he so chooses, and he can do so arbitrarily. Hoping that I have made it at least plausible that we should leave open the possibility that God could select among multiple best possible worlds if there is no uniquely best possible world, I now turn to explaining why I believe the notion of a best possible world is meaningful – and here, having once been persuaded by Reichenbach, I have returned to Leibniz.

Reichenbach's thought-provoking position can be gathered from the closing words of his 1979 article, 'Must God Create the Best Possible World?'

> We have argued that the notion of the best possible world is meaningless, because for any world which might be so designated, there would always be another which was better, either in being populated by beings with better or a greater quantity of good characteristics, or else by being more optimific. For any world that is chosen, there is a better world conceivable. If we are correct on this point, then it would be impossible for God to create a best possible world. Consequently, it would be meaningless to inquire whether he must create the best possible world; the very concept of such a world is a chimera.   (211–12)

A year later Reichenbach defended this position against criticisms by David Basinger (Basinger 1980; Reichenbach 1980); after two more years his position remained unchanged, as can be seen in his *Evil and a Good God*. I agree that Basinger's points against Reichenbach are ineffective, but there are other points that do seem effective. Here I take my cue from the closing paragraphs of Leibniz's essay, 'On the Ultimate Origination of the Universe.'

Speaking of the universe in his inclusive sense of "world," Leibniz writes: "As the climax of the universal beauty and perfection of God's works, it must also be recognized that the total universe is engaged in a perpetual and spontaneous progress, so that it always advances toward greater culture" (93). He concludes with this paragraph:

> To the best possible objection that thus the world would of necessity have long ago turned into a paradise, it is easy to reply: Many substances already may have attained great perfection; yet, the continuum being infinitely divisible, there will always remain in the unfathomable depth of the universe some somnolent elements which are still to be

awakened, developed, and improved – in a word, promoted to a higher culture. This is why the end of progress can never be attained.   (94)

From this point, taken together with Leibniz's inclusive definition of "world," I believe that a refutation of Reichenbach's position can be constructed.

When Reichenbach says that for any world we might conceive we can conceive of a greater one, he is apparently thinking of static worlds, worlds in which the furniture and/or the inhabitants are fixed. That is, he seems to believe that for every possible world either there is a limit to how much pleasure its inhabitants can enjoy, or there is a limit to how much pleasure its parts can provide, or both, such that for any possible world A we can think of a greater one B, i.e., one the inhabitants of which by virtue of greater powers of enjoyment could get more pleasure out of A, or one the parts of which would provide more pleasure to the inhabitants of A, or both.

If I have understood Reichenbach's position correctly, it is based on the assumption that, no matter how happy any given creature is, it could always be happier. This seems false because creatures have saturation points, i.e., points beyond which they cannot enjoy food anymore, or sex, or companionship, or philosophy, etc. One might reply, "But we can conceive of them being able to enjoy those things even longer." To do so, however, would be mistaken because it would involve thinking of those creatures as having capacities that they do not in fact have. The question is whether any given creature *as it is* in constitution at the moment has an infinitely progressive capacity for enjoyment of a certain thing or group of things.

Empirical evidence in the form of satiation indicates that none does, and conceptual analysis of what it means to be a creature, and therefore finite, provides at least *prima facie* support for the notion that a creature, as finite, cannot have a limitless capacity for enjoyment of a specific thing. From this I believe it follows that all creatures have limits such that it would be possible for them to be made perfectly happy, i.e., to be made so happy that they would not want to be happier and could not in fact be made happier at t_1 given their constitution at t_1. I am proposing, then, that any finite creature will have limits of discrimination and absorption such that changes beyond a certain point would go unnoticed by him or unappreciated by him or would turn pleasure to discomfort or pain, as too much food can do no matter how excellent it is.

Reichenbach might reply that his point still stands because, even if it is true that *in* any given world the creatures by virtue of their specific and finite constitutions will have limits of happiness beyond which they are not capable of experiencing greater happiness, still it is possible to imagine *another* world in which there exist creatures identical to those in the first world except that they have some gift for enjoyment (intensive or extensive) that the creatures in the first world do not, so that the first world could not be correctly described as "a best possible world." To be sure, we could stipulate that the creatures in either world would be perfectly happy with their lives in a subjective sense, but we should acknowledge that in an objective sense the creatures in the second possible world would be better off because their happiness would consist of a more intense or discriminating enjoyment of the same types of objects as exist in the first world, or because their happiness would derive at least in part from enjoyment of additional and perhaps superior objects, so that their happiness would be richer and perhaps more elevated.

As an example consider one world in which all of the creatures are monocular and another world in which they are all binocular and therefore enjoy the pleasures and benefits of depth vision. Consider two more worlds in which everything is identical except that in one of them all vision is in black and white whereas in the other the full range of our color spectrum is experienced. Finally, consider two more worlds in one of which there are creatures like ourselves except that they have no capacity for friendship whereas in the other there is a capacity for the highest level of friendship. For any given world, it seems, we can conceive another in which the creatures are happier in an objective, if not a subjective, sense.

The preceding point that in its objective respect the happiness of creatures is always surpassable – a point that I have been developing on Reichenbach's behalf – would discredit the coherence of the notion of a best possible world if God could create nothing but a static world, i.e., a world the subjects and objects of which were unalterably fixed in nature. But it is not so. Because God is omnipotent, therefore he can create a dynamic world, i.e., a world in which objects of enjoyment develop in ways that afford more and more pleasure to its inhabitants, in which new objects that afford new pleasures emerge, in which the subjects develop greater and greater capacities for enjoyment of old objects, and in which the subjects develop new capacities for enjoyments of which they were not before capable.[6]

Our world seems to be such a world, both in phylogeny and ontogeny, and so can be used to illustrate these notions. As to the phylogeny, as best we can tell there once were no creatures that could enjoy playfulness or mathematics; now there are such creatures. As to ontogeny, puppies cannot immediately upon birth enjoy the pleasures of vision; lepidoptera cannot immediately enjoy the pleasures of flight; humans cannot immediately enjoy the pleasures of language or sex. In most, and perhaps all, of these cases an organic change must take place before the said enjoyment can occur; it is not merely a matter of cultivating an already existent capacity to enjoy the said pleasure. We have, then, clear examples ready to hand of (1) ways in which capacities for new enjoyments have arisen with new species, (2) ways in which capacities for new enjoyments have developed in individuals, and (3) ways in which established capacities for enjoyment have been enhanced in the same individual. Hence, with regard to the ways in which God might cause the progressive increase of an individual's ability to enjoy itself, others, and God, the end of progress, as Leibniz says, can never be attained. Surely that is a wonderful thing.

With a Leibnizian notion of a dynamic world in our background, I am now prepared to attempt a theistic description of the best possible world, i.e., a world than which God could have created none better. First it would be a world in which there is no evil at all or else no evil the prevention of which would have been compatible with so great a good as will obtain. Second, it would be a world in which free creatures freely choose to be there. They would not be there by coercion, threat, or unwitting manipulation. Hence, the best possible world requires an initial phase during which MFCs choose for or against existence under God's rule, and which is, therefore, a phase during which innocent suffering is a real possibility insofar as MFCs choose for or against God's kingdom by how they relate to one another.[7] Third, the best possible world is one in which, after the preceding decision has been made, those who choose God's kingdom become characterized everlastingly by two things. On the one hand each will always be perfectly happy subjectively, i.e., each will be perfectly satisfied with herself and her state of affairs, wanting nothing more than she has.[8] On the other hand, God will cause the saved everlastingly to enjoy higher and higher levels of bliss by either improving old objects or creating new objects for their enjoyment, or improving existing faculties or creating new faculties by means of which they can enjoy old things more or new things at all, or both.[9]

Such a two-phase world, I submit, in which free, intelligent creatures freely enjoy perfect happiness at all times and on higher and higher levels, such that they are always perfectly content on any given level, yet from the next higher level can appreciate that they are even happier than they were, is a world than which none better can be conceived. Such a world, I submit, God could create. *Contra* Leibniz, however, I believe there are infinitely many forms that such a world could take. God is free to actualize any one of them (though only one of them) or none of them. *Contra* Adams, if God actualizes a world at all, he will actualize one of the best possible worlds. To be sure, because of his omnipotence, he could do something less, but because of the excellence of his nature he will not. Therefore, as Leibniz argues, we can be confident that, if there is a God, we are living not only in a good world but in a best possible world, an equallable but unsurpassable world, a world than which none better could have been created by God.

Now let us look at three criticisms that might be leveled at my claim that the best possible world has just been described. First, one might say, "But for any world you conceive, I can conceive a better one because the world you conceive will necessarily be in some state or other and I will be able to conceive a better state." This criticism is based on a misconception of what I am proposing. To be sure, there will be temporal states of the world I am proposing, and of any one of those states it would be correct to say, "But I can conceive of a better one." That, however, would not be to conceive of a better world. The world of which I speak is one in which, at least during its second phase, each of its temporal states is perfectly suited to the subjective happiness of its inhabitants and each of its states is always followed by another that is objectively even better for the same inhabitants. Hence, of a dynamic possible world such as I am proposing, it is not relevant to say of any of its states, "But there could be a better one than this one," because there will be. Such a world, then – though not any one of its stages – would be not only good but unsurpassably good. To infer from the surpassability of each of the stages of such a world the surpassability of that world would be to commit the fallacy of composition.

Having seen the significance of the progressive nature of such a world, the critic should abandon his effort to construct a better world by trying to include a better state than the other world has; an everlastingly progressive world can always include any good state that another has, or at least include an axiologically equivalent state. The critic might, however, claim that the very progressiveness of such a world would imply that it was surpassable: "For any possible dynamic world, another can be conceived which is superior to it because, though it is identical to it in every other respect, God leads its creatures more swiftly to higher and higher levels of happiness than he does in the first possible world."

Initially this seems to be a point with merit, but upon analysis its seeming merit vanishes. The faster rate of transcendence from level to level of happiness is a difference that makes no significant difference because (1) creatures in both worlds will proceed through all the same levels of happiness, (2) creatures in the slower world will not be unhappy by virtue of not moving more quickly, and (3) creatures in the faster world will not be happier by virtue of transcending more quickly. Indeed, one could argue that moving more slowly would be better because it would allow more time to savor the delights of each level.

Yet neither argument, for fast or slow, would be conclusive. Surely God can arrange things so that, no matter the speed of transcendence, there is never unhappiness because the previous level was left too soon or the next level is too long in coming. Hence, the infinite range of speeds of transcendence does not imply incoherence in the notion of a best possible world. That the rate of transcendence is faster in W_2 than in W_1 does not entail that W_2 is a better world. As there are an infinite number of unsurpassable worlds among which God may choose arbitrarily, there are an infinite number of possible speeds of transcendence (including variable speeds) among which God may choose arbitrarily because they are all compatible with a best possible world.

Third, one might say, "Okay, the speed of transcendence is irrelevant to the notion of a best possible world, but for any world that God actualizes I can conceive of another world that is identical in all respects except that in it God's kingdom starts at a higher level of happiness than that at which it starts in the first world. Obviously the second world would be better than the first world because there God's kingdom would start at a higher level of happiness and thereby not include the inferior level(s) of happiness on which God's kingdom would start in the first world."

This strikes me as a more difficult objection than the first, but not as intractable. First, it would be irrelevant to the subjective happiness of creatures on which level God started his kingdom. The citizens of his kingdom will be equally satisfied on all levels. Hence, the differences made by starting on a higher level would have to be on the objective side of happiness – higher levels of happiness being distinguished by greater or new capacities for enjoyment or new or better objects of enjoyment. But, for my second point, W_2 would not contain any level of happiness that W_1 did not contain, so W_2 could be objectively superior to W_1 only by virtue of *not* containing the lower level(s) of W_1. How this omission in and of itself would make W_2 superior to W_1 is not clear. One might even argue that W_1 is a better world than W_2 because its inhabitants would be able to appreciate having moved from the level that it does not share with W_2 to the levels that it does share with it, thereby bringing into play the axiological principle of contrast. Yet even this rings hollow because in any best possible world God's kingdom will have to begin arbitrarily at some level and then proceed through an infinite number of higher levels. Because of the infinite progression in every best possible world, no best possible world will proceed through more levels or higher levels than another. Hence, given that all levels of God's kingdom in any world will be good and adequate causes of perfect subjective happiness and given that the more inclusive world would contain all the same levels of happiness as the less inclusive world, I see no good reason to think that a world in which God's kingdom starts on a higher level of happiness would be superior to one that starts on a lower level.

Even if the preceding arguments are sound, one might wonder whether I have built them on a principle pernicious to an earlier part of my position. I have attempted to achieve my ends in this chapter by distinguishing between the subjective and objective sides of happiness, pointing out that God can make us unsurpassably happy subjectively but that he cannot make us unsurpassably happy objectively. But does this not imply that the notion of unsurpassable happiness taken as a whole is an incoherent notion and that, therefore, God's own happiness must be surpassable, and that, since on my reckoning God's inner life is immutable, therefore the surpassability of his happiness must be dependent on the world, and therefore he must be passible in feeling? I think not – at least if the notion of essential happiness is a coherent one.

Necessarily God, as a supremely perfect being, is subjectively happy. This alone does not rule out the possibility that God's happiness may everlastingly transcend from level to level, but, when we consider that if God had not created a world, he would nonetheless have had to be perfectly happy in all respects, and he would have had to be so in the absence of any individual other than himself, it seems clear that his happiness, both subjectively and objectively, must be from himself, so that he depends on nothing else for the fact of his happiness or the unsurpassability of his happiness. There can be no object of value higher than or equal to God, so the idea of there being anything that could increase his happiness is a chimerical one. It is by virtue of our finitude that our happiness is infinitely surpassable on its objective side; it is by virtue of his infinitude that God's happiness is essentially perfect and unsurpassable.

Now I would like to argue that, if there is a God such as I have described, then there is a sense in which this is, after all, *the* best possible world. If by "possible" we mean "all that is or can yet be" (as distinguished from what is logically conceivable), then, inasmuch as only one world can ever be actual, it follows that when one possible world is actualized all other possible worlds are rendered impossible, i.e., they neither are nor can be. To be sure, they remain possible in the sense of "logically conceivable," but they cease to be possible in the sense of "actual or able to be actualized." Therefore, once God actualizes a possible world, it becomes the only possible world. Further, inasmuch as God would – as argued earlier – actualize only an unsurpassably good world, it follows that any world that God actualizes will be not only the only possible world but also the best possible world, since it will be an unsurpassably good world and no other world will be possible.

Whether Leibniz had anything like the preceding in mind, I do not know. And though it may sound as though it provides support to his theological rationalistic determinism, it does not. Ours is in fact the actual world and therefore is, on the preceding reasoning and the assumption that there is a God, the best possible world. That our world is *now* the best possible world would not, however, have provided God with a reason for choosing our world to actualize. Our world did not become the best possible world until God actualized it. The formal value of the possible world of which this one is the actualization is identical to that of an infinite number of other best possible worlds. Hence, God did not select this world to become actual because it was the best of all possible worlds; rather, it became the best of all possible worlds – indeed, the only possible world – because God chose it. Had he chosen any other best possible world for actualization, as he could have done with equally good reason, it would have become the actual world, the only possible world, the best possible world (within the limits established earlier). Hence, the unique supremacy of our world over all other conceivable unsurpassably good worlds derives entirely from God having actualized it.

It seems, then, that the notion of a best possible world is coherent, that God could create such a world, that if God were to create a world at all he would create such a world, that at most he could create one such world, and that, since there is a world, those who believe that there is a God should also believe that this is a best possible world, indeed, the best possible world – at least as far as God could make it. The fact that believers should also hold that God had arbitrarily to select this world from among an infinite number of other possibilities should not be seen as detracting from his rationality. The fact only reveals the richness of the freedom and the power within which divine rationality operates.

Finally, is this our world the best possible world? The form of Reichenbach's argument that it cannot by experience be proved not to be such can be used equally effectively, as he notes, to show that neither can it by experience be proved to be such. It is only by proof of the existence of God that we could know, by inference, that this is the best possible world. Those who have not been smitten by such a proof can still hope and pray for faith that there is a God and that, therefore, this is the best possible world, a world ideally fitted to its purposes, providing unsurpassable opportunities that lead to an unsurpassable good, a world the possible sufferings of which are necessary for the reality of that great end, and the actual sufferings of which will be overwhelmed by the good that is revealed to those who choose the kingdom of God.

12

Conclusion

THE LENGTH AND COMPLEXITY of this essay may have caused the reader to lose a sense of its overall configuration and how its various parts fit together. I would like, therefore, to draw together the results of the preceding chapters.

We noted first that the question of God's passibility or impassibility turns upon whether God can be changed by the world or not. We noted next that there are four respects in which God might be passible or impassible. Hence, we must examine each of them rather than saying indiscriminately that God is passible or impassible. The four respects in which God can be considered to be passible or impassible are his nature, will, knowledge, and feeling. It seems uncontroversial that God must be impassible, indeed, immutable, in nature. His status as God must not be something that could be changed by anything.

God's impassibility in will follows from his omniscience and omnipotence. In his omniscience he knows all that can be done and all that he can do. He knows these things by virtue of knowing the plenum and his power in relation to it. The notion of the plenum was posited because of the incoherence of the doctrine of creation *ex nihilo*. The plenum is the passive side of the absolute; God is the active side; and the absolute is that which exists primordially and necessarily. God knows the potentialities of the plenum not in the form of discrete possibilities; that would be impossible. Rather, he knows them by means of ranges of potentiality; ultimately, I suspect, he knows them by means of one grand range of potentiality, viz., the range of potentiality of contingent being.

God's eternal knowledge of the plenum means that nothing ever comes to pass the possibility of which he was not already familiar with. Hence, God never has to wait on actuality in order to decide his will. Given his eternal knowledge of all possibilities, our most plausible assumption is that he has eternally indexed his will to all possibilities. Hence, he never has to wait until after we do something in order to decide his response to it. He has eternally decided his response to all that we might do.

Further, God does not need to change in order to implement his decisions once we act. He can have eternally disposed his will and the world such that whatever his will is for us, it will be implemented without change on his part. Hence, as far as his existence, knowledge of basic possibilities, and will are concerned, God is related externally, i.e., impassibly, to the world. No change in his action is required or need be caused by whatever happens in order for his providence to be appropriate and adequate.

There is, however, a respect in which it appears that God cannot be impassible, and that is in his knowledge of what is happening in the world. It cannot be an illusion that change is occurring in this world, and change cannot be known adequately except by an awareness that undergoes a corresponding change caused by the thing of which one is aware. This is a metaphysical principle to which there can be no exception. Hence, the Boethian conception of eternality according to which changing things are changelessly present to God is mistaken. If it were true, then the appearance of change would be an illusion; but this cannot be, so the Boethian doctrine of divine eternality is mistaken.

This does not mean, however, that God is essentially temporal. Things that are essentially temporal are things whose existence is contingent, i.e., things whose duration depends on something other than themselves. Hence, temporality is not the mode of God's existence. God's existence, his knowledge of basic possibilities, and his will are eternal, i.e., noncontingently actual, but his knowledge of the world cannot be eternal. Because the world is distinct from God, God must be passive to what is going on in the world, even when what is going on in the world is determined entirely by his will. God's knowledge of what is happening is determined by what is happening. Were he to know what was happening in the world merely by knowing his will for the world, then he might know all that was happening in the world, but he would not know those things themselves. He is omniscient, though, so he must know those things themselves, and therefore he must be passive to them as they come into existence, change, and pass out of existence.

The doctrine of divine foreknowledge implies passibility in God's knowledge of the world because it is predicated on the distinction between what is actual and what is not actual but will be. Surely God must be passible to the world in order first to know it as not containing something that he knows it will contain, and then to know it as containing it. However, in its all-inclusiveness the doctrine of divine foreknowledge implies that humans are not subjectively free, so libertarians reject it.

The effort to save God's knowledge of our future free actions by means of the concept of middle knowledge, i.e., knowledge of what we would do, proves unsuccessful because it has no way of making intelligible how God could know that one possible world would be actualized rather than another when the alternative turns not on God's will but on a creature's free will. At best the doctrine of middle knowledge is a sophisticated begging of the question of God's knowledge of future free creaturely actions. But if divine eternality, divine foreknowledge, and middle knowledge are rejected, there seems to be no further way to compatibilize human freedom and divine omniprescience. It seems, then, that God has no such knowledge. That is no strike against this conception of God; the future free actions of creatures are something that in principle cannot be known.

God's lack of such knowledge does not imply delay or difficulty in his decision-making *vis à vis* the world. Because of his eternal knowledge of all basic possibilities, he has eternally resolved his will regarding all that we might do. Now he waits and watches and accompanies us as we make our decisions and experience his will. He is with us as solicitously as any parent has ever been with his children, but he is not continually deciding what to do next in response to what we have done. He has decided his will eternally. Our relationship to the world and to him is now up to us – within the parameters of the possibilities afforded to us by his grace, and as modified by the decisions of other free creatures.

If I am correct that God must be passible in his knowledge of what is going on in the world, it follows that he must be passible to what we are doing and experiencing; therefore he must be passible to the evil that we do and suffer. Is it not the case, then, that inasmuch as God loves us dearly, he must suffer because of our sufferings and sins, and therefore be passible in feeling? For three reasons I have argued that this is not so. First, it is intelligible that a being is blissful by nature, and therefore God, a perfect being, should be thought of as such. God is dependent on no other individual for the actuality or perfection of his existence or happiness.

Second, God has created free creatures that they might choose for or against his kingdom, wherein lie everlasting life and happiness. Such a serious choice requires adequate opportunity for deliberation; we can be confident that God will provide it. God provides for every morally free creature to choose his kingdom, but he honors the decisions of those who choose otherwise. Because the fundamental purpose of God's granting subjective freedom to creatures is to enable them to make a radical choice for or against his kingdom, and because he knows he can honor their choice without breaching his goodness or the happiness of himself or of those who choose his kingdom, he is not grieved by those who choose against his kingdom.

Third, though God would rather that no one suffer innocently and involuntarily, he knows that the possibility of such suffering is a necessary condition of the great good that will obtain in his kingdom, and that those who choose his kingdom will find it to be such a great good that they would be willing, knowing what they will know then, to go through all their previous suffering again if it were necessary to achieve and enjoy that great good everlastingly.

We have, then, the basis of a theory as to why God created the world. It is a theory that attributes its creation to the sheer magnanimity of God, who in no way needs the world for his own happiness, but who in liberality creates it that there might also be others to enjoy the great good of existence under his sovereignty.

Must God create a world? To be sure, God must make a decision among his own possibilities, i.e., he must be creator of himself insofar as determination of his possibilities is concerned, but he can be creator of himself as not-a-creator-of-a-world or as creator-of-a-world. Hence, he must be a creator, but not necessarily of a world. He can choose to leave the potentialities of the plenum entirely unactualized. If he does create a world, it is not the case that his knowledge alone will be the cause of the world's existence. God's knowledge informs him of the range of his possibilities; actualization of possibility requires that his knowledge be supplemented by his will choosing among the alternatives of which his knowledge informs him.

If God creates a world from the plenum, and therefore from no individual, can he create an individual that is subjectively free? This is a difficult question, but it appears plausible that he can; indeed, it appears necessary that such creatures be created by God if their existence is to be intelligible. However, because subjective freedom is an essential characteristic of any creature that it qualifies, each subjectively free creature must be free from the very first moment of its existence. Because it cannot bring itself into existence, it is necessary that in its first moment of existence its creator create it as decided-but-deciding, i.e., as definite in all appropriate respects but also as deciding whether to maintain, modify, or reject that definiteness in any respect.

God having chosen magnanimously to afford the enjoyments of existence to individuals other than himself, what kind of world would he create for them? Surely he would create a good world, i.e., a world in which evil would be possible only insofar as its possibility was a necessary condition of a good so great that those who suffer evil innocently would agree that its permission was justified for the sake of so great a good.

But could God create a world than which none better could be conceived – a world the inhabitants of which would everlastingly transcend from level to level of happiness? I have argued that he could. Further, if there is a God, then because of his perfect goodness, wisdom, and power, we can be confident that this is such a world. Surely God would not do less than that which is fitting to his excellence.

Notes

1 THE ISSUE OF DIVINE IMPASSIBILITY

1 For a thorough examination of God and emotions, see 'God and Emotions,' a 1975 dissertation by Janine Marie Idziak, directed by Jack W. Meiland at the University of Michigan.

2 Some people try to make themselves emotionally impassible by taking drugs that make them feel imperturbably happy or peaceful or numb, or that make nearly everything seem funny or aesthetically fascinating.

3 Gregory of Thaumaturgus' treatise on divine passibility is in Syriac. Apparently the only translation of it into a modern language is the German translation (1880) by Victor Ryssel. There is also, however, a fine Latin translation by Paulus Martinus, and a fairly detailed summary in French by Henri Crouzel. See the bibliography for details. I thank Michael Slusser of The Catholic University of America for this and other valuable references on Gregory and the issue of impassibility in the early church.

2 DIVINE IMPASSIBILITY IN NATURE AND WILL

1 A will that is free cannot be passible because it must by definition be self-determining, but I do not believe that a will is necessarily free.

2 I thank Norman Kretzmann for this reference and the translation.

3 For classical statements on God's knowledge of possibility see St Augustine's *De Trinitate* VI, 10, and XV, 13, and Thomas Aquinas' *Summa Contra Gentiles* I, 66.

4 Hartshorne's position on divine resolution and foreknowledge can be found in *Man's Vision of God*, 328–39. His understanding of God's knowledge of possibilities is set forth at length in his 'Santayana's Doctrine of Essence.' See also his early reflections on continuity and possibility in *Beyond Humanism*, chs. 8, 9, and 16.

5 For another recent statement of the position that God's intentions can be eternally "indexed to, or conditional upon, contingencies arising in the created universe," see Thomas V. Morris, 'Properties, Modalities, and God,' esp 47–8. I thank Stephen Schwartz for bringing this article to my attention.

6 I do not want to take on here the question as to whether God *can* change his mind. That is a question that I hope to take up elsewhere in the broader context of potentiality in God. Here I am limiting my deliberations to whether God might *want* to change his mind.

7 See Isaiah 25.1, and recall Carl Henry's sentiment: "... a redeemer and judge of mankind ... whose purpose may vacillate, is not a deity in whom we can ever be religiously at rest" (1982: 288).

8 I am using c_1 instead of t_1 because I believe it is more plausible to think of God's will as relativized to circumstances (past and present) than to time – a topic to which we will return in Chapters 5 and 6.

9 Not all of God's willing need be understood in this way, of course. The laws of nature seem to be willed by God independently of human behavior – unless the Garden of Eden story or something like it is literally true. If it is, then though the laws of nature are stable now, as best we can tell, their present form is partially dependent on how Adam and Eve behaved.

10 The "pre" in "presponses" can be interpreted logically, to suit classical eternalists, or temporally, to suit temporalists. If this is not acceptable to eternalists because of the heavy temporal connotations of "pre," then inasmuch as "*responses*" also suggests temporality, perhaps eternalists would prefer to speak of "*inde*sponses," i.e., responsive actions decided upon and implemented *inde*pendently of actuality.

11 Leibniz objected correctly to the implication of occasionalism, and by anticipation modern process philosophy, that God is incessantly making billions of decisions every millisecond in response to what is happening in the world. Such a conception of God seems unnecessarily complex.

12 I would like to thank James Keller of Wofford College for the criticisms to which I have been responding in the last two paragraphs.

13 See Thomas Aquinas' *Summa Contra Gentiles* II, 11–14, and *Summa Theologiae* Ia, q. 13, a.7, and q. 28. In Chapter 5 I will argue that God's relation to us cannot be entirely external.

14 T. P. Smith argues in his 'On the Applicability of a Criterion of Change,' 325–33, that a Cambridge change implies a change in the subject when the predicate is non-relational, e.g., "moves," "begins to intend," "becomes square," but does not entail a change in the subject when the predicate is relational, e.g., "begins to be to the right of," "becomes greener than," "begins to taste awful." Obviously all statements about God's relations to changes in the world are relational and so do not entail changes in God – though by themselves they do not exclude them either.

15 Richard Swinburne, *The Coherence of Theism*, 214 and 218. In this section Swinburne shuttles quickly between his own views and the views of others whom he finds compatible. I believe he intends in the quotations above to express his own views as well as the views of others, such as biblical figures and Paul Tillich.

16 In *The Coherence of Theism*, 221, Swinburne seems to switch to the position that the idea of volitional impassibility is incoherent. However, his statements are qualified such that he seems to be toying with the position rather than adopting it. He writes that "superficially" the idea "seems incoherent" – which suggests that after all it is not; he adds that in order to defend this idea the theist would have to allow that he is using such phrases as "brings about" in a very different sense from the normal sense – but classical theists ordinarily make such an allowance anyway, and Swinburne agrees that to do so is at least sometimes legitimate. In fairness it should be noted that in this passage Swinburne is attacking the notion of God's utter timelessness, which he definitely believes to be incoherent. Hence, because of the qualifications in this passage, and because of its dissonance with *Coherence* 214–15 and *Existence* 238–9, it seems most reasonable to hold that Swinburne recognizes the idea of volitional impassibility as coherent, but rejects it because he believes it would stifle our emotional relationship with God.

17 Professor Keller of Wofford College has through generous correspondence sharpened my understanding of process philosophy and contributed to the refinement of my position by challenging it in numerous perceptive ways. I thank him.

Readers should see his examination of basic differences between classical and process metaphysics (Keller, 1982: 3–20).

18   See also Eleonore Stump's excellent article, 'Petitionary Prayer,' 81–91.

3 CONTINUITY, POSSIBILITY, AND OMNISCIENCE

1   See, for example, Aquinas' *Summa Theologiae* 1a, 14.9.

2   These remarks are contained in a letter dated December 16, 1980, from Professor Hartshorne to me. See also Hartshorne 1970: 122, and 1972: 59.

3   Readers familiar with Alvin Plantinga's *The Nature of Necessity*, ch. 8, will recognize in this quotation the distinction that Plantinga adopts under the terminology of "predicative and impredicative propositions."

4   Lewis Ford has pointed out in correspondence that Whitehead would disagree with the last statement.

5   Readers unfamiliar with A. N. Whitehead should note that Hartshorne disagrees sharply with his theory of possibility. See Lewis Ford's 'Whitehead's Differences from Hartshorne.'

6   Since to most people the denial of possible individuals is initially preposterous, I am surprised that Hartshorne does not follow Henri Bergson in smoothing the way by playing up the contrast between two very different senses of "x was possible," one sense being retained and the other rejected. See Bergson 1965: 21.

7   Hartshorne's paper was read in response to my paper, 'Impassible Love.' The meeting was held in Wilmington, North Carolina.

8   See John Morreall's interesting discussion of Hume's missing shade of blue in *Philosophy and Phenomenological Research*. Morreall argues that our ability to fill in a missing shade of blue is destructive of Hume's copy theory of thought but is compatible with his empiricist framework.

9   The first and last phrase are from Hartshorne's *Anselm's Discovery* 196–7. The clause is from his letter to me. I would like to thank Professor Hartshorne for reading an earlier draft of this expository part of the present chapter to help ensure that it is correct.

10   Phil Weiss seems also to have arrived at this conclusion in his analysis of the theories of possibility of David Lewis, Nicholas Rescher, and Justus Buchler. See his 'Possibility: Three Recent Ontologies.'

11   Whether we should hold that there are an infinite number of basic continua is an interesting question that I will not take up. Hartshorne does not seem disposed to think that there are, and neither am I.

12   For interesting statements by Aquinas on God's knowledge of possibilities see his *Summa Contra Gentiles* 1, 50(7–9), 51(1), and 54(5).

13   Strictly speaking, we cannot slice a continuum at a point because there are no points, in the sense of joints, in a continuum. Rather, the point is created by the slice.

14   Lest it seem that in speaking of whisking away perceptual handkerchiefs or rubbing away a patina I am setting up straw-men that need not be taken seriously, consider the following statements from George Berkeley's *Three Dialogues*: "When things are said to begin or end their existence, we do not mean this with regard to God, but his creatures. All objects are eternally known by God, or, which is the same thing, have an eternal existence in His mind: but when *things, before imperceptible to creatures, are, by a decree of God, made perceptible to them; then are they said to begin a relative existence*, with respect to created minds" (emphasis

mine). Also, "nothing is new, or begins to be, in respect of the mind of God." Beginnings and endings, therefore, are to be understood entirely in respect to finite spirits. ". . . things, with regard to us, may properly be said to begin their existence, or be created, when God decreed they should become perceptible to intelligent creatures, in that order and manner which he then established, and we now call the laws of nature" (84, 85).

15 For Blanshard's distinction between general and specific universals, see his *The Nature of Thought*, ch. 17, and *Reason and Analysis*, ch. 9.

16 James W. Felt, S.J., is moving in a direction similar to mine in some ways, but is more sympathetic to Hartshorne in other ways. See Felt's distinctions between possibilities, Possibility, and potentiality, in his 'Impossible Worlds' and 'God's Choice'.

17 Given Hartshorne's belief that becoming is discrete, not continuous, I believe he would say that there can be no such thing as an actual continuum; any seemingly actual continuum would be illusory. See his, 'A Revision of Peirce's Categories,' esp. pp. 286 ff.

18 My argument should be acceptable to classical theists. Process theists may rejoin that God's knowledge of his power is general not specific; that is, God knows *that* his cooperation with other entities is a necessary condition of, for example, new colors coming to pass, but prior to their actualization God is not familiar with the colors that, with his cooperation, will come to pass.

19 Interestingly, for Hartshorne God's power exceeds his knowledge, i.e., he can do things that he does not know he can do. My position is the opposite: God's knowledge is greater than his power, i.e., he can know of more than he can do, e.g., he knows of the possibility of free actions by creatures but he cannot cause them to perform particular free actions.

20 Eugene Peters' 'Hartshorne on Actuality,' is the only piece I know of, other than my own, that is exclusively devoted to critical evaluation of Hartshorne's theory of possibility. However, the articles by David Griffin and Lewis S. Ford in *Two Process Philosophers* (1973) are excellent expository background and contain some critical remarks, especially by Ford. See also Theodore Vitali's 'The Peirceian Influence on Hartshorne's Subjectivism', and Barry L. Whitney's 'Does God Influence the World's Creativity? Hartshorne's Doctrine of Possibility.' Relevant to the type of analysis that I shall give is Ford's use of set theory in 'God Infinite? A Process Perspective.'

21 Barry L. Whitney argues in similar fashion that the infinitude of our alternatives and freedom can be trivialized in Hartshorne's system. It is of little significance that our alternatives are always infinite in number if they fall within a very narrow range. For example, if the "infinite" dial on our kitchen stove were limited to temperatures between 200 and 201 degrees fahrenheit, we would not be happy with it, infinite though the possible settings be. See Whitney's 'Does God Influence the World's Creativity? Hartshorne's Doctrine of Possibility' and his 'Process Theism: Does a Persuasive God Coerce?'

22 Perhaps on this topic we would be best advised to follow the Wittgensteinian counsel of Peirce in 6.508. 'God's knowledge is something so utterly unlike our own that it is more like willing than knowing. I do not see why we may not assume that He refrains from knowing much. For this thought is creative. But perhaps the wisest way is to say that we do not know how God's thought is performed and that [it] is simply vain to attempt it. We cannot so much as frame any notion of what the phrase 'the performance of God's mind' *means*. Not the faintest! The question is gabble.'

23 Lewis Ford notes this problem in his article, 'Whitehead's Differences from

Hartshorne,' 78–9. See Barry L. Whitney's attempt to defend Hartshorne in his 'Does God Influence the World's Creativity?'

24 Process philosophers believe that the real individuals, as distinguished from societies of individuals, of which reality consists are tiny events, "actual occasions," that flash into and out of existence quickly. None of these events ever returns to existence, but each is succeeded by another event that inherits the experience of the earlier event and adds its own contribution, every actual occasion having some level of experience and some degree of freedom. See A.N. Whitehead's *Process and Reality* or Donald W. Sherburne's *A Key to Whitehead's 'Process and Reality'*.

25 Hartshorne surprisingly almost says as much, in contradiction to the many passages quoted earlier, in 'The God of Religion and the God of Philosophy.' He writes there, "Consider the totality of possible world states. This is 'infinite' if the word means anything. Not only does God know this infinite totality, but he could and would know the realisation of any of the possibilities were it to be realised" (163). If pressed, Hartshorne might reply, "Well, God only knows the infinite totality in a vague way," but he seems to mean something more here.

26 I say this on the assumption that Hartshorne, if forced to choose, would prefer the position that God's memory moves away from the truth systematically, e.g., by becoming increasingly more vivid or less vivid than the truth, rather than randomly, e.g., by being more vivid than the truth at one moment but less vivid at the next, etc.

27 Lewis Ford in 'Whitehead's Differences from Hartshorne' notes this problem but passes it by as a "tension" in Hartshorne's position. I see it as a contradiction that cannot, like a tension, be retained by means of a mediating principle.

28 Rem Edwards takes the latter position in his 'The Human Self: An Actual Entity or a Society?,' 195–203, but elsewhere he seems to accept Hartshorne's analysis of possibility. John B. Cobb, Jr, in *A Christian Natural Theology*, esp. pp. 155–6 and ch. 5, takes Whitehead's position on possibility but Hartshorne's position on the social nature of God.

29 Because our willings are free and have temporal beginnings, and because we are ignorant and fickle, we sometimes discover that, when a moment of decision comes, we do not will what we had thought we would. If my argument in Chapter 2 is correct, then God can never be ignorant or mistaken about what he will will because he is always willing all that he ever will will. There is no futurity to God's will as far as his deciding it is concerned or as far as his implementing it is concerned. The only futurity to God's will concerns how it is chosen by us into our lives. God's eternal, freely chosen will, as I will argue more fully in Chapter 7, is to provide a state of affairs for us to choose in relation to. Hence, God's purpose is not to achieve something in the future. The future is relevant to us but not to God. God, then, is not without a purpose, but he is without a future-oriented purpose that is significant for himself. What God purposes is fully accomplished in his eternal willing.

30 Readers should see James Keller's 'Continuity, Possibility, and Omniscience: A Contrasting View,' *Process Studies* (forthcoming, 14/3). It is a knowledgeable and valuable critique of an abridged version of this chapter that was published in *Process Studies* in 12/4 (1982), 209–31.

4 GOD, PLENUM, WORLD

1 Historical aspects of the notion of creation *ex nihilo* are pursued more fully in *Creation: The Impact of an Idea*, ed. Daniel O'Connor and Francis Oakley. The

epilogue by Hans Jonas is especially valuable. See also *Schöpfung aus dem Nichts: Die Entstehung der Lehre von der Creatio ex Nihilo* by Gerhard May.

2   The term "basic action" was coined by Arthur Danto. See his articles 'What We Can Do,' *The Journal of Philosophy*, 60 (1963), 435–45, and 'Basic Actions,' *American Philosophical Quarterly*, 2 (1965), 141–8. The term is now common coin, but its explication is a matter of dispute. See, e.g., Alvin I. Goldman's *A Theory of Human Action* (Englewood Cliffs, N.J., Prentice-Hall, Inc., 1970), and A. Baier, 'The Search for Basic Actions,' *American Philosophical Quarterly*, 1971. Roughly, a basic action is an action involving the agent only and that is not causally generated by anything other than the will of the agent; the agent just does it – such as holding one's breath or waving one's hand. Richard Swinburne applies this notion to God in his *The Coherence of Theism*, pp. 102f and 132–8.

3   As can be seen in Chapter 2, I agree with orthodoxy that there are no potentialities of God's will that remain to be actualized; all potentialities yet to be actualized must reside in something distinct from God.

4   Something that exists is not a possibility; it is an actuality, either necessary or contingent. Something which cannot be is not a possibility; it is an impossibility. Something which cannot not be is not a possibility; it is a necessity.

5   My colleague Stephen Schwartz has suggested that the plenum might better be named "the void" or "the plenum-void." I shy from "void" because it suggests emptiness, vacuity, and nothingness, whereas the plenum is exhaustively rich in non-divine possibilities. I shy from "plenum-void" merely because it is an awkward expression, but it does capture well the notion of an infinitely fecund but unfertilized womb of finite being. Perhaps "the void-plenum" does so even better.

6   However, the existence of the plenum does not imply the existence of a world. God needs the plenum in order to be God, but he does not need a world in order to be God. The world, unlike God and the plenum if they exist, is not self-explanatory. The explanation of its existence must lie outside it, and if in God and the plenum, then in both of them and not in just the one or the other. These points will be expanded in Chapter 9.

7   That God is the only conceivable form of omnipotence I will leave unargued here, though it is certainly controversial. As my colleague Stephen Schwartz has pointed out, perhaps several weaker individuals could together have enough power to actualize the entire range of the plenum, so that "in the beginning" were x, y, z (the weaker beings), no God, and the plenum.

8   With regard to God and the plenum, then, I am sympathetic to Whitehead's claim that the fundamental notions of speculative philosophy "presuppose each other so that in isolation they are meaningless" (1951: 5). With regard to two of those fundamental notions, God and eternal objects, Whitehead states that God does not create the eternal objects, "for his nature requires them in the same degree that they require him" (1951: 392). Joseph Donceel makes a similar point by reference to Hegel's principle of universal correlativity: 'Everything is itself by being related to something else' (1979: 166). God, I am arguing, is himself by being related to the plenum, and vice-versa.

9   It does not follow, however, that all possibilities have to become actual. The principle of plenitude violates logic by dictating that what cannot be done will be done (all possibilities will be actualized), and violates God's freedom by dictating that God must actualize all possibilities, thereby making him a slave of the principle of plenitude.

10 The notion of something like the plenum seems implicit in humankind's fascina-

tion with magic. This can be seen clearly in Christopher Marlowe's late-sixteenth-century play, *Doctor Faustus*. At the beginning of the play Faustus has despaired of satisfying his considerable passions by means of ordinary human activities. An angel urges him to go beyond the ordinary: BAD ANGEL: "Go Forward, Faustus, in that famous art [magic] wherein all nature's treasury is contained. Be thou on earth as Jove is in the sky. Lord and commander of these elements." Faustus, sensing the vastness of the control that he would have over the treasury of nature, replies, "How am I glutted with conceit of this! Shall I make spirits fetch me what I please, resolve me of all ambiguities, perform what desperate enterprise I will?" Later it turns out, of course, that his control would be only temporary and not immediate – Mephistophilis being the intermediary who, for a price, would do Faustus' bidding for a while. But during his period of power Faustus rules over nature's treasury like God over the plenum. His will is instantly and perfectly effective. In this respect Faustus is a fascinating example of Jean-Paul Sartre's claim that man is the desire to be God, to rule over the realm of possibility according to his will. See Christopher Marlowe's *Doctor Faustus* and Sartre's *Being and Nothingness*.

11 It seems to me that critics of the argument from contingency to the existence of God are correct that it does not succeed upon the assumption of CEN because something cannot return to absolutely nothing any more than it can come from absolutely nothing. However, if we understand that the argument from contingency refers to the existence of individuals as individuals, and if we predicate it upon the plenum rather than CEN, then, I believe, it succeeds because the existence of contingent individuals presupposes the existence of a necessary individual who is the efficient cause of their existence but who himself exists by virtue of his own essence.

12 Hartshorne makes similar statements in his essay on Santayana, cited in the bibliography to Chapter 3. On 141 he states that the "absolute infinite of the determinable" presupposes that there exists "some substance whose determinability is absolute in its range." My plenum is such an absolutely infinite determinable – though I shrink from calling it a substance. On 167 Hartshorne says, "If the foregoing account of continuity is correct, then pure being is the only essence that is eternal, the continuum of undifferentiated potentiality (the bare power of God) that alone precedes every event whatever." Here Hartshorne has introduced the notion of the necessity of an active power, namely God, relative to "the continuum of undifferentiated potentiality." He is correct that there must be an active and a passive side to pure being. If there were no active side, potentiality would just sit there – indeed for a lack of power that could actualize it, it would not be potentiality. At best we could say that it would have been potentiality had there been something that could actualize it. Similarly if there were no passive side to pure being, the active side would be unable to do anything, making it meaningless to call it active even in the sense of meaning that it had the power to act. At best we could say that it could have been active had there been something that it could have actualized. Apart from the plenum, then, God could not be God, and, apart from God, the plenum could not be a plenum. In Tillich's terminology perhaps we could say that God is the active ground of being and the plenum is the passive ground of being. These reflections should help satisfy the legitimate insistence of Peter Bertocci (1969: 200) and W. Norris Clarke, S.J., that an ultimately dualistic or pluralistic theory of the absolute should make intelligible the affinity of the ultimates for one another. See Clarke's *The Philosophical Approach to God*, 72–4.

13 See also James Felt's 'Impossible Worlds,' 265.

14 Recall Danto's notion of a basic action and see *Three Philosophers* by G. E. M. Anscombe and P. T. Geach, pp. 107–8.

15 Aristotle's other two types of cause are also applicable here. The formal cause of the existence of a contingent individual has roots in both God and the plenum. It exists in the plenum as the possibility of the actualization of that form and it exists in God as his awareness of the possibility of the actualization of that form. The final cause of the existence of a contingent individual is God's reason for actualizing it, perhaps together with the intentions of other free agents, such as parents.

16 For extensive discussion of the concept of matter, see the two volumes *The Concept of Matter in Greek and Medieval Philosophy* and *The Concept of Matter in Modern Philosophy*, edited by Ernan McMullin. See also Barrington Jones' 'Aristotle's Introduction of Matter.' According to Jones, Aristotle's concept of matter is "a purely 'formal' notion." That is, "matter" is a relational term rather than a natural kind term. The matter of something is that (whatever it might be) from which the something has come to be. Stone is the matter of a certain statue; an embryo is the matter of a human; and so on. Hence, there may be no single stuff of which all physical objects are constituted, and it may be that every physical object is *outcome* relative to something that precedes it (which something would be its matter) and *matter* relative to some physical object that will succeed it. In this sense the plenum is prime matter, i.e., that which is not individual but is pure potentiality for the emergence of individuals, their properties, and relations. I thank Lewis Ford for bringing this article to my attention.

17 For a valuable explanation of the concept of natural kinds see Stephen P. Schwartz's introduction to his anthology of papers by leading thinkers on this and related topics: *Naming, Necessity, and Natural Kinds*.

18 See G. E. M. Anscombe's analysis of Aristotle's concept of matter in *Three Philosophers*, 52–3. She says that according to Aristotle the concept of prime matter is intelligible, yet we cannot in the ordinary way say what prime matter is because the ordinary way of saying what a thing is is to state its form, but prime matter is that which has no form of its own. It is, rather, the pure capacity for forms, "the capacity of being now of this, now of that substantial kind."

19 If we use the term "exist" to refer to things that stand out from the plenum, i.e., that exist contingently, then it follows that God does not exist even if he is real; it follows also that the plenum does not exist even if it is real. God does not stand out from the plenum; he stands over against the plenum. The plenum does not stand out from God; it stands over against God; but it does not stand over against God in a limiting way; it stands over against God in a complementary way, as the convex side of a curve stands over against the concave side.

20 I would like to thank my student, Erik Wikstrom, for causing me to see that the biblical "without form and void" is relative in meaning, not absolute.

5 DIVINE IMPASSIBILITY IN KNOWLEDGE

1 Thomas Aquinas, *Introduction to Thomas Aquinas*, trans. Anton C. Pegis, New York, Modern Library, 1948, pp. 134–5. *Summa Theologiae* 1a. q. 14, a.5.

2 In this regard see George Berkeley's *Principles of Human Knowledge*, par. 16 of "Introduction" and par. 126 of "Principles."

3 Norman Kretzmann has argued recently that careful analysis shows that from Aquinas' two principles that "God is goodness itself, and goodness is *essentially* ...

diffusion of itself and being" that necessarily God creates a world. This is a startling, intriguing point, but I believe that if Aquinas had been confronted with it he would have modified or rejected the second principle, viz., the Dionysian principle, in favor of God retaining his freedom to create or not create a world. See Kretzmann's 'Goodness, Knowledge, and Indeterminancy in the Philosophy of Thomas Aquinas,' 631–49.

4   Lewis Ford has developed the second point very effectively in *Two Process Philosophers*, pp. 62–3. It is also assumed and developed by James Keller in his 'Continuity, Possibility, and Omniscience: A Contrasting View.'

5   For criticism of Hartshorne's theory of logical possibility and its relation to God, see Henry L. Ruf, 'The Impossibility of Hartshorne's God,' 345–63, and R. L. Purtill's 'Ontological Modalities,' 306–7, and 'Hartshorne's Modal Proof,' *The Journal of Philosophy* (1966), 408. My reply to Ruf, and perhaps Purtill, would proceed from points made in the paragraph above.

6   That God's knowledge of free creaturely actions is passive is sensitively considered and acknowledged by William J. Hill, O.P., in his 'Does the World Make a Difference to God?,' 146–64. Hill insists, correctly, I believe, that this passivity in God's knowledge entails no diminution of the powers or integrity of God's nature. Soon I shall argue that from the *passiveness* of God's knowledge of free creatures we can infer the possibility of the divine nature in this respect, i.e., God's knowledge of free creatures is not only passive but is also subject to change. Hill, assuming the concept of divine eternality, does not go so far.

7   I am quite sympathetic to Nicholas Wolterstorff's argument for this kind of position in his 'God Everlasting,' esp. secs. II–III. This is, I believe, the tack that Geach must take to resolve the structural stress pointed out in *God and the Soul*, 93, and *Providence and Evil*, 57 – though it is a tack that can be taken only at the price of acknowledging that God's knowledge is not entirely unchangeable.

8   See selections from Edwards' *Freedom of the Will* in *Jonathan Edwards* (1962). Anthony Kenny's 'Divine Foreknowledge and Human Freedom' is an excellent source from which to become familiar with much of the terminology used in contemporary discussions of divine foreknowledge. See his *Aquinas: A Collection of Critical Essays*, 255–70.

9   For expositions and analyses of Molina and middle knowledge, see John A. Mourant, 'Scientia Media and Molinism,' pp. 338–9; Robert Adams, 'Middle Knowledge and the Problem of Evil,' 109–17; Anthony Kenny, *The God of the Philosophers*, pp. 62–71; and James W. Felt, S.J., 'Impossible Worlds,' esp. 260–1.

10 Alvin Plantinga explicates this notion in his *God, Freedom, and Evil* and *The Nature of Necessity*.

11 See Alfred J. Freddoso, 'Accidental Necessity and Logical Determinism,' 257–78. In this article Freddoso's objective is to undermine logical determinism by developing a middle knowledge position based on Ockham rather than Molina. I do not believe that his position succeeds, nor that such a position can be used, as he suggests at the end of his article, to reconcile divine foreknowledge and human freedom. The crucial point that Freddoso fails to see – a point that I shall develop in the text – is that, when the actual world includes free agents, the possible world of which it is the actualization cannot be decided unilaterally by God. It is decided cooperatively by God eternally (as described in Chapter 2) and by free creatures temporally, i.e., at each moment. Hence, which actions *will* be performed by free creatures cannot be known, not even by God.

12 J. R. Lucas and Richard Swinburne have tried to escape the problem by saying that

God *could* foreknow the future but refrains from doing so in order that we might be free. I agree with Anthony Kenny that this strategy does not work. It is like saying, "If God peeks at what we will do, we will not be free to do it or not do it, whereas if he does not peek, we will be free." But if God *could* peek, then there must be something to peek at, i.e., something that I will do. But, if there is already something that I will do, then whether God knows what it is or not is irrelevant to whether it will be done – and so we would still have the issue of logical determinism to deal with. See Lucas' *Freedom of the Will*, ch. 14, Swinburne's *The Coherence of Theism*, 174–8 and 289, and Kenny's *The God of the Philosophers*, 60–1. Freddoso's article, cited above, is a valuable explication of the problem of logical determinism.

13 For a similar but briefer statement of the nature of eternity that has the additional value, for our purposes, of being developed in the context of a Thomistic analysis of process philosophy, see W. Norris Clarke, S.J., *The Philosophical Approach to God*, 94–6.

14 My position is similar to that of Peter Geach in his 'Some Problems About Time,' esp. pp. 311–12. There Geach rejects the triadic understanding of simultaneity and points out that basic analysis of the notion of simultaneity belongs to logic, not physics.

15 Peter Geach provides such a proof in 'Some Problems About Time,' 305–6, and *God and the Soul*, xvi and 92. See also *Providence and Evil*, 42–3.

16 If Geach's analogy of God-as-chess-master is not meant to imply that God knows our every move because he can and does ensure that we will will as he wills us to, even though we are free, but only that no matter how we will we can neither surprise, baffle, nor defeat him, then I do not disagree with Geach. He seems, however, to be taking the stronger position.

17 I do not believe that every individual must be free; it seems conceivable that there could be a creature whose changes were completely under the control of the will of God, and that God could create such a creature, but I will not take up this issue here.

18 Some say that a parallel analysis reveals that either God's decision-making must be temporal or it is not free. I hope to take up this issue elsewhere.

6 GOD, TIME AND ETERNITY

1 The mistake that I believe Boethian-eternalists make is to treat eternality not only as the mode of God's existence and will, but also as the mode of all of his knowledge.

2 See Aquinas' *Summa Theologiae*, 1a.13.7; *Summa Contra Gentiles* II.11–14; *On Truth* IV.5.

7 DIVINE IMPASSIBILITY IN FEELING

1 This is a statement that I have seen attributed to St Bonaventura, but without a specific citation. My research indicates that it is probably a mistaken attribution.

2 If God did have to suffer infinitely in order to be worthy of worship, I would think that, like the man who had been tarred and feathered and was being carried out of town on a rail, he would, if asked, "Well, how do you feel now?", reply, "If it weren't for the honor, I would just as soon have missed the occasion."

3 Whether God can know everything about himself is a question that I explore in 'Can God Know That He Is God?,' 195–201.

4 This is Hartshorne's explicit position, but it is not strictly true that the only source

of suffering to Hartshorne's God is the world. As a good Buddhist would point out, it is God's caring about the world that causes him to suffer in response to it. If God did not care about the world, it could not cause him to suffer. Hence, an aspect of God's essence is a contributory cause of his suffering.

8   EVIL, MORALITY, REDEMPTION

1   I will not in this book review Hartshorne's arguments against the possibility of everlasting life for humans, nor will I argue for that possibility. Obviously, though, this is an issue that I need to address.

2   See Schopenhauer's essay 'On the Vanity and Suffering of Life,' in his *The World as Will and Idea*, Book v, supplements. An English source is cited in my bibliography. Richard Swinburne provides valuable reflections in *The Existence of God* on the problem of the quantity of evil, which he calls "the crux of the problem of evil" (218–21, 223–4).

3   For statements of Hick's universalist position see his *Death and Eternal Life*, 250–9, *The Center of Christianity*, 89–90, and *God and the Universe of Faiths*, 70–3.

4   I am sympathetic to many of Richard Swinburne's ideas as to why people do or do not go to heaven. See his *Faith and Reason*, 134–5, and ch. 6. For perceptive, imaginative reflections on hell, see Peter Geach's *Providence and Evil*, 123–49. Geach, as do Swinburne and I, rejects Hick's universalism.

5   I first employed this Thomistic distinction between the intensive and the extensive aspects of happiness in a paper titled 'Happiness and Resurrection: A Reply to Morreall.' W. Norris Clarke, S. J., seems to be making a similar distinction in *The Philosophical Approach to God*, 98. By contrast, James Felt, S. J., proposes that God freely diversifies the intensity of his feelings for different people (Felt 1974: 259–61). Hence, he accepts a theological version of the second form of passibility cited in *The Oxford Dictionary of the Christian Church* (1974: 694).

6   Peter Geach expresses similar sentiments in *Providence and Evil*, 124 – sentiments that are quite the opposite of Hartshorne's.

7   Richard Swinburne says there is good reason "to maintain that not all fates are sealed at death. Some persons may have the opportunity in some further world to work out further their ultimate destiny" (1981: 169). John Hick's universalism obviously requires such an opportunity until everyone is saved (1976: 250–9; 1978: 88–90).

8   Bruce Reichenbach in his article 'Natural Evils and Natural Laws: A Theodicy for Natural Evils,' argues, successfully I believe, that it is impossible to prove on the basis of experience that ours is not an unsurpassably good world. G. W. Leibniz makes this point in his *Theodicy*, par. 194.

9   John Hick claims that "no theodicy is possible" if personal consciousness is obliterated forever at death (1978: 89). Given the history of human suffering, I agree. Hence, from the tragedies of this life grows the confidence of the classical theist that, if there is a God, then there is life after death.

10   For an explanation of the italicized terms and several others of relevance, see Roderick M. Chisholm's 1969 presidential address, 'The Defeat of Good and Evil.' The points I am making by means of Chisholm's concepts may not be points to which he would agree.

11   My colleague Stephen Schwartz has pointed out that the innocent, involuntary suffering of those who reject the kingdom of God would not be redeemed. That

seems correct, but because it would be the free choice of those very individuals that their suffering not be redeemed in the only way it could be, viz., in the kingdom of God, that state of affairs would not seem to be a good reason to fault God morally.

12 St John expressed a related sentiment when he said in 1 John 4.20, "...he who does not love his brother whom he has seen, cannot love God whom he has not seen."

13 Parenthetically, the tragedy of the cross was not the tragedy of God suffering. It was the tragedy of a man suffering – a man who was tender and compassionate, whose concern was for the sick, the weak, the downcast and the outcast – a man who in no way deserved the pain and abuse that were inflicted upon him. If that man was also God, that does not deepen the tragedy of the cross. Rather, it saves it from being an absolute tragedy.

14 There may be physical reasons why it is not possible for a human to avoid emotional disturbance altogether in an emergency situation. If so, that does not entail that such disturbance is unavoidable on the part of God.

15 All that I have said in the paragraph above is not enough to satisfy some people. My wife, Diane, has pointed out that sometimes what most helps people in grief is for their friends to cry with them. Reverend Douglas Greene insists, in the tradition of Gregory of Thaumaturgus, that though we cannot *make* God suffer, he can *choose* to suffer with us. Michael Slusser has said in correspondence that, "The nub of the matter for Christians is whether impassibility excludes voluntary passibility," i.e., voluntary passibility in feeling. If God can choose to suffer, perhaps out of love he does choose to suffer with those who need him to do so.

16 See *The Teachings of the Compassionate Buddha*, ed. E. A. Burtt (New York, Mentor, 1955), 43–6; *Apology* by Plato, 35e–42a; The Gospel according to Luke 23.34.

   Those who say, "But Jesus did despair on the cross. He asked God, 'Why have you forsaken me?',", should read the triumphant remainder of the psalm of which those words are the opening statement – Psalm 22. If Jesus had been really despairing, as, for example, Lewis Ford claims in *The Lure of God*, I believe he would have been more original in his expression of that fact rather than citing the opening words of a psalm the remainder of which every good Jew would know. With the little strength he had Jesus prayed for forgiveness for his executioners, put his mother into the care of one of his disciples, comforted a dying thief, and by citing the opening words of Psalm 22 pointed his disciples toward a perspective-inducing song that begins with the grief they were feeling but ends on notes of triumph and majesty.

9 WHY DOES GOD CREATE?

1 E. L. Mascall has worded this point nicely: "...since the act of creation does not confer any benefits upon beings who already exist but gives them their very existence, if God had not created finite beings there would be no finite beings to suffer from not being created" (1949: 126–7). See Richard Swinburne's expression of this point in his 1979: 130–1, and recall Hartshorne's repudiation of Whitehead's sentiment that possibilities haunt reality, begging for instantiation (1970: 59).

2 Norman Kretzmann has argued recently that Thomas Aquinas' position entails divine creation of a world because of its assumption of the Dionysian principle that good is necessarily diffusive of itself and of being (Kretzmann 1983: 631–41).

3 According to Peter Geach, Aquinas also held this position, at least about contingently existing individuals (Geach 1961: 70–1).

4   According to Lewis Ford, Whitehead, as distinguished from Hartshorne, took a position similar to the one I am developing here. "Unlike Hartshorne," Ford writes, "Whitehead assumes that alternative metaphysical structures are consistently conceivable, for he insists that we must look to experience to discover which one is in fact actual. If so, God could have created an alternative metaphysical structure, including one whereby his own act of existence would completely exhaust all creativity, permitting him to exist in his solitary splendor. In this sense God is free to create or not to create the world" (Ford: 1977: 184–5; also 1970: 148).

5   I say "arbitrary, within limits" because later I will argue against Leibniz that, if God chooses to create a world, he will create a best possible world, but there are an infinite number of these best possible worlds among which he must choose arbitrarily.

6   Richard Swinburne develops this point nicely in *The Coherence of Theism*, 141–6, and *The Existence of God*, 152–4. In *Coherence*, 145–8, and *Existence*, 154–60, he reflects on why God creates animals and men.

7   Aristotle said it well in his *Eudemian Ethics* 1245^{b}19: "... with us welfare involves a something beyond us, but the deity is his own well-being." See *The Works of Aristotle Translated into English*, ed. W. D. Ross (12 vols., Oxford, Oxford University Press, 1915). vol. IX.

8   Thomas Aquinas says basically the same thing in his *Summa Contra Gentiles* 1.93.7. There he says that God's creation of the world is "an act of liberality" which is done "not for the sake of some benefit expected from the giving, but because of the goodness and befittingness of the giving." However, if Norman Kretzmann is correct that Aquinas accepts the Dionysian principle, and therefore believes in a God who must create a world, then the notions of liberality and magnanimity cease to tell us why such a God creates the world; they tell us only how he creates it, viz., bountifully and multifariously.

10   CREATION AND FREEDOM

1   Aquinas adds valuable illustrations to this distinction in 1964: 1a.14.8. The translations in the paragraph above are by Norman Kretzmann.

2   The quoted material consists of Anthony Kenny's paraphrases of Luis de Molina's conception of two of God's three types of knowledge – the third type being God's "free knowledge," i.e., "his knowledge of what will actually happen after the free divine decision has been taken to create certain free creatures and to place them in certain circumstances" (Kenny 1979: 62). For reasons stated in the fourth paragraph of this chapter, I believe this three-part distinction of God's knowledge is an improvement over Aquinas' two-part distinction.

3   It is interesting to note that on this analysis the actual occurrence of a free human action is doubly contingent. It is contingent in the first place because the human agent could have chosen not to perform that action. It is contingent in the second place because God could have chosen not to actualize any world in which the agent freely performs that action. Hence, both the human and God have to will freely the occurrence of that action in order for it to come to pass.

I, too, believe that free human actions are doubly contingent, but because I also believe that God cannot know our future free actions, I hold that a human free action will not be contingent upon God having willed *it*; rather, it will be contingent upon God having willed freely a world in which that action could be freely chosen.

4   Readers should consult Peter Geach's defense of *scientia dei, causa rerum*
    (1972: 324–7; 1977: 57, 141), and Anthony Kenny's criticism of it (1979: 34, 36,
    62–71). Having said much on this topic already, I will resist the urge to present and
    examine what Geach and Kenny say.

5   Whitehead's theory to this effect is reminiscent of Frederick Hoyle's continuous-
    creation-of-the-universe theory according to which new molecules of hydrogen are
    inexplicably continuously popping into existence, thereby causing the continuous
    expansion of the universe. See the first edition of Hoyle's *The Nature of the
    Universe* (New York, Harper and Brothers, 1950).

6   Victor Lowe makes this point in his 1951: 408. John Stacer, S. J. elaborates the
    point in his 1981: 362 and 372.

7   Lewis Ford suggests that, if God creates us *ex nihilo*, then we in relation to God
    would be analogous to the figments of our imagination relative to our minds
    (1977: 187). This is a tempting analogy that I used before finding it in Ford, but I
    now believe it is too problematic for use without considerable qualification. It
    points out correctly one relation of man to God, viz., man can no more exist apart
    from God than the contents of our imaginations can exist apart from our thinking
    them, but Ford's more important point is that, if we were figments of God's
    imagination, we could not be free because we would in every respect be entirely a
    creation of God's. I see the point but I balk at the analogy because, at least in my
    own case and apparently that of James Thurber, the figments of human imagin-
    ation form and perform independently of conscious control to a considerable
    extent.

8   I examine Sartre's position at more length in my article, 'Atheism and Freedom'.

9   Ford and Sartre seem to agree to this without realizing it. For Sartre man is the will
    to be God; for Ford man is a self-creator. Are these not essences?

10 A popular saying states: "What you are is God's gift to you. What you make of
    yourself is your gift to God." Process philosophers are very fond of the idea in the
    second sentence, but, I have argued, they have an insufficient appreciation of the
    idea in the first sentence. I am happy to add, however, that my conception of divine
    creation and human freedom is richly complemented in some ways by the process
    conception of the objectives and methods of God's presence in history.

11   HOW TO CREATE THE BEST POSSIBLE WORLD

1   Peter Geach also has affirmed that the notion of the best possible world is
    incoherent. He was convinced of this by James McTaggart. See Geach's *Provi-
    dence and Evil*, 125–6, and *Virtues*, 98.
        Norman Kretzmann argues that this point can be found also in Aquinas. See
    Kretzmann's 1983: 638–41 and Aquinas' 1964: 1a.25.6.3. Anthony Kenny pro-
    vides a similar analysis of Aquinas in Kenny 1979: 113–15. Kenny and Kretzmann
    seem correct in their exposition of Aquinas' position. I will not respond here to
    what they and Aquinas say about this issue, but by the end of the chapter it should
    be fairly clear what I would say.

2   Kretzmann, on behalf of Aquinas, calls this an "optimally composed" world,
    relative to its inhabitants, and adds that necessarily God must create an optimally
    composed world (1983: 640–1).
        Anthony Kenny also notes this distinction in Aquinas, viz., whichever world
    God creates, *it* could not have been made better, but whichever world God creates,
    God could have created a better one than that (1979: 113–15).

3   Michael Sean Quinn also argues that, if God creates a world, he will create the best possible world. Quinn, however, seems to make this a matter of moral obligation on the part of a perfect moral agent, viz., God. I, too, believe that if God creates a world he will create an unsurpassably good world, but, as I have argued, I do not believe that he has a moral obligation to do so. I believe he will do so because of his personal excellence (Quinn 1973: 2–8).

4   Richard Swinburne develops this point nicely in *Faith and Reason*, 170–1.

5   Peter Abelard insisted that God is bound by his goodness to do what is best and therefore could not do otherwise than he has done. For this he was condemned at the Council of Sens (1140). I believe he was correct that, because of God's goodness, God will do only what is best. Unfortunately Abelard did not see that what is best, i.e., unsurpassably good, might take various forms, thereby leaving God freedom of choice among unsurpassable contraries (Kenny 1979: 9).

6   Richard Swinburne depicts heaven in a similar way in *Faith and Reason*, 135.

7   See, for example, Exodus 20.8–17; Micah 6.6–8; Amos 5.11–24; Matthew 25.31–46; 1 John 4.20–1. An eloquent development of the idea that we choose for or against God by how we relate to other people can be found in Arthur C. McGill's *Suffering: A Test of Theological Method*.

8   Augustine develops a related point in *The City of God*, bk. XXII, ch. 30. There he states that, because it is the City of God, every citizen will be perfectly happy, but because of different degrees of merit resulting from their earthly lives some individuals will enjoy a clearer, fuller vision of God. Still, no one will be jealous of anyone else's happiness or in any way discontent with his own state of bliss. Note that in Augustine's vision of the city of God creaturely happiness is static objectively as well as subjectively.

9   I do not mean to suggest that all enjoyments in the kingdom of God will be passive. Participation in the actualization of good can itself be experienced as good, even though the participation be at the expense of considerable voluntary exertion and even pain.

Bibliographies

1 THE ISSUE OF DIVINE IMPASSIBILITY

Abramowski, Luise. 'Die Schrift Gregors des Lehrers "Ad Theopompum" und Philoxenus von Mabbug,' *Zeitschrift für Kirchengeschichte*, 89 (1978), 273–90.

Bache, Christopher M. 'The Logic of Religious Metaphor,' Providence, Rhode Island, Brown University, 1978.

Bertocci, Peter. *Introduction to Philosophy of Religion*, New York, Prentice–Hall, 1951, ch. 18.

'The Person God Is,' in *Talk of God*, Royal Institute of Philosophy Lectures, vol. II, London, Macmillan, 1969, pp. 185–206.

Brasnett, Bertrand. *The Suffering of the Impassible God*, London, Society for Promoting Christian Knowledge, 1928.

Cross, F. L., and Livingston, E. A., eds. *The Oxford Dictionary of the Christian Church*, 2nd edn, Oxford, Oxford University Press, 1974, p. 694.

Edwards, Rem B. 'The Pagan Dogma of the Absolute Unchangeableness of God,' *Religious Studies*, 14 (1978), 305–13.

Elert, Werner. 'Die Theopaschitische Formel,' *Theologische Literaturzeitung*, 75 (1950), 195–206.

Der Ausgang der altkirchlichen Christologie, Berlin, Lutherisches Verlagshaus, 1957.

Franks, Robert S. 'Passibility and Impassibility,' in *The Encyclopedia of Religion and Ethics*, ed. James Hastings, New York, Charles Scribner's Sons, 1951, vol. IX, pp. 658–9.

Grant, Robert M. *The Early Christian Doctrine of God*, Charlottesville, University of Virginia, 1966.

Gregory of Thaumaturgus. 'Die Schrift an Theopompus über die Leidensunfähigkeit und Leidensfähigkeit Gottes,' in *Gregorius Thaumaturgus: Sein Leben und seine Schriften*, trans. Victor Ryssel, Leipzig, Verlage von L. Fernau, 1880, pp. 71–99. Ryssel's seems to be the only translation of this 3rd-century essay into a modern language from the original Syriac, though there is a Latin translation, 'Ad Theopompum: De Passibili et Impassibili in Deo,' by J. P. Paulinus Martinus in *Analecta sacra spicilegio solesmensi parata*, ed. J. B. Pitra (8 vols., Farnborough, England, Gregg Press, 1966), vol. IV, pp. 363–76. A detailed summary has been published in French by Henry Crouzel: 'La Passion de l'Impassible,' in *L'Homme devant Dieu. Mélanges offerts au Père Henri de Lubac*, Paris, Aubier, 1963, vol. I, pp. 269–79.

Hartshorne, Charles. *Man's Vision of God*, New York, Harper and Row, 1941.

The Divine Relativity, New Haven, Yale University, 1948.

The Logic of Perfection, LaSalle, Ill., Open Court, 1962.

A Natural Theology for Our Time, LaSalle, Ill., Open Court, 1967.

Hartshorne, Charles, and Reese, William L. *Philosophers Speak of God*, Chicago, University of Chicago Press, 1953.

Henry, Carl F. H. *God, Revelation and Authority*, 6 vols., Waco, Texas, Word Books, 1982, vol. v.

Hügel, Baron Friedrich von. 'Suffering and God,' in *Essays and Addresses in the Philosophy of Religion*, Second Series, London, J. M. Dent and Son, 1926.

Idziak, Janine M. 'God and Emotions,' Ann Arbor, Michigan, University of Michigan, 1975.

Lee, Jung Y. *God Suffers For Us: A Systematic Inquiry into a Concept of Divine Passibility*, Hinfam, Mass., Martinus Nijhoff, 1974.

Mozley, J. K. *The Impassible God*, Cambridge, Cambridge University Press, 1926.

Noro, Yoshio. 'Impassibilitas Dei,' Th.D. Thesis, Union Seminary, New York, 1955.

Ottolander, P. Den. *Deus Immutabilis*, N.V., Van Gorcum, 1965.

Owen, H. P. 'God, Concepts of,' in *The Encyclopedia of Philosophy*, 8 vols., ed. Paul Edwards, London, Collier Macmillan, 1967, vol. iii, pp. 344–8.

Concepts of Deity, New York, Herder and Herder, 1971.

Prestige, G. L. *God in Patristic Thought*, London, Society for Promoting Christian Knowledge, 1952.

Russell, John T. 'The Doctrine of Divine Impassibility in Modern Thought, 1926–1963,' Sewanee, Tennessee, The University of the South, 1964.

Slusser, Michael. 'Theopaschite Expressions in Second-Century Christianity as Reflected in the Writings of Justin, Melito, Celsus and Irenaeus,' Oxford, Oxford University Press, 1975.

'Docetism: A Historical Definition,' *The Second Century*, 1/3 (Fall 1981), 163–72.

2 DIVINE IMPASSIBILITY IN NATURE AND WILL

Aquinas, Thomas. *Summa Theologiae*, 60 vols., Cambridge, Blackfriars, 1964.

Summa Contra Gentiles, 4 vols., trans. Anton C. Pegis, F.R.S.C., Notre Dame, Ind., University of Notre Dame, 1975.

Augustine. *The Trinity*, The Fathers of the Church, vol. xlv, trans. Stephen McKenna, C.SS.R, Washington, D.C., Catholic University of America, 1963.

Brasnett, Bertrand. *The Suffering of the Impassible God*, London, Society for Promoting Christian Knowledge, 1928.

Coburn, Robert C. 'Professor Malcolm on God,' *Australasian Journal of Philosophy*, 40–1 (1962–3), 143–62. The notion of God-as-person is rejected in section 15 as incoherent.

Geach, Peter T. *God and the Soul*, London, Routledge and Kegan Paul, 1969.

'God's Relation to the World,' in *Logic Matters*, Berkeley, University of California, 1972, pp. 318–27.

Providence and Evil, Cambridge, Cambridge University Press, 1977.

Grant, Robert M. *The Early Christian Doctrine of God*, Charlottesville, University of Virginia, 1966, pp. 14–33 and 111–14.

Hartshorne, Charles. *Beyond Humanism*, Lincoln, University of Nebraska, 1968; originally published 1937; chs. 8, 9, and 16.

Man's Vision of God, New York, Harper and Row, 1941.

'Santayana's Doctrine of Essence,' in *The Philosophy of George Santayana*, ed. Paul Schilpp, New York, Tudor, 1951, pp. 135–82.

Anselm's Discovery, LaSalle, Ill., Open Court, 1965.

A Natural Theology for Our Time, LaSalle, Ill., Open Court, 1967.

Creative Synthesis and Philosophic Method, LaSalle, Ill., Open Court, 1970.

Reality as Social Process, New York, Hafner, 1971.

Henry, Carl F. H. *God, Revelation and Authority*, 6 vols., Waco, Texas, Word Books, 1982, vol. v.

Keller, James A. 'Some Basic Differences Between Classical and Process Metaphysics and Their Implications for the Concept of God,' *International Philosophical Quarterly*, 22/1 (March 1982), 3–20.

Kenny, Anthony. *The God of the Philosophers*, Oxford, The Clarendon Press, 1979.

Kneale, William and Martha. *The Development of Logic*, Oxford, The Clarendon Press, 1962.

Lee, Jung Y. *God Suffers For Us: A Systematic Inquiry into a Concept of Divine Passibility*, Hinfam, Mass., Martinus Nijhoff, 1974.

Morris, Thomas V. 'Properties, Modalities, and God,' *The Philosophical Review*, 93/1 (Jan. 1984), 35–55.

Mozley, J. K. *The Impassible God*, Cambridge, Cambridge University Press, 1926.

Mühlen, Heribert. *Die Veränderlichkeit Gottes als Horizont einer zukünftigen Christologie*, Munster, Aschendorff, 1969.

Owen, H. P. *Concepts of Deity*, New York, Herder and Herder, 1971.

Pike, Nelson. *God and Timelessness*, New York, Schocken, 1970.

Smith, T. P. 'On the Applicability of a Criterion of Change,' *Ratio*, 15 (1973), 325–33.

Swinburne, Richard. *The Coherence of Theism*, Oxford, The Clarendon Press, 1977.
The Existence of God, Oxford, The Clarendon Press, 1979.

3 CONTINUITY, POSSIBILITY, AND OMNISCIENCE

Aquinas, Thomas. *Summa Theologiae*, 60 vols., Cambridge, Blackfriars, 1964, 1a.14.9.
Summa Contra Gentiles, 4 vols., trans. Anton C. Pegis, F.R.S.C., Notre Dame, Ind., University of Notre Dame, 1975, secs. 1.50.7–9; 1.51.1; 1.54.5.

Bergson, Henri. *The Creative Mind*, Totowa, N.J., Littlefield, Adams, and Co., 1965, pp. 17–26 and 91–106.

Berkeley, George. *Three Dialogues*, ed. Robert M. Adams, Indianapolis, Ind., Hackett, 1979.

Blanshard, Brand. *The Nature of Thought*, 2 vols., London, George Allen and Unwin, 1939, vol. i, ch. 17.
Reason and Analysis, LaSalle, Ill., Open Court, 1964, ch. 9.

Cobb, John B., Jr. *A Christian Natural Theology*, Philadelphia, Westminster, 1965.

Edwards, Rem. B. 'The Human Self: An Actual Entity or a Society?', *Process Studies*, 5 (Fall 1975), 195–203.

Felt, James W., S.J., 'Impossible Worlds,' *International Philosophical Quarterly*, 23/3 (Sept. 1983), 251–65.
'God's Choice,' *Faith and Philosophy*, 1 (1984: forthcoming issue 3 or 4).

Ford, Lewis, S. 'Whitehead's Differences from Hartshorne,' in *Two Process Philosophers*, American Academy Studies in Religion, No. 5, ed. Lewis S. Ford, Missoula, Montana, 1973, pp. 58–83.
'God Infinite? A Process Perspective,' *The Thomist*, 42/1 (June 1978), 10–13.

Griffin, David R. 'Hartshorne's Differences from Whitehead,' in *Two Process Philosophers*, American Academy Studies in Religion, No. 5, ed. Lewis S. Ford, Missoula, Montana, 1973, 35–57.

Hartshorne, Charles. *Man's Vision of God*, New York, Harper and Row, 1941.
'Santayana's Doctrine of Essence,' in *The Philosophy of George Santayana*, ed. Paul Schilpp, New York, Tudor, 1951, pp. 135–82.
Anselm's Discovery, LaSalle, Ill., Open Court, 1965.

'The God of Religion and the God of Philosophy,' in *Talk of God*, Royal Institute of Philosophy Lectures, vol. II, London, Macmillan, 1969, pp. 152–67.

Creative Synthesis and Philosophic Method, LaSalle, Ill., Open Court, 1970.

Whitehead's Philosophy: Selected Essays, 1935–70, Lincoln, University of Nebraska, 1972.

'A Revision of Peirce's Categories,' *The Monist*, 63/3 (July 1980), 276–89.

'A letter to the author,' December 16, 1980.

Keller, James A. 'Continuity, Possibility, and Omniscience: A Contrasting View,' *Process Studies* (forthcoming, 14/3).

Morreall, John. 'Hume's Missing Shade of Blue,' *Philosophy and Phenomenological Research*, 42/3 (March 1982), 407–15.

Peirce, Charles S. *Collected Papers of Charles Sanders Peirce*, 6 vols., ed. Charles Hartshorne and Paul Weiss, Cambridge, Mass., Harvard University, 1960.

Peters, Eugene H. 'Hartshorne on Actuality,' *Process Studies*, 7/3 (Fall 1977), 200–4.

Plantinga, Alvin. *The Nature of Necessity*, Oxford, The Clarendon Press, 1974, ch. 8.

Sherburne, Donald W. *A Key to Whitehead's 'Process and Reality,'* New York, Macmillan, 1966.

Vitali, Theodore R., C.P. 'The Peirceian Influence on Hartshorne's Subjectivism,' *Process Studies*, 7/4 (Winter 1977), 238–49.

Weiss, Phil. 'Possibility: Three Recent Ontologies,' *International Philosophical Quarterly*, 20/2 (June 1980), 199–219.

Whitehead, Alfred N. *Process and Reality*, New York, Harper and Brothers, 1957. See also the corrected edition, ed. David Ray Griffin and Donald W. Sherburne, New York, Free Press, 1978.

Whitney, Barry L. 'Process Theism: Does a Persuasive God Coerce?', *Southern Journal of Philosophy*, 17 (1979), 133–43.

'Does God Influence the World's Creativity? Hartshorne's Doctrine of Possibility,' *Philosophy Research Archives*, vol. VII, microfiche 7 (July 1981), E8 to F3.

4. GOD, PLENUM, WORLD

Anscombe, G. E. M. 'Aristotle,' in *Three Philosophers* by G. E. M. Anscombe and P. T. Geach, Ithaca, New York, Cornell University, 1961, pp. 3–63.

Aquinas, Thomas. *Summa Contra Gentiles*, 4 vols., trans. Anton C. Pegis, F.R.S.C., Notre Dame, Ind., University of Notre Dame, 1975, I.43.6 and II.16.3 and 9.

Bertocci, Peter. *Introduction to Philosophy of Religion*, New York, Prentice-Hall, 1951, ch. 18.

'The Person God Is,' in *Talk of God*, Royal Institute of Philosophy Lectures, vol. II, London, Macmillan, 1969, pp. 185–206.

Clarke, W. Norris, S.J. *The Philosophical Approach to God*, Winston-Salem, N.C., Wake Forest University, 1979, pp. 66–109. Clarke's footnotes on pp. 105–9 are rich in good references.

Donceel, Joseph. *The Searching Mind*, Notre Dame, Ind., University of Notre Dame, 1979.

Felt, James W., S.J. 'Impossible Worlds,' *International Philosophical Quarterly*, 23/3 (Sept. 1983), 251–65.

Geach, Peter T. 'Aquinas,' in *Three Philosophers* by G. E. M. Anscombe and P. T. Geach, Ithaca, New York, Cornell University, 1961, pp. 67–125.

'Causality and Creation,' *Sophia*, 1/1 (April 1962), 1–8.

Gilkey, Langdon. *Maker of Heaven and Earth*, Garden City, New York, Doubleday, 1959.

Jonas, Hans. 'Jewish and Christian Elements in the Western Philosophical Tradition,' in *Creation: The Impact of An Idea*, ed. Daniel O'Connor and Francis Oakley, New York, Charles Scribner's Sons, 1969, pp. 241–58.

Jones, Barrington. 'Aristotle's Introduction of Matter,' *The Philosophical Review*, 83/4 (Oct. 1974), 474–500.

Marlowe, Christopher. *Christopher Marlowe's Doctor Faustus*, ed. Irving Ribner, New York, Odyssey Press, 1966.

Mascall, E. L. *Existence and Analogy*, New York, Longmans, Green and Co., 1949.

May, Gerhard. *Schöpfung aus dem Nichts: Die Entstehung der Lehre von der Creatio ex Nihilo*, Berlin, Walter de Gruyter, 1978.

McMullin, Ernan, ed. *The Concept of Matter in Greek and Medieval Philosophy*, Notre Dame, Ind., University of Notre Dame, 1965.

The Concept of Matter in Modern Philosophy, Notre Dame, Ind., University of Notre Dame, c.1978.

Plantinga, Alvin. *Does God Have a Nature?*, Milwaukee, Wisc., Marquette University, 1980.

Sartre, Jean-Paul. *Being and Nothingness*, trans. Hazel E. Barnes, New York, Washington Square, 1966, pt. 2, ch. 1.

Schwartz, Stephen P., ed. *Naming, Necessity, and Natural Kinds*, Ithaca, New York, Cornell University, 1977.

Swinburne, Richard. *The Coherence of Theism*, Oxford, The Clarendon Press, 1977.

The Existence of God, Oxford, The Clarendon Press, 1979.

Tillich, Paul. *Systematic Theology*, 3 vols., Chicago, University of Chicago, 1967, vol. 1.

Whitehead, Alfred N. *Process and Reality*, New York, Harper and Brothers, 1957. See also the corrected edition, ed. David Ray Griffin and Donald W. Sherburne, New York, Free Press, 1978.

5 DIVINE IMPASSIBILITY IN KNOWLEDGE

Adams, Robert M. 'Middle Knowledge and the Problem of Evil,' *American Philosophical Quarterly*, 14/2 (April 1977), 109–17.

Aquinas, Thomas. *The Disputed Questions on Truth*, trans. Robert W. Mulligan, S.J., Chicago, Henry Regnery, 1952, vol. 1.

Summa Theologiae, 60 vols., Cambridge, Blackfriars, 1964, 1a.14.5 and 1a.84.6–8.

Berkeley, George. *Principles of Human Knowledge*, in *Principles, Dialogues, and Philosophical Correspondence*, ed. Colin Murray Turbayne, Indianapolis., Ind., Bobbs-Merrill, 1965. See 'Introduction,' par. 16, and 'Principles,' par. 126.

Boethius. *The Consolation of Philosophy*, trans. Richard Green, Indianapolis, Bobbs-Merrill, 1962, bk. v.

Clarke, W. Norris, S.J. *The Philosophical Approach to God*, Winston-Salem, N.C., Wake Forest University, 1979, pp. 66–109.

Edwards, Jonathan. *Jonathan Edwards*, ed. Clarence H. Faust and Thomas H. Johnson, New York, Hill and Wang, 1962.

Felt, James W., S.J. 'Impossible Worlds,' *International Philosophical Quarterly*, 23/3 (Sept. 1983), 251–65.

Ford, Lewis S. 'Whitehead's Differences from Hartshorne,' in *Two Process Philosophers*, American Academy Studies in Religion, No. 5, ed. Lewis S. Ford, Missoula, Montana, 1973, pp. 58–83.

'Can Freedom Be Created?', *Horizons*, 4/2 (1977), 183–8.

Freddoso, Alfred J. 'Accidental Necessity and Logical Determinism,' *The Journal of Philosophy*, 80/5 (May 1983), 257–78.

Geach, Peter T. 'Aquinas,' in *Three Philosophers* by G. E. M. Anscombe and P. T. Geach, Ithaca, New York, Cornell University, 1961, pp. 67–125.

God and the Soul, London, Routledge and Kegan Paul, 1969.

'God's Relation to the World,' in *Logic Matters*, Berkeley, University of California, 1972a, pp. 318–27.

'Some Problems About Time,' *Logic Matters*, Berkeley, University of California, 1972b, pp. 302–18.

Providence and Evil, Cambridge, Cambridge University Press, 1977.

Hill, William, J., O.P. 'Does the World Make a Difference to God?', *The Thomist*, 38/1 (Jan. 1974), 146–64.

Keller, James A. 'Continuity, Possibility, and Omniscience: A Contrasting View,' *Process Studies* (forthcoming, 14/3).

Kenny, Anthony. 'Divine Foreknowledge and Human Freedom,' in *Aquinas: A Collection of Critical Essays*, ed. Anthony Kenny, Notre Dame, Ind., University of Notre Dame, 1976, pp. 255–70.

The God of the Philosophers, Oxford, The Clarendon Press, 1979.

Kretzmann, Norman. 'Goodness, Knowledge, and Indeterminancy in the Philosophy of Thomas Aquinas,' *The Journal of Philosophy*, supplement to 80/10 (Oct. 1983), 631–49.

Lewis, C. S. *Miracles*, New York, Macmillan, 1947.

Lucas, J. R. *The Freedom of the Will*, Oxford, The Clarendon Press, 1970, ch. 14.

Mourant, John A. 'Scientia Media and Molinism,' *The Encyclopedia of Philosophy*, 8 vols., London, Collier Macmillan, 1967, vol. VII, pp. 338–9.

Plantinga, Alvin. *God, Freedom, and Evil*, New York, Harper, 1974.

The Nature of Necessity, Oxford, The Clarendon Press, 1974.

Purtill, R. L., 'Hartshorne's Modal Proof,' *The Journal of Philosophy*, 63 (1966), 408.

'Ontological Modalities,' *The Review of Metaphysics*, 21 (1967), 306–7.

Ruf, Henry L. 'The Impossibility of Hartshorne's God,' *The Philosophical Forum*, 7/3–4 (Spring–Summer 1976), 345–63.

Stump, Eleonore, and Kretzmann, Norman. 'Eternity,' *The Journal of Philosophy*, 78/8 (August 1981), 429–58.

Swinburne, Richard. *The Coherence of Theism*, Oxford, The Clarendon Press, 1977.

Westphal, Merold. 'Temporality and Finitism in Hartshorne's Theism,' *The Review of Metaphysics*, 13 (1966), 550–64. Westphal defends Aquinas. See Hartshorne's reply in issue no. 82, *Rev. of Meta*.

Whitehead, Alfred N. *Process and Reality*, New York, Harper and Brothers, 1957. See also the corrected edition, ed. David Ray Griffin and Donald W. Sherburne, New York, Free Press, 1978.

Wolterstorff, Nicholas. 'God Everlasting,' in *Contemporary Philosophy of Religion*, ed. Stephen M. Cahn and David Schatz, New York, Oxford University Press, 1982, pp. 77–98.

6   GOD, TIME, AND ETERNITY

Aquinas, Thomas. *The Disputed Questions on Truth*, trans. Robert W. Mulligan, S.J., Chicago, Henry Regnery, 1952, vol. I.

Summa Theologiae, 60 vols., Cambridge, Blackfriars, 1964.

Summa Contra Gentiles, 4 vols., trans. Anton C. Pegis, F.R.S.C., Notre Dame, Ind., University of Notre Dame, 1975.

Geach, Peter T. 'God's Relation to the World,' in *Logic Matters*, Berkeley, University of California, 1972, pp. 318–27.

Kneale, Martha. 'Eternity and Sempiternity,' *Proceedings of the Aristotelian Society*, New Series, 69, London, 1968–9, pp. 223–38.

Kneale, William. 'Time and Eternity in Theology,' *Proceedings of the Aristotelian Society*, New Series, 61, London, 1960–1, pp. 87–108.

Philo. 'On the Unchangeableness of God,' in *Philo*, The Loeb Classical Library, trans. F. H. Colson and G. H. Whitaker, Cambridge, Mass., Harvard University, 1930, vol. III, pp. 11–101, sec. 277.32.

Plotinus. 'Time and Eternity,' in *Plotinus: The Enneads*, 3rd edn, trans. Stephen MacKenna, New York, Pantheon, 1959, third ennead, ch. 7. For the Greek text and a translation by A. H. Armstrong see *Plotinus* in The Loeb Classical Library, Cambridge, Mass., Harvard University, 1967, vol. III, ch. 7.

Shoemaker, Sydney. 'Time Without Change,' *The Journal of Philosophy*, 66/12 (June 1969), 363–81.

Stump, Eleonore, and Kretzmann, Norman. 'Eternity,' *The Journal of Philosophy*, 78/8 (August 1981), 429–58.

Swinburne, Richard. *The Coherence of Theism*, Oxford, The Clarendon Press, 1977, pp. 172–8 and 210–29.

Wright, G. H. von. *Time, Change, and Contradiction*, Cambridge, Cambridge University Press, 1968.

7   DIVINE IMPASSIBILITY IN FEELING

Amory, Cleveland. 'When Faith Is Triumphant: A Portrait of Rose Fitzgerald Kennedy,' *People Magazine* (June 3, 1983), pp. 4–6.

Baker, John Robert. 'The Christological Symbol of God's Suffering,' in *Religious Experience and Process Theology*, ed. Harry James Cargas and Bernard Lee, New York, Paulist Press, 1976, pp. 93–105.

Brasnett, Bertrand. *The Suffering of the Impassible God*, London, Society for Promoting Christian Knowledge, 1928.

Dougall, Lily. *Voluntas Dei*, London, Macmillan, 1912, esp. ch. 19.

Fretheim, Terence E. *The Suffering of God: An Old Testament Perspective*, Philadelphia, Fortress, 1984.

Galot, Jean, S. J. *Dieu souffre-t-il?*, Paris, Lethielleux, 1975.
  'La Réalité de la souffrance de Dieu,' *Nouvelle Revue Théologique*, 101 (1979), 224–44. A summary of recent literature plus replies to criticisms of his book.

Hartshorne, Charles. *Man's Vision of God*, New York, Harper and Row, 1941.
  Creative Synthesis and Philosophic Method, LaSalle, Ill., Open Court, 1970.

Hartshorne, Charles and Reese, William L. *Philosophers Speak of God*, Chicago, University of Chicago Press, 1953.

Hinton, James. *The Mystery of Pain: A Book for the Sorrowful*, New York, Mitchell, Kennerley, 1914. Originally published 1866.

Keller, Helen. *My Religion*, Garden City, N.Y., Doubleday, 1927.

Küng, Hans. 'Exkurs 2: Kann Gott Leiden?', *Menschenwerdung Gottes*, Freiburg, Herder, 1970, pp. 622–37.

Kushner, Harold S. *When Bad Things Happen to Good People*, New York, Avon, 1981.

Lactantius. 'A Treatise on the Anger of God,' in *The Ante-Nicene Fathers*, ed. Alexander Roberts and James Donaldson, Grand Rapids, Michigan, Wm. B. Eerdmans Publishing Company, 1979 reprint, vol. 7, pp. 259–80.

Leibniz, Gottfried Wilhelm von. 'A Vindication of God's Justice Reconciled with His Other Perfections and All His Actions,' in *Monadology and Other Philosophical Essays*, trans. Paul and Anne Martin Schrecker, Indianapolis, Bobbs-Merrill, 1965, pp. 114–47.

McConnell, Francis John. *Is God Limited?*, New York, Abingdon, 1924, ch. 23.

Ogden, Schubert M. *The Reality of God*, New York, Harper and Row, 1963.

Owen, H. P. *The Christian Knowledge of God*, London, Athlone, 1969.

Pollard, T. E. 'The Impassibility of God,' in *The Scottish Journal of Theology*, 8 (1955), 353–64. Contrasts Greek to Hebrew view.

Randles, Marshall. *The Blessed God: Impassibility*, London, Charles H. Kelly, 1900.

Robinson, H. Wheeler. *Suffering: Human and Divine*, New York, Macmillan, 1939, esp. 139–200.

Soelle, Dorothee. *Suffering*, Philadelphia, Fortress, 1975.

Swinburne, Richard. 'The Problem of Evil,' in *Reason and Religion*, ed. Stuart Brown, Ithaca, New York, Cornell University Press, 1977, pp. 81–102.

    The Existence of God, Oxford, The Clarendon Press, 1979.

Vann, Gerald, O.P. *The Pain of Christ and the Sorrow of God*, Springfield, Ill., Templegate, 1947.

Williams, Daniel Day. *The Spirit and the Forms of Love*, New York, Harper and Row, 1968.

Woollcombe, Kenneth J. 'The Pain of God,' in *The Scottish Journal of Theology*, 20 (1967), 129–48. A wide-ranging survey of theological literature.

8   EVIL, MORALITY, REDEMPTION

Aquinas, Thomas. *Summa Theologiae*, 60 vols., Cambridge, Blackfriars, 1964a.

    Treatise on Happiness, trans. John A. Oesterle, Englewood Cliffs, N.J., Prentice-Hall, 1964b.

Baker, John Robert. 'The Christological Symbol of God's Suffering,' in *Religious Experience and Process Theology*, ed. Harry James Cargas and Bernard Lee, New York, Paulist Press, 1976, pp. 93–105.

Brasnett, Bertrand. *The Suffering of the Impassible God*, London, Society for Promoting Christian Knowledge, 1928.

Caldwell, Taylor. *Answer as a Man*, New York, Fawcett Crest, 1980, esp. 115–23.

Chisholm, Roderick M. 'The Defeat of Good and Evil,' *Proceedings and Addresses of the American Philosophical Association*, vol. XLII, 1968–9, pp. 21–38.

Clarke, W. Norris, S.J. *The Philosophical Approach to God*, Winston–Salem, N.C., Wake Forest University, 1979.

Creel, Richard E. 'Happiness and Resurrection: A Reply to Morreall,' *Religious Studies*, 17/3 (Sept. 1981), 387–93.

Dostoyevsky, Fyodor. *The Brothers Karamazov*, trans. Constance Garnett, New York, Modern Library, n.d.

Dougall, Lily. *Voluntas Dei*, London, Macmillan, 1912, esp. ch. 19.

Felt, James W., S.J. 'The Temporality of Divine Freedom,' *Process Studies*, 4/4 (Winter 1974), 252–62.

Geach, Peter T. *Providence and Evil*, Cambridge, Cambridge University Press, 1977.

Hartshorne, Charles. 'Whitehead and Berdyaev: Is There Tragedy in God?', *The Journal of Religion*, 37/2 (April 1957), 71–84.

Hick, John H. *God and the Universe of Faiths*, New York, St Martin's, 1973.
Death and Eternal Life, San Francisco, Harper and Row, 1976.
The Center of Christianity, San Francisco, Harper and Row, 1978.

Hügel, Baron Friedrich von. 'Suffering and God,' in *Essays and Addresses in the Philosophy of Religion*, Second Series, London, J. M. Dent and Son, 1926.

Kaufmann, Walter. *The Faith of a Heretic*, Garden City, New York, Anchor Books, 1963, pp. 370–6.

Leibniz, Gottfried Wilhelm von. *Theodicy*, ed. Diogenes Allen, Indianapolis, Bobbs-Merrill, 1966.

Madden, Edward H., and Hare, Peter H. *Evil and the Concept of God*, Springfield, Ill., Charles C. Thomas, 1968.

Mascall, E. L. *Existence and Analogy*, New York, Longmans, Green, and Co., 1949.

Morreall, John. 'Perfect Happiness and the Resurrection of the Body,' *Religious Studies*, 16/1 (March 1980), 29–35.

Randles, Marshall. *The Blessed God: Impassibility*, London, Charles H. Kelly, 1900.

Reichenbach, Bruce. 'Natural Evils and Natural Laws: A Theodicy for Natural Evils,' *International Philosophical Quarterly*, 16 (1976), 179–96.

Schopenhauer, Arthur. 'On the Vanity and Suffering of Life,' in *The Will to Live: Selected Writings of Arthur Schopenhauer*, ed. Richard Taylor, New York, Frederick Unger, 1967, pp. 199–214.

Swinburne, Richard. *The Existence of God*, Oxford, The Clarendon Press, 1979.
Faith and Reason, Oxford, The Clarendon Press, 1981.

Williams, Bernard. 'The Makropoulos Case: Reflections on the Tedium of Immortality,' in *Problems of the Self*, Cambridge, Cambridge University Press, 1973, ch. 6.

9   WHY DOES GOD CREATE?

Aquinas, Thomas. *Summa Contra Gentiles*, 4 vols., trans. Anton C. Pegis, F.R.S.C., Notre Dame, Ind., University of Notre Dame, 1975.

Augustine. *The City of God*, trans. Marcus Dods, New York, Modern Library, 1950.

Donceel, Joseph. *The Searching Mind*, Notre Dame, Ind., University of Notre Dame, 1979.

Ford, Lewis S. 'The Viability of Whitehead's God for Christian Theology,' *American Catholic Philosophical Association: Proceedings*, 44 (1970), 141–51.
'Can Freedom Be Created?', *Horizons*, 4/2 (1977), 183–8.

Geach, Peter T. 'Aquinas,' in *Three Philosophers* by G. E. M. Anscombe and P. T. Geach, Ithaca, New York, Cornell University, 1961, pp. 67–125.

Hartshorne, Charles. *Man's Vision of God*, New York, Harper and Row, 1941.
'Whitehead and Berdyaev: Is There Tragedy in God?', *The Journal of Religion*, 37/2 (April 1957), 71–84.
Creative Synthesis and Philosophic Method, LaSalle, Ill., Open Court, 1970.

Kretzmann, Norman. 'Goodness, Knowledge, and Indeterminacy in the Philosophy of Thomas Aquinas,' *The Journal of Philosophy*, supplement to 80/10 (Oct. 1983), 631–49.

Mascall, E. L. *Existence and Analogy*, New York, Longmans, Green, and Co., 1949.

Philo. 'On the Unchangeableness of God,' in *Philo*, The Loeb Classical Library, trans. F. H. Colson and G. H. Whitaker, Cambridge, Mass., Harvard University, 1930, vol. III, pp. 11–101, sec. 277.32.

Swinburne, Richard. *The Coherence of Theism*, Oxford, The Clarendon Press, 1977.
    The Existence of God, Oxford, The Clarendon Press, 1979.

10   CREATION AND FREEDOM

Aquinas, Thomas. *The Disputed Questions on Truth*, trans. Robert W. Mulligan, S.J.,
    Chicago, Henry Regnery, 1952, vol. I.
    Summa Theologiae, 60 vols., Cambridge, Blackfriars, 1964.
    Summa Contra Gentiles, 4 vols., trans. Anton C. Pegis, F.R.S.C., Notre Dame, Ind.,
    University of Notre Dame, 1975.
Augustine. *The Trinity*, The Fathers of the Church, vol. XLV, trans. Stephen McKenna,
    C.SS.R., Washington, D.C., Catholic University of America, 1963.
Creel, Richard E. 'Atheism and Freedom: a Response to Sartre and Baier,' *Religious
    Studies*, 20/2 (June 1984), 281–91.
Ford, Lewis S. 'Can Freedom Be Created?', *Horizons*, 4/2 (1977), 183–8.
    The Lure of God, Philadelphia, Fortress, 1978.
Geach, Peter T. 'God's Relation to the World,' in *Logic Matters*, Berkeley, University of
    California Press, 1972, esp. pp. 324–7.
    Providence and Evil, Cambridge, Cambridge University Press, 1977, esp. pp. 57 and
    141.
Kenny, Anthony. *The God of the Philosophers*, Oxford, The Clarendon Press, 1979, esp.
    pp. 34, 36, and 62–71.
Kretzmann, Norman. 'Goodness, Knowledge, and Indeterminacy in the Philosophy of
    Thomas Aquinas,' *The Journal of Philosophy*, supplement to 80/10 (Oct. 1983),
    631–49.
Leibniz, Gottfried Wilhelm von. 'What Is Nature,' in *Monadology and Other Philo-
    sophical Essays*, trans. Paul and Anne Martin Schrecker, Indianapolis, Bobbs-
    Merrill, 1965, pp. 101–12, esp. secs. 8, 13, and 15.
Lowe, Victor. 'Alfred North Whitehead: Introduction,' in *Classic American Philoso-
    phers*, ed. Max Fisch, New York, Appleton–Century-Crofts, 1951, pp. 395–417.
Plato. *Statesman* in *The Collected Dialogues of Plato*, ed. Edith Hamilton and
    Huntington Cairns, New York, Pantheon, 1963, pp. 1018–85.
Sartre, Jean-Paul. *Existentialism and Human Emotions*, New York, Philosophical
    Library, 1957.
    Being and Nothingness, trans. Hazel E. Barnes, New York, Washington Square, 1966.
Stacer, John R., S.J. 'Integrating Thomistic and Whiteheadian Perspectives on God,'
    International Philosophical Quarterly, 21/4 (Dec. 1981), 355–77.

11   HOW TO CREATE THE BEST POSSIBLE WORLD

Adams, Robert M. 'Must God Create the Best?', *The Philosophical Review*, 81/3 (July
    1972), 317–32.
Aquinas, Thomas. *Summa Theologiae*, 60 vols., Cambridge, Blackfriars, 1964.
Augustine. *The City of God*, trans. Marcus Dods, New York, Modern Library, 1950,
    bk. XXII, ch. 30.
Basinger, David. 'Must God Create the Best Possible World? A Response,' *International
    Philosophical Quarterly*, 20/3 (Sept. 1980), 339–45.
Donceel, Joseph F., S.J. *The Searching Mind*, Notre Dame, Indiana, University of Notre
    Dame, 1979.
Geach, Peter T. *Providence and Evil*, Cambridge, Cambridge University Press, 1977.

Virtues, Cambridge, Cambridge University Press, 1977.

Kenny, Anthony. *The God of the Philosophers*, Oxford, The Clarendon Press, 1979.

Kretzmann, Norman. 'Goodness, Knowledge, and Indeterminancy in the Philosophy of Thomas Aquinas,' *The Journal of Philosophy*, supplement to 80/10 (Oct. 1983), 631–49.

Leibniz, Gottfried Wilhelm von. 'On the Ultimate Origination of the Universe,' in *Monadology and Other Philosophical Essays*, trans. Paul and Anne Martin Schrecker, Indianapolis, Bobbs-Merrill, 1965, pp. 84–94.

Theodicy, ed. Diogenes Allen, Indianapolis, Bobbs-Merrill, 1966.

Mackie, J. L. 'Evil and Omnipotence,' *Mind*, 64 (1955), 200–12.

McCloskey, H. J. *God and Evil*, The Hague, Nijhoff, 1974.

McGill, Arthur C. *Suffering: A Test of Theological Method*, Philadelphia, Westminster, 1982.

Quinn, Michael S. 'Mustn't God Create for the Best?', *The Journal of Critical Analysis*, 5/1 (July/October 1973), 2–8.

Reichenbach, Bruce R. 'Must God Create the Best Possible World?', *International Philosophical Quarterly*, 19/2 (June 1979), 203–12.

'Basinger on Reichenbach and the Best Possible World,' *International Philosophical Quarterly*, 20/3 (Sept. 1980), 339–45.

Evil and a Good God, New York, Fordham University, 1982.

Swinburne, Richard. *Faith and Reason*, Oxford, The Clarendon Press, 1981.

Index